American Standard

# American Standard

## The Bible in US Popular Culture

*Robert Paul Seesengood*

*Drew Theological School*
*Drew University*

*Registered Offices*

John Wiley & Sons, Inc., 111 River Street, Hoboken, NJ 07030, USA

John Wiley & Sons Ltd, The Atrium, Southern Gate, Chichester, West Sussex, PO19 8SQ, UK

For details of our global editorial offices, customer services, and more information about Wiley products visit us at www.wiley.com.

*Library of Congress Cataloging-in-Publication Data Applied for:*

Paperback ISBN: 9781118361566

Cover Design: Wiley

Cover Image: © Joanna McCarthy/Getty Images

Set in 9.5/12.5pt STIXTwoText by Straive, Pondicherry, India

*For Maisie Faye*

# Contents

# Acknowledgments

This book took too long to write. When I began it, I was intending to produce a book on cultural studies and biblical studies that married the theory-focus and consistency of a single-author title with the breadth of content and cultural review that comes from multiauthor collections. I still like that idea, but now understand precisely how long it will take for a single person to acquaint themselves with such a huge array of theory. Even a meager volume such as this would not be possible without the generous insight and conversation of many scholarly friends. Most all these chapters first appeared as presentations to regional or national professional meetings and campus lectures; I benefited greatly from key questions, suggestions, and ideas from an array of collaborators and more. To mention just a few, I have serious debts to Rhonda Burnette-Bletsch, Dan Clanton, Jr., Jason Cocker, Laura Copier, James Crossley, Steed Davidson, Scott Eliot, Rhiannon Graybill, Maia Kotrosits, Joseph Marchal, Stephen Moore, Brent Plate, Matt Rindge, Peter Sabo, Donovan Schafer, Greg Seigworth, Linda Schearing, Ken Stone, Hannah Strømmen, Jay Twomey, Richard Walsh, and Andrew Wilson. Some material was also read and reacted to by students at Albright College and in Kesher Zion Synagogue's adult education program. I'm grateful to all for the fine, honest questions they brought, as well. When I began this project, so long ago, I was faculty and administration at Albright College in Reading, PA. As I do final drafts and edits, I am administration and faculty at the Theological School of Drew University in Madison, NJ. Thanks are due to my colleagues in Religious Studies at Albright College for their unflagging support: Charles Brown, Victor Forte, Midori Hartman, Mel Sensenig, Andrew Mbuvi – and especially Jennifer Koosed, my colleague and partner in nearly everything. I'm overwhelmed with gratitude to my many fine colleagues at Drew, as well. I'm particularly grateful for my partners in Academic Affairs – Edwin Aponte, Tanya Bennett, Meredith Hoxie-Schol, Kathie Brown, Hilary McKane, Beth Babcock, and Nancy Keats – as well as the always stimulating conversation partners among the faculty in Bible and Cultures – Stephen D. Moore, Danna Nolan Fewell, Melanie Johnson-Debaufre, Kenneth Ngwa, Althea Spencer-Miller, and Dong Sung Kim.

Previous versions of Chapters 3, 6, and 8 appeared as "The Bible as Graphic Novel: When the Word Becomes (Affecting) Image" (*Bible & Critical Theory* 14.1 [2018]: 87–101), "'Do Not Forsake Me': Biblical Motifs in Zinnemann's *High Noon*" (*SBL Forum* May–June 2009) and "Documentaries." In: *Biblical Reception in Film*, Vol. 1 (ed. R. Burnette-Blestch), 193–208. Handbooks on Biblical Reception, 2; Leiden: de Gruyter, 2016; and some paragraphs of "Publishing in the Bible and American Popular Culture." In: *The Oxford Handbook of the Bible and American Culture* (ed. D. W. Clanton, Jr. and Terry Clark), 537–552. New York: Oxford University Press, 2021; and "Wrestling with the 'Macedonian Call': Pauline Scholarship in the Nineteenth-Century Colonial Missions." In: *The Colonized Apostle: Paul Through Post-Colonial Eyes* (ed. C. Stanley), 189–205. Minneapolis, MN: Fortress Press, 2011, reappear in Chapters 1 and 2. Chapter 10 was originally published as "Bespoke Words: The Bible, Fashion, and the Mechanism(s) of Things" (*Bible & Critical Theory* 16.2 [2020]: 50–58).

Finally, I need to thank Jennifer, Abby, Simon, and Ben for years of support, patience, love, and curiosity. I'm more grateful than I can ever express. This is what I was thinking about and working on all those times. I hope you like it.

*For Maisie Faye*

# 1

# A General Introduction to Cultural Studies and Cultural Studies Approaches to the Bible

## Spreading the Word: The Bible's Viral Encounter with US Pop Culture

During the pandemic of 2020, cloistered inside my "bubble" of immediate family, with my books, the internet and this (proto)manuscript as company, I was struck by a metaphor for the Bible's prevalence in US culture: its influence is actually, not metaphorically, epidemic. Thinking so much of contagion and transmission, I simply can't imagine a person living in the United States for a year without, at some point, physically encountering a Bible or spending 15 minutes in proximity of someone who owned a Bible. The Bible, like a cultural pandemic, ripples through nearly every aspect of US history, media, and society. Bibles can be found everywhere, even in a winterized, backwoods cabin in Centre County, PA, in dozens of translations and editions. Bibles and Bible commentary flood the internet. Even during a pandemic, copies of the Bible are given away on street corners by earnest missionaries on (even largely empty) college campuses and (surreally quiet) city streets. The Bible permeates not only America's mass culture, but even its physical space. It's physical presence, like a virus, both produces and testifies to the influence of its effectiveness.

Viruses, like Bibles, are strange. Viruses are the margins of matter and "living." They are a complicated, though small, "text" of genetic code that, when "read," replicates its message. As the novel coronavirus Covid-19 has shown, again and again, a virus beguiles us into language of will and sentience (a "crafty" variation). Viruses, like Bibles, cannot travel alone; they need a host. But viruses, like Bibles, function by convincing their host to assist their spread. When one encounters a virus, "touches" it, the exchange – a moment of reading and interpretation and influence – begins.

I touch the Bible, open on the table beside me. It, like a virus, can be understood in a myriad of ways. One can trace its genealogy, its evolution, its mutations, its

*American Standard: The Bible in US Popular Culture*, First Edition. Robert Paul Seesengood.
© 2024 John Wiley & Sons Ltd. Published 2024 by John Wiley & Sons Ltd.

processes; it can be understood in its lexemes and grammar, in terms of its affinity – or uniqueness – to other books (ancient and contemporary), in terms of its bookishness or in terms of its history of transmission, transcription, translation. It can be read by the devout as a message of spiritual truth, of divine importance, or it can be read with detachment, in terms of its impact on individual readers or upon whole streams of culture, present or historic. It is a book one can touch with one's hand, a physical thing, but it is also a breathtakingly effective meme.

This book, *American Standard,* a title that blends reference to one of the first best-selling translations of the Bible indigenous to the United States with acknowledgement of the Bible's central role in the US cultural repertoire, is in part an introduction to scholarship that blends biblical studies with the study of pop culture and mass media (particularly in a US context). The book offers both an introduction and theoretical framing for study of the Bible in/and/as popular culture, and a selection of essays performing that analysis in a variety of ways. For the critical theory, I have chosen to focus on classical and foundational authors and texts for the field of cultural studies. For engagement with popular culture, I have consistently erred to the side of accessibility, hopefully choosing moments of popular culture with sufficient cultural breadth and potential "staying power" to be recognizable to a wide variety of readers.

I am imagining readers who are trained in biblical studies meeting cultural studies, in an organized way, for the first time, but also readers well-versed in cultural studies who might be curious about Bible. I will argue that biblical scholarship on cultural studies can be grouped into three methodological categories that emerge, roughly, sequentially from the mid-twentieth century until the early twenty first, each in conversation with the one preceding it. I am arguing that the dialog between Bible and media/cultural studies both follow broader postwar transitions in humanities scholarship, moving from a defense of "high" culture to a sense of cultural Marxism then through into postmodern or late capitalist intertextuality and finally coalescing in affect studies and posthumanism. In this book, alongside this evolutionary taxonomy of method, I will present three sets of three essays, grouped and ordered to demonstrate those three methodological lenses (displaying both their independence and their inter-animation with one another). *American Standard* is divided into three sections with three chapters each. This introduction provides an overview of the lens for each section in the triad that follows; the essays will be a demonstration or example of that lens.

The first methodological lens is the development of "culture" and "cultural studies" as typified by the work of the Birmingham Centre for Contemporary Cultural Studies (CCCS). This work (which I will discuss in Section 1.2 of this introduction) argued that popular or mass culture, previously seen as "vulgar" or beneath serious attention, was actually apt for serious scholarly critique. It further developed notions of how both "high" and "low" culture (and their designations) function(ed) to create hierarchies in culture, creating hegemonic systems with clear winners and losers. This work, in Britain, was heavily Marxist. As it migrated to the United States, and to the late twentieth century and "postmodern" scholarship, many of its themes and interests coalesce in Fredrick Jameson's "culture of Late Capitalism" which also marks a transition, in North American scholarship, to a sort of "postmodern" intertextuality. Section 1.2 of this introductory chapter will survey some examples of biblical scholarship in direct continuity with the Birmingham Centre and that resonate with Jameson's critique. Chapters 2–4 of this book will feature essays contiguous with this approach.

When cultural studies began to gain ground among US biblical scholars, it did so, as we will see, without the overt Marxist focus found in earlier British work. In Section 1.3 of this introduction, I will argue that, for American biblical scholars, intertextuality, as voiced for by Fernando Segovia, was a much more important, though often unacknowledged, influence. Much (I would argue, the vast majority) of US-based scholarship on the Bible and popular culture unveils interconnections between seemingly disparate works, reveling in the productive comparison of art generated across vast differentials of time, culture, and community. Sometimes this unveiling is the articulation of ways the Bible or the cultural product draw directly upon other subjects. Within this broad intertextual set of readings lies yet another trend in scholarship on Bible and popular culture; reviewing contemporary (mass market) use of the Bible is, itself, a form of biblical interpretation, a type of biblical scholarship. This critical approach examines Bible in popular culture to see how contemporary people are (or have been) understanding – or better: creating – biblical meaning. In a few other cases, this examination of intertextuality is fully Kristevan – an exploration of how the modern reader (here, often, the scholar) creates (or discovers) meaning by the juxtaposition of the Bible and modern mass culture, interrogating the definitions of "author," "reader," and "text." Section 1.3 of this introduction will survey some examples of this work in contemporary biblical scholarship. Chapters 5–7 of this book are examples of it as well.

Finally, work emerging in the early twenty-first century is not only contiguous with these prior methodological lenses, but also reflects emerging interests across the humanities in post-humanism (particularly new materialism) and in affect criticism. The Venn diagram of these two scholarly conversations overlap in the work of Giles Deleuze. Deleuze articulated the concepts of "the assemblage" and the book as "machine." Both of these concepts are used by modern critics to discuss how the Bible (or culture) makes or manufactures "meaning" (among groups or for individual readers). Deleuze also developed the idea of juxtaposition and "becomingness," of affect – the precognitive cognition of discovery and intersection. All of these concepts have been used by contemporary critics of Bible and popular culture. Section 1.4 of this introductory chapter will explain these ideas further and will cite some examples among modern scholars. Chapters 8–10 of this book will be essays examining Bible and popular culture through this methodological lens.

As a beginning reader of modern biblical interpretation quickly learns, the nineteenth century of biblical scholarship is synonymous with the growth of "higher criticism" among European (largely German) scholarship. The early twenty-first century will be known for scholarship on the Bible and popular culture (its broader genus: "reception criticism"), particularly among Anglophone scholarship. Germanic higher criticism reflected larger academic and cultural values of its era; for example, a growing valuation of "scientific" or "reasoned" criticism in the humanities; assumptions about cultural evolution and social Darwinism; and the methodological refinement of supporting disciplines such as sociology, archaeology, linguistics, and philology. As I will argue, scholarship on Bible and mass culture reflects our (post)modern moment through shifting assumptions of authority and semiotic and literary "meaning": analysis of cultural structures and power, keen interest in subjectivity and aesthetics, the sophistication inherent in consumption, and the assertion of complexity in what seems superficial and ephemeral. The study of Bible in/and/as popular culture is a hallmark of contemporary biblical scholarship.

The balance of this introduction is an overview of the origins of popular cultural studies, noting the broader transition of cultural studies from the late twentieth century until today, mapping briefly the intrusion of cultural studies into biblical studies, reviewing the migration of that work from British to US context, and exploring the Americanized versions, infused with intertextuality and affect, all set against broader intellectual trends at play in US academic work in the humanities. I want to proceed less as annotated bibliography and more as literature and contextual analysis. While I will offer an overview of the field (citing some representative examples), it is not a catalog of work that pretends to be exhaustive. In review and in example, I hope to trace what I would identify as three major theoretical foci of current work on Bible and pop culture. There are additional characteristics of US work that I will highlight.

## Old School: Birmingham, Marxism, and Late Capitalism

Study of the Bible in/and mass, popular culture is a scholarly trend that presumes many (but by no means all) assumptions, methods, and queries from British-style "cultural studies" of the 1960s and 1970s, as well as American interest in mass media and internet culture. Despite some notable exceptions (which I highlight subsequently), there is disproportionate attention in biblical studies to film, television, and visual culture and much less on other questions common to British-style cultural studies such as material culture (or "new materialism"), race and ethnicity (until very recently), food culture, civic practice, family and community studies (beyond race, class and gender), affect criticism, or cultural ideologies. Publication and dissemination of scholarship in popular culture are, however, growing rapidly in biblical scholarship, with the support of major scholarly societies (such as the Society of Biblical Literature), the focus of several journals (many published only electronically), significant – and extremely ambitious – new reference works, and several new monograph series.

The critical field of cultural studies begins with the question: What do we mean by "culture" and "popular/mass culture."[1] Prior to Emile Durkheim, "society" referred to the economic and political elite, to "high society." Durkheim transformed this term into our more modern usage of groups with common ideologies, technologies, etc. In a similar way, "culture" was redefined in the twentieth century. As the century dawned, "culture" referred to high art activities – say, opera, museums, serious plays and literature. Now, we understand culture to be ubiquitous, those elements of language, material, art, custom and values that are produced by, consumed by and defining of a given society (as per Butsch 1990 or Surdam 2015).

Culture is, indeed, difficult to define, largely because it is so encompassing. Kroeber and Kluckholm (1952, p. 104) describe it as a total system of negotiated interexchange – including language, religion, education, art, and more. Culture is material and systemic, but it is also ephemeral and ideological. It includes, as notes Schein (1984, 1990) broad values, norms, and assumptions alongside observable actions, legal and social bodies, and material objects. Tyler (1974), one of the originators of the concept, describes "culture" as a "complex whole which includes knowledge, belief, art, morals, law, custom, and any other capabilities and habits acquired by Man [sic] as a member of society." (1974, p. xx). Culture, by the late twentieth century, was understood as everything produced by humans, including scholarship of culture, which, as Culture's product itself, adds to culture's complexity, ambiguity, and variation.

The definition of both "society" and "culture" did not emerge overnight, nor by happenstance. Further, the transition (fueled by a growing middle and

---

1 A great deal of the following is outlined in Moore 1998a, pp. 1–32. Slightly more oriented toward historical development of the theory would be Exum and Moore 1998a, pp. 20–45. Strong outlines of methodology, though not as oriented to history of development or as explicitly rooted in continental thought, can also be found in Sawyer 2006, pp. 1–8. A briefer review of highlights is in Wainwright 2010, pp. 1–12. Of significant value for the background and basic assumptions of cultural studies and the CCCS, discussed later, see During 1993, 1996, 53–83; Hall 1980, pp. 57–72; 1982, pp. 56–90.

university class, post World War II) brought debates over whether there was merit (or even sense) in the scholarly analysis of "low" or "popular" forms of culture – items (chiefly entertainment, media, and consumables) notable for their popular appeal, but deemed "lower" or less worthy of serious analyses or enjoyment by educated classes.

For example, in the 1930s, F. R. Leavis argued (persuasively at the time) that education should consist of cultivating "proper" leisure and exposure to the mainstays of western literature, art, or music. The properly educated person avoided crass "mass" culture (1930). Richard Hoggart's *Uses of Literacy* (1957) offered an alternative perspective. Hoggart analyzed how, where, why and what "working class" Britons read; he challenged much of the idea and content of "high" culture, celebrating instead working-class values, even as he also challenged a singular, homogenous "mass culture." Raymond Williams's *Culture and Society* took the argument further, arguing that differences between "high" and "low" culture are social norms designed to perpetuate and protect class divisions and distinction (Williams 1958; also of interest 1996, pp. 168–177). Understanding "low" or mass culture, they argued, was critically important, and popular or "pulp" culture was as worthy of rigorous scholarly attention as "mass" culture, and in many ways more revealing.

Hoggart founded the CCCS in the early 1960s to study, rigorously and seriously, mass culture as means of understanding present British society; the CCCS was led through the 1960s and 1970s by Stuart Hall (for an overview of Hall's tenure and perspective(s) on his influence, see Radway 2016, 2, pp. 312–321). In these years, general Marxist assumptions were dominant, as the CCCS tended to assume elite social classes (normally, but not exclusively, the wealthy) maintained their social privilege by the exploitation of the labor and productivity of lower classes and used popular media to either create or to perpetuate these systems (note the array of essays and influences in Munns and Rajan 1995). Embedded within popular culture were the structures, and sometimes the mechanisms, of class distinction and social inequity. The CCCS was exploring how these social divisions were reflected in ideas of "culture" and how "culture" worked to create and perpetuate these distinctions.

The work of neo-Marxist philosophers Antonio Gramsci (particularly as represented in the collections Gramsci 1971, 1978) and Louis Althusser (most frequently engaging Althusser 1969 and Althusser and Balibar 1968) were particularly important. Gramsci argued for what he called cultural "hegemony" where subdominant social groups (the "subaltern") participate willingly in the construction of systems that keep them oppressed (perpetuating, for example, systems of racism, gender control, religious persecution, etc.). Althusser argued that social structures called "institutions" (religion, family, the military, education) are constructed to perpetuate the social hierarchy on the whole. This of necessity means that they will perpetuate forms of social domination, and this domination was created, maintained, and mediated via the vehicle of "culture," particularly mass culture (note, also, Adorno 1991, which assumes this, throughout).

In the 1980s the Marxist focus of cultural studies (as practiced at the CCCS) became more tenuous. There were three general reasons for this. First, politically, the United States and Britain, led by conservative neoliberals Ronald Reagan and Margaret Thatcher, were experiencing rapid expansion in financial markets with a rapidly growing difference in wealth, and, in both nations, there was less interest in traditional Marxist ideology. The "middle class" was going away, and wealth has a vested interest in perpetuating economic and political structures. There was also a rise in nationalism. Fewer academics were interested in exploring Marxist questions (or, perhaps more cynically: fewer academic programs, grantors and book publishers were interested in their faculty pursuing Marxist questions); those who were met frequent pushback. A second, more intellectual reason is the sudden growth of a global perspective facilitated by new technologies that, with the rising suspicion of simple explanation inherent in postmodernity, revealed that the equation of state-vs.-worker or bourgeoisie-vs.-proletariat were too simple. "Bourgeoisie" with respect to whom? Subaltern where? Simple Marxist systems did not work as readily in the emerging complexity of both perspective and structure that globalism created.[2]

Cultural studies has shifted intellectual focus from professional scholars to public intellectuals and from exclusive attention to elite "culture" toward functions of mass culture. It looks at widely popular expressions of culture (including, indeed often seeking out, the "vulgar"). These are then interrogated for how they construct/reflect (often at once) popular assumptions that empower/disempower (often at the same time) particular groups and how they perpetuate/refute (again, often at once) particular ideologies. In the case of cultural studies and the Bible: what, precisely, are we doing when we study "the Bible and cultural studies?" Are we studying the Bible, using the insights of cultural studies or mass use, or are we studying mass culture via analysis of how the Bible floats through its various strata? Certainly, the latter is possible. Few books have been more "popular" (in the sense of widely known) in western culture. The Bible is also used as an instrument of control and restriction (say,

---

2 Marxist structures have had a resurgence in scholarly and popular thinking in the early twenty-first century. Part of this resurgence arises from general dissatisfaction with neoliberalism and traditional US and UK liberalism, particularly in its failure to best outright emerging conservative nationalism (and fascism). Part also arises from the use of Marxist structures to underpin contemporary critical race theory (especially as advocated by Derek Bell and Harvard University Law School), where racial privilege/subalterity replaces hegemonic tensions of bourgeoisie/proletariat.

opposition of some clergy to LGBTQ issues) and as a basis for arguments of liberation (as by Martin Luther King, Jr.). It is used in/as a variety of forms of art. It is dominator and dominated at once. For many (using a division articulated by Durkheim who argued that "religion" is exactly and always opposite the "profane" or ordinarily secular) the Bible cannot be "mass culture," but it is little else. The use of the Bible is always-already a form of biblical interpretation. Its use reveals what someone wants or imagines the Bible to say and to be. In other words, observing the Bible in pop culture is the observation of significant and substantial political expression.

When cultural studies immigrated to the United States from the United Kingdom, it rapidly began to lose its historic connection to Marxism and theory even as it widely (and wildly) expanded its review of mass culture. Cultural studies is not a method, per se. In the diffuse context of America, it is also not really a common set of questions and assumptions. Instead, it tends to become a generic orientation (to revelation of systems of interpretation and structures that construct social organizations) turned to mass culture items. Cultural studies in biblical scholarship tends even further from political and theoretical analysis in recent literature, focused on questions of how/why biblical text, in its "use" in pop culture is a form of interpretation.

North American scholarship has tended to embrace the arguments from cultural studies regarding the dissolution of "high" vs. "popular," formal vs. mass production of cultural artifacts and general art and literature. Cultural studies after the fashion of Hoggart, Hall, and others entered critical biblical scholarship in the 1990s. Ironically, however, biblical cultural studies very often moves on to critique the limits of the pop interpretation, implicitly re-inscribing a hierarchy of "professional" vs. "mass" interpreter, of "right" vs. "wrong" readings (where more often than not professional interests and "right" readings perpetuate the systems that privilege the professional biblical scholar making the argument). In other words, the lack of attention to methodological history often ends up with the biblical-cultural-studies essay reinscribing systems of domination, privilege, hegemony, hierarchy, and ideological oppression that the discipline of cultural studies was initially designed to at least expose (if not correct).

The majority of the US contribution to cultural studies is interwoven with postmodern criticism and philosophy. The late twentieth century saw a transition away from modernity toward "postmodernity." In simplest terms, "postmodern" as an ideology can be summed up in a deliberate turn from high confidence in the values and ideals of modernity. One philosopher, J. E. Lyotard, defined postmodernism as a "suspicion of all metanarratives." (Lyotard 1984). By "metanarratives," Lyotard meant the large stories we construct, as a society, to explain and understand reality.

Perhaps. Yet a clear and substantive description of what postmodernity *is* (apart from an articulation of what it *isn't*) has remained problematic. Most everyone concedes a definition of "modernity," and most also acknowledge that by "post," we mean we are in an era where the assumptions and assertions of modernism are under interrogation and reassessment. Yet there are real challenges to be made against assertions that postmodernity is a radical break. Perhaps a healthy suspicion of metanarrative is, itself, the apex of modernist thought; perhaps, far from being replaced, modernity is simply reaching its fullest expression.

In 1984, Frederick Jameson published an article, "Postmodernity: Or, the Cultural Logic of Late Capitalism," which he later expanded and used as the central chapter of a book of the same title (Jameson 1984, pp. 59–92; 1991). Jameson accepts the view of thinkers such as Lyotard that the present moment does, indeed, seem to reject the absolutes of modernity. He also concedes arguments about the destabilization of confidence in large, systemic metanarrative. For Jameson, however, Lyotard's insistence upon rejection of *all* metanarrative doesn't destabilize confidence at all. We have not, really, rejected metanarrative. Indeed, much the opposite seems to be the case; we have radically proliferated metanarratives and often become polemic in our defense of them (certainly this describes twenty-first century US social media). Late capitalism rejects *exclusive* metanarratives, but not metanarrative, per se. Multiple, even contradictory, metanarratives may coexist. Ideology does not cease in postmodernity; it becomes even more central and volatile. We chose ideology (or identity) from a marketplace of sorts. Epistemology and economics merge. For Jameson, these changes are the essential characteristics of "late capitalism." The continuity with modernity results from capitalism's integral relationship to the products of modernism. The "post" results in the natural breakdown of confidence and continuity resulting from the types of changes that global capitalism produces. Jameson sees the culture of late capitalism as one that foregrounds superficiality. His book, after laying out his initial premises, explores postmodernity/late capitalism in broader ideology, video, architecture, literature, "utopian" expectations, critical theory (epistemology), economics, and film. Through the examination of popular and mass culture, Jameson argues for:

> [T]he following constitutive features of the postmodern: a new depthlessness, which finds its prolongation both in contemporary "theory" and in a whole new culture of the image or the simulacrum; a consequent weakening of historicity, both in our relationship with public History and in the new forms of our private temporality, whose "schizophrenic" structure (following Lacan) will determine new types of syntax or syntagmatic relationships in the more temporal arts; a whole new type of emotional ground tone – what I will call "intensities" – which can best be grasped by a return to older theories of the sublime; the deep

constitutive relationships of all this to a new technology, which is itself a figure for a whole new economic world system.

(Jameson 1991, p. 6)

Postmodernity is, indeed, a move away from metanarrative, but the move is an intentional separation from previous systems of mooring. The postmodern is defined by intentional superficiality, and this superficiality, Jameson argues, is a direct result of "late capitalism." Capitalism's ultimate expansion has, as we have seen, destabilized expectations of "truth." It has also celebrated systems of competition which results in ethical strain and in a particular type of rootlessness where emphasis lies on result more than history or process. It has also, finally, resulted in expectations of consumption and, most critically, in choice. For Jameson, late capitalism and postmodernity are the rootlessness arising from dissolving confidence in metanarrative at the exact opportunity that consumption is most prized and most available. "Depth" is the antithesis of the postmodern.

Biblical scholarship that engages popular culture has expanded exponentially in the first decades of the twenty-first century. Much of the early, critical work positioned itself as inheritor of classic, CCCS scholarship; much of the contemporary work sees itself as the natural outgrowth of postmodernity and late capitalism having their influences upon the field. Stephen D. Moore and Yvonne Sherwood have argued the present turn toward cultural studies by biblicists is the natural end of postmodern literary criticism in general and biblical studies, in particular; they also assert that, as a development, it is the future of biblical scholarship (Moore and Sherwood 2011).

At minimum, a cursory review of the shifting nature of biblical criticism reveals that some sort of encounter between cultural studies and modern, academic biblical scholarship would seem inevitable.[3] Indeed, "reception critical" methodologies may be the capstone of modern, secular biblical criticism. Biblical scholarship that attends to or draws comparison with popular, mass culture is not the antithesis of "scholarly," or "scientific" higher criticism; it is its perfection.

Late Renaissance/early Enlightenment scholars such as Hugo de Groot and Erasmus famously began to read the Bible according to the norms and standards of any other book from antiquity. The Bible was not read, primarily, as a book opened only via divine or supernatural guidance, read solely within the protected confines of dogma and community. Instead, it was subject to "normal" critical

---

3 For a quick review of what follows, consult Legaspi 2010. Readers will note, though his survey of the history and development of modern biblical studies is quite accurate, Legaspi, a theologian, clearly laments the loss of biblical authority resulting from the transition. Not all critics agree this loss – or perhaps better, "transformation" – is detrimental. For a manifesto for secular or political readings of the Bible unbeholden to Christian or Jewish theology, see Boer 2007 and Berlinerblau 2005.

techniques of historical analysis and grammatical review. This seed germinated in the nineteenth century via "higher criticism" – where scholars intentionally set aside allegiances to faith and read the Bible as a historical text, asking sometimes rude questions about the Bible's historical reliability, textual integrity or even claims to authorship and authority. By early twentieth century, these secular critiques were assumed: the Bible was a book from history, written by other humans within history, and best read according to the norms of reading, more generally. Scholars sought the "meaning" of the Bible not in spiritual revelation or disclosure, but by painstaking reconstruction of content and what scholars posited that the original authors most likely intended the text to mean. Nearly from its beginning, then, critical biblical studies has focused, at least in part, on the interpreter, the history of text and scholarship, and the reception of biblical text. Reception criticism *is* modern, secular biblical studies. By mid-to-late twentieth century, schooled against high modernism's intellectual overconfidence in its own, purely rational dispassion, scholars were increasingly aware of the role of the interpreter's bias in any reading – including in the reconstruction of the historical context(s) and "meaning" of the Bible. No longer confident a text can "mean" what an author intended, scholars looked more and more into analysis of how culture and bias shaped Bible readers (or how the Bible was used to construct cultures or defend biases). Cultural studies informed biblical criticism and continues this late-capitalist critique of Bible and its influence(s).

For example, Roland Boer's *Knockin' on Heaven's Door* (1999; a book in many ways prefaced by Boer 1997) was an early, full-length monograph devoted to the study of the Bible in/and mass culture. Boer notes that a handful of volumes preceded his own work, largely edited volumes of collected essays that did not engage the broader history of cultural studies. Boer is a Marxist, arguing societies are divided, hierarchically, into categories of production and consumption where higher, more altern (to use Althusser's term) groups enjoy privilege and benefit from the labor and production of subaltern groups. The subaltern communities are often exploited, though, as Gramsci has observed, and often also are participating themselves, willingly, in the system(s) of exploitation.

Boer outlines the general history of cultural studies as represented by the classic CCCS literature. He notes that the academic field of religion, particularly theology and biblical studies, historically is mother to numerous other academic subfields, and these fields generated the field of cultural studies. Cultural studies was coming home. For Boer, biblical scholarship is (and always is) cultural studies. Boer seeks to undermine the "censor" of broader culture – the cultural norms (often driven by implicit metanarratives) that determine what is "high" and "low" culture, what is "vulgar" and what is "refined," what is "correct" and "incorrect" in interpretation, what is "sacred" and what is "profane," – as he reads the Bible alongside popular fiction, rock-and-roll music (including heavy metal), pornography, and the fast-food industry.

Another significant scholar of this early work is Stephen D. Moore. Moore began his work exploring postmodern modes of reading, and as his work developed during his years on the faculty of the University of Sheffield, his interest shifted from analysis of language and theory of interpretation to exploration of popular modes of biblical appropriation and interpretation, with specific interest in cultural constructions of gender and power/hierarchy. Alongside editing two significant early collections of general scholarship on Bible and popular culture (Exum and Moore 1998b; Moore 1998b), Moore explored biblical depictions of the form/image of God and their popular appropriations in his (1996) *God's Gym*. His interest was how these images inscribe gender identity for God and how this inscribed gender identity appropriated by popular culture both created and perpetuated expectations of both divine and masculine power. Moore followed this with his 2001 *God's Beauty Parlor*.[4] Many of the same themes (gender, power, cultural constructions of hierarchy) persist in this work, as well. Moore's focus moves toward Jesus and toward explicit analysis of gender, sexuality, and sexual preference with a particular focus on what culture deems as "queer" sexual identity. Examining "queerness" reveals cultural modes of constructing "normal" identity and expression that, in turn, reveals systems of cultural domination. Moore's work is characterized by a relentless interest in and precision toward theory.

## It's in the Mix: Cultural Studies as Intertextuality

In American biblical criticism on popular culture and cultural studies, it would be difficult to underestimate the influence of Fernando Segovia. Writing in 1995, he defined and defended cultural studies of the Bible, grounding it within traditionally "postmodern" and literary approaches to biblical criticism. For Segovia, cultural studies is an opportunity for the critic to examine her own context-driven reading assumptions and investment(s).

> It is the role assigned to the reader that, without doubt, most sharply differentiates cultural studies from other competing paradigms in contemporary biblical criticism. For cultural studies the reader does not and

---

4 A significant hallmark of Moore's work during this period was his use of autobiographical criticism and his interest in the emerging methodology of "new historicism." The former foregrounded the experience of the critic-as-reader in overt ways; the latter famously foregrounds the interpretive significance of "popular" or mass history and experience. Cultural studies, in many ways, fused these interests around questions of subjectivity and "meaning." One could argue that contemporary work in affect criticism is the continuation of all these various strands. Notably, Moore is a major contributor to the development of affect theory in/ and biblical scholarship.

> cannot remain … in the background, even if so wished and attempted, but is actively and inevitably involved in the production and meaning of "texts" and history.[5]

Segovia argued that cultural studies readings of the Bible expose the way systems and ideologies worked to create culturally altern groups – specifically via colonial engagement and race and ethnicity. Following the work of the CCCS, biblical scholarship has maintained a principal focus on contemporary popular culture (vs. examination of ancient mass culture, as one might anticipate among biblicists. Exum and Moore 1998a, p. 39; Moore 1998a, pp. 2–3). In part, I would argue that this is because of the way Segovia's seminal definition justifies cultural criticism by embedding it in the experience of the (contemporary) Bible reader, but also because his rationale, within the field of biblical studies, was itself an implicit rejection of traditional historical-grammatical exegetical work (which often asserts that the reader/interpreter is merely a conduit, neutrally discerning "meaning" after scholarly reconstruction of both text and context).

Segovia was reflecting a long conversation in the humanities surrounding the growing complexity of thought regarding "meaning" in texts and language. Under modernism, structuralist approaches to language (and critical theory) sought out the inherent "structures" in language, literature, indeed even in human thought itself. Human communication (and culture) produced a series of signs and signifiers. The task of the interpreter was to deduce the Signified. This worked on macro level (to interpret a document, story, narrative, etc.) and on the level of individual word (or, indeed, any specific Sign). The process of encoding and decoding Signs and Signifiers revealed a universalism, a commonality in human cognition.

Reflecting, however, notions of the *post*modern (such as Lyotard), *post*structuralism emerged in continental philosophy and critical theory in the late twentieth century. Essentially, these approaches denied any sense of universality in cognition, meaning or communication, challenging systems that simplified signifier–sign relationships. "Meaning" was a process, a construction, that varied from encounter to encounter. What a Sign (or a text) might "mean" varied based upon the interpreter, who brought her own sets of skills, insights, information, ignorance, and agendas to the process of interpretation. Meaning was constructed and constantly varied.

The Russian linguist and critical theorist Mikhail Bakhtin argued that language and meaning were dialogic. Bakhtin noted that words most commonly get

---

5 Segovia 1995, Vol. 2, p. 12. Segovia would later refine this, writing that cultural studies is a "joint critical study of texts and readers," 2000, p. 30.

their meaning from their use in context (much more than from their codification in "standard" lists or lectionaries. Indeed, good lectionaries collect usages and determine word definitions from those contexts). Bakhtin (see esp. Bakhtin 1994) argued that a sentence is a "conversation" between its words, larger (external) grammar systems, histories of interpretation, scholarship and more – these latter mitigated through the experience of the reader. In an act of interpretation, there are three "voices" in dialog – text, author, and reader – but each node of this conversation is, itself, enmeshed in a series of contexts and conversations.

Bakhtin was a key influence on Roland Barthes. Barthes famously wrote his pivotal essay "death of the author" ("le mort de l'auteur") in 1967 (note as well Logic 2013 for helpful overview). This essay was originally published as a pamphlet in a "journal" that was really a series of items – of signifiers – collected in a box. Ironically, in its own context, Barthes's essay was the most conventional, at least in form. Barthes argued that authors (he preferred the term "scriptor") vanish after writing. Meaning was a construction of the reader who brought their own experiences, insights, and ideas – including the influence of all other things, all other Signs and Signifiers, they knew and had "read."

Julia Kristeva was a student of Barthes, attending his Paris seminar on Bakhtin. In her own work on Bakhtin (Kristeva 1969) she argued for interpretation as a form of "intertextuality." A reader brings with her all the other "texts" she has encountered in her construction of reading. Signs (in our case, "texts" or items in culture) are actually vast networks of other signs (for us, other texts or items of culture) linked by the experience and engagement of the reader. Readers create meaning, but do so via the dialog of all semiotic exchange. For many biblical scholars "intertextuality" is reduced to an analysis of the ways in which one biblical text cites or quotes another text. An obvious moment would be the use of Hebrew Bible in the writings of Paul, or the use of written sources, such as Q, by the gospel authors. More subtle would be the appearance of Bible in subsequent western art, literature, film and mass culture. Such can be (indeed often is) little more than an analysis of where and how the Bible is cited (often with critique as to whether Bible is being used "correctly"). It may also, however, influenced by Kristeva and the conversation among poststructuralists before her, be an example of Segovia's challenge – where modern Bible readers are acknowledging that the "meaning" of a biblical book is constructed in the viewer via the interanimation of encounter – that the "signifier" and "signified" are dialogic. Many critics don't realize it, but they are doing an intertextual reading – pointing out how culture does or doesn't use the Bible, but quietly evaluating the same, generally based on the way they as interpreters have been trained to read, in order to produce readings of both Bible and culture that reflect their own roles as interpreters.

The changes to cultural studies among biblical scholars, which were anticipated by Exum and Moore, have been revealed to be the combination of

Segovia's interest in the location of the reader (a reader herself embedded in, and influenced by, mass culture) wedded to work also drawing from Kristeva's notion of "intertextuality."[6] Moving beyond the individual and her role as reader (and the attendant emphasis upon contemporary culture), a second line of scholarship has focused on reception history or "biblical afterlives," looking at systems of interpretation and ideological engagement with the Bible.

Kristevan "intertextuality" as a mode of scholarship on Bible and/in mass culture explores the inter-animation of "texts." Often highly disparate works – separated from one another by varied genre, chronology, language, or purpose – reflect or reveal a mutual interest in theme, ideology, and even structure. This may be because of intentional citation or allusion, but it is often via the analysis and close reading of a reader who brings her own interests and creates her own resonances and connections. Intertextuality is intentional "eisegesis" via comparative reading (though, most intertextual critics would argue all exegesis is, in the end, eisegetical). As intertextuality has entered cultural studies the meaning of "text" has been expanded to include recorded music, film, still image, web text, and more. Analogous to the knowledge potentially gained by comparative anatomy, the examination of moments of Intertextuality can reveal "this is that" analogies and parallels exposing implicit themes, ideas, or motives in both works; it can also clarify how more transparent structures "work" to create meaning. Intertextual approaches, rooted in scholarship of subjectivity, frequently took gender and feminist interests as a critical lens for examination of Bible in/and mass culture. Feminism has had a particular interest in the way images in general and film in particular construct and reflect popular ideas of the feminine ideal and gendered behavior, particularly asking (sometimes pointed) questions about the location of the viewer's "gaze." Images of women both create and perpetuate cultural norms about feminine beauty, for example. Yet, these images, as images, also draw the viewer/consumer into participation in this construction. As we watch or gaze, we become collaborators with the perpetuation of these larger cultural norms.

Yvonne Sherwood's (2001) analysis of the "afterlives" of the biblical character Jonah – how Jonah's myth and image were used in later Judeo-Christian art to create or reinforce ideology of later generations – is an example and early landmark in the formal development of "reception criticism" (on "reception history"

---

6 For early work, see Bach 1994, 1996, 1997. Much of this work arose from studies devoted to exploring the Bible in visual images and in film and had a notably feminist interest, as per Exum 1998, pp. 3–4; Pippin 1996; Aichele and Pippin 1997. Bach's early work in advancing cultural studies and popular culture among biblical scholars is difficult to underestimate. She founded, for example, the journal *Biblicon* for this express purpose and was early, and vocally, engaged in creating space for such work at the annual meeting of the Society of Biblical Literature. On intertextuality and cultural studies readings, note in particular Aichele 2000.

note, to begin, England and Lyons 2015). Some key studies consider popular or mass cultural items from the past (See, for examples, Seesengood and Koosed 2013; Koosed 2011; Clanton 2006; Conway 2017). Reception criticism has become an increasingly broad approach to biblical criticism, generating major reference and research works such as The Blackwell Bible Commentary[7] or the impressively ambitious *Encyclopedia of the Bible and Its Reception* published by Walter de Gruyter and the SBL Press series The Bible and Its Reception.[8]

Work on the Bible in popular culture has expanded dramatically. The annual meeting of the Society of Biblical Literature now has several sections dedicated to popular culture, cultural studies, and the Bible in various forms of modern media. As I will discuss, several new monograph series with a focus on various aspects of Bible and popular culture/cultural studies have emerged. As this work has expanded, methodological structure has become even more diffuse, though still tending to orbit around issues of discovery of "meaning" and interpretation(s) of/in biblical text, the role of Bible in popular culture for the construction of identity (particularly gender), and center largely on visual images, film (including television), and music. This latter focus has foregrounded, for some, questions about the borders between work that is categorized as "high" and "low/mass" culture and the difference and similarity between "professional" and "popular/mass" interpretation.

On survey of some contemporary work in Bible and popular culture we find elements of "popular culture" examined by biblical scholars vary widely, but cluster (when they do) around (contemporary) mass entertainment. For example, Sawyer's *The Blackwell Companion to Bible and Culture* demonstrates the breadth of the influence of the Bible in various forms of popular culture such as film, literature, music, and the visual arts, but also theater, architecture, and the Victorian circus (Sawyer 2006). Timothy K. Beal (2012) has written on the Bible as a cultural and mass publishing phenomenon, and has also examined the Bible and its role in American folk religion and tourism (2005). These themes echo work on the current state of popular "biblical literacy" (Edwards 2015; note, as well, Elliott and Boer 2012) and in critique of the American Bible tourism destination without equal: the Museum of the Bible (Baden and Moss 2017). Scholars have examined the role of the Bible in popular political rhetoric in America

---

7 Blackwell Bible Commentaries, edited by John Sawyer, Christopher Rowland, Judith Kovacs and David M. Gunn. Each of the 28 individually authored volumes is subtitled "Through the Centuries."

8 *The Encyclopedia of the Bible and Its Reception*, ed. Christine Helmer, Steven Linn McKenzie, Thomas Chr. Römer, Jens Schröter, Barry Dov Walfish, and Eric Ziolkowski. It is published in print, but latest versions are available online at https://www.degruyter.com/view/db/ebr.

(Berlinerblau 2008) and in England (Crossley 2014, 2018). The Bible's role in selling more than just political ideology – indeed, its place within the crass, very mass, world of modern advertising – has also received notice (Edwards 2012). Much work has been devoted to the Bible in various mass entertainment media, from comic books (Clanton 2012) to pop music (Gilmour 2005, 2004, 2009; Clanton 2009; Leneman 2007) but especially to film.[9]

Despite long-running interest at Society of Biblical Literature meetings and conferences, little of this scholarship, to date, has trickled down into the society's premier journal: the *Journal of Biblical Literature*. A number of essays, however, have appeared in the society's monograph series Semeia Studies. Some significant journals that have been leaders in reception criticism and popular culture are *Biblical Interpretation* and *Bible and Critical Theory*. Surprisingly, much of the work on the Bible and popular culture appears in various monograph series. Indeed, these are, at the time of this writing, not only prominent but proliferating. Some series titles include Biblical Intersections (Gorgias), The Bible and Its Reception (Society of Biblical Literature), The Bible and the Moving Image (Walter de Grutyer), Biblical Reception and The Bible in the Age of Capital (Rowman & Littlefield) and The Bible in the Modern World (Sheffield Phoenix). In the late 1990s, major publishers included Routledge, T & T Clark, Continuum, and Sheffield Academic Press.

## Assembling the Pieces: Reception, Deleuzian Machines, Affect

The first waves of CCCS and Marxist-influenced Bible and cultural studies criticism looked at *why* the Bible was used in/as culture, at what was produced, arguing that the goal was creation and regulation of group status and systems of (hegemony) and control. Via attention to intertextuality, cultural studies has unveiled with increasing depth and acumen *where* and *when* Bible appears, noting how the juxtaposition is, itself, a form of interpretation and meaning making. An emerging body of work, focused upon affect and the creation of cultural meaning-making "machines" has taken on the question of *how* these intertextual moments produce meaning.

"Affect" in cultural or literary criticism may, superficially, be taken to mean the emotional significance and impact of a given work. It is rooted, however, in

---

9 The study of film and television is, without serious challenge, the broadest category of work on Bible and popular culture. A very select review of recent, methodology/survey oriented work (particularly multiauthor collections, which are good places for beginning reading) should include Burnette-Bletsch 2016; Copier and Vander Stichele 2016; Reinhartz 2012, 2013; and Walsh 2018.

psychology, particularly the work of Silvan Tomkins. Tomkins (Tomkins 1962–1992) identified a series of precognitive reactions, functioning as memes or ciphers for engaged thought. Tompkins would eventually collect his thinking into nine affects: distress-anguish, interest-excitement, enjoyment-joy, surprise-startle, anger-rage, fear-terror, shame-humiliation, disgust, and dissmell (avoidance). These reactions are innate and from birth. They are not, in themselves, emotions or feelings; "feeling" is our term for our awareness of them. Awareness of affect (feeling) plus memory produces emotion. Affect is inherent in an object, as well. It is an involuntary response. Something has affected us, producing a cascading avalanche of affect-memes, feelings, memories, emotions and finally thoughts (and actions).

Tomkins's work has influenced critical theory and the humanities via two general streams (see, in general Gregg and Seigworth 2009; Kotrosits 2016 or Koosed and Moore 2014b). The first, crystalized in the work of Eve Sedgwick, focuses on the psycho-biological aspects of affect (esp. Sedgewick 2003). Her work, and those influenced by it, is particularly interested in the way we construct a sense of identity and self. Literary and cultural studies influenced by her (particularly biblical scholarship that engages pop culture) examine the way meaning is broader than "reasoned" or "rational" aware engagement – that bodies, traumas, memories, and emotions are both influencing us as readers *and* embedded in books and culture themselves.

A second is work drawing from Giles Deleuze and Felix Guattari (Deleuze and Guattari 1980; seen by some as the natural extension of "postmodern" biblical criticism, e.g. Moore 2023). Deleuze concentrates on the moment of encounter and exchange between object and its perception – the potential in the moment of juxtaposition and exchange, the transfer of the affect. Appropriately, Deleuze has been quite influential on an array of work engaging the "posthuman" – scholarship that looks at how items in culture, cultural systems, and other "nonhuman" things (including, most obviously, the natural world and the animal) possess a form of agency and autonomy. Culture is produced by humans, yet it also, itself, *produces* humans – both making them, as an organism, "human" (as opposed to just another ape) *and* scripting to/for a culture what it recognizes and values as humane.

Three essay collections have been crucial to the introduction of affect criticism into biblical studies. Moore and Bray have edited a collection of essays by leading scholars in affect, encouraging each to think specifically about how their work intersects with religious studies (Bray and Moore 2020). Emerging from this theory work are two specific collections on affect in biblical studies – one edited by Jennifer Koosed and Stephen Moore (Koosed and Moore 2014a), the other edited by Fiona Black and Jennifer Koosed (Black and Koosed 2019; note also Kotrosits 2015).

Scholarship in posthuman studies has entered biblical scholarship initially via work on animals and animality (note, for example, Schaefer 2015). What does it mean to describe one being as "animal" and the other as "human?" What are the differences (or lack of difference) between their forms of cognition and experience? What are their obligations to one another (and in what ways do culture – and Bible – create ideologies or structures that affect planetary life? Should they?)? Both Hannah Strømmen (Strømmen 2018) and Ken Stone (Stone 2017) have written effectively on these questions, and the collection edited by Moore assembles an array of critical work by biblical scholars (2014). Koosed expands this collection, and augments it with work moving more toward general "posthuman" studies in her edited collection of 2016 (Koosed 2014).

In thinking of the agency of Things – what can, for example, a Bible *do* in culture? Is it completely inert or does it have a form of agency in the communities it constructs? – nods again to the work of Giles Deleuze. Deleuze and Guatarri somewhat famously have referred to books (and other items such as music, painting, film, etc.) as meaning generating machines. Constructed by "authors" the book fuses an array of cultural symbols, signs, codes, memories, and more in affective ways. The Book is not invested with meaning; the Book becomes an assemblage, a machine that functions together to create "meaning."

Again, several recent works of biblical scholarship explore the notion of the agency of Things (and of Bibles). Seesengood and Wilson have collected a series of essays exploring object-oriented ontology or "new materialism" in biblical studies (Seesengood and Wilson 2020a, b). Their essays take seriously the meaningfulness of Things (and question the limits of what we intend by "agency" and "action"). Two extremely provocative studies of Bible and New Materialism are those by Anne Elvey (Elvey 2005, 2011) and Maia Kotrosits (2020). Elvey demonstrates the transition from posthuman through ecofeminism to arrive at new materialism in her 2005 "Matter, Freedom and the Future." Kotrosits (long a leading voice in affect and biblical studies) turns her attention to the affective agency of Things in her 2020 *The Lives of Objects*. Affect, posthumanism, animal studies, and new materialism have, more and more often, begun to coalesce in studies of mass culture (see Sencindirer 2017; Grusin 2015; Coole and Frost 2010; Bennett and Joyce 2010); we may expect the same in biblical studies.

## The Plan of This Book

*American Standard* is a series of essays, case studies, that demonstrate all these methodological lenses in cultural studies by a series of essays ranging across several aspects of twentieth and early twenty-first century American pop culture. I will sort these essays into three major sections, each exploring one of the critical lenses (classical CCCS and Marxist, intertextuality, and affect/posthuman studies). The essays will review methodology, literature, and assumptions but will do so via an original reading and interpretation of Bible. In each section, the three essays are sequenced from simpler to more nuanced methodology and subtlety; each runs a bit further afield into critical theory than the last, and the third essay is often a bridge into the next triad. The book will end with a conclusion that reviews the sweep of the all the work presented in the book and that suggests ways to integrate methods/foci into a productive reading of Bible in US mass culture, with a particular focus on race and political division the current crisis points in US culture.

Part I, "From CCCS to Late Capitalism" collects three essays that each draw from themes set by landmark CCCS scholarship or themes (or "CCCS adjacent" for the case of Chapter 3) and benefit from the CCCS attention to Gramsci and Althusser and Jameson's "late capitalism." All three (at least implicitly) rely on Marxist structures and logics (if not, necessarily, explicit argument). All three foreground the CCCS focus on the false binary of "high" and "low" culture, with attention to mass consumption and "popular" items being as meritorious as attention to – and scholarly rigor regarding – protected, "canonical" high or classical culture (in this case, we are also explicitly engaging with Bible and biblical scholarship). The essays take as their inspiration such foundational classical studies worthies as F. R. Levis, Richard Hoggart, Stuart Hall, and Michel de Certeau.

Chapter 2 is "Reading Readers: Modern Evangelicalism's Material (Biblical) Renaissance." If the Bible's (self?) designation as The Good Book is challenged by some, there is little question that publishing Bibles (and books about the Bible) has been good for the book business. There is an abundance of printed Bibles to line the shelves of stores or pages of web-catalogs. Bibles are produced in a variety of English translations. Many have special notes or reference systems to lead readers into the secrets of the Bible's meaning. Bibles are marketed to specific markets – men, women, youths, to a variety of denominations, racial and sexual identities, even to non-believers. Bible production – and Bible *consumption* – form a major segment of the US book market, and have been for centuries. This chapter will argue that, in the US context, individuals and communities often define themselves by the items they consume. This seems particularly true of evangelicals, one of the largest Bible-buying segments in the United States. Using Jameson's notion of late capitalism, this essay will examine Bibles, themselves, as cultural products and will read Bible production, and consumption, as a device for identity and culture construction.

Chapter 3 is titled "Graphic Bibles: The Word Becomes (Affecting) Image." Drawings and paintings have been used to represent biblical stories and characters for nearly as long as there has been a Bible. Contemporary scholarship has explored several genres of graphic representation of the Bible: "Bible-zines," "children's" Bible illustrations, evangelistic tracts (ChickTracks), and more. The Bible has also been rendered as a graphic novel. One very recent and very engaging Bible-comic is Robert Crumb's *Genesis*. When artists make the necessary decisions for depicting a biblical scene or story, they must make interpretations. What race, for example, were Adam and Eve? In this chapter, I will be exploring how Crumb "translates" biblical text into a new medium.

Chapter 4 takes up de Certau's notion of "everyday life" in/and cultural studies. "'Eat This Book': The Bible and the American Diet," will explore the notions of "biblical eating," an increasingly complex matrix of issues and concerns. Recent scholarship, for example, has addressed: the origins and transformation of the food production companies of Kellogg's and Welch's, the changing definition of kosher and kosher demarcation, the recent rise of "biblical vegetarianism," the Bible's role in contemporary discussions over the environment and animal rights, modern weight loss-via-Bible-guidance movements (Weigh Down Watchers, etc.) and contemporary evangelical "reclamation" of biblical kosher regulations. The chapter will explore several of these food-Bible intersections and will ask what these modern engagements reveal about the structure, content, and practicality of biblical instructions regarding food.

In Part II, "The Intertextual Bible," Chapters 5–8, I will be looking at Bible and cultural studies as a moment of intertextuality. For the most part, these essays will conform to what one finds in the majority of US criticism of Bible in pop culture that is emerging from biblical studies circles. In general, this work is looking at ways Bible appears in mass culture (with a focus on film and television), and comparing this use to formal scholarship of the Bible (noting either commonalities, correcting pop culture, or demonstrating pop culture is a form, itself, of interpretation). These essays will proceed from those more explicit in their invocation of Bible to the more allusive. As before, these essays will largely demonstrate their critical underpinning via an original reading of both Bible and US mass culture. As we progress, as well, the essays will argue more and more that attention to intertextual engagement with the Bible in media can not only tell us how the Bible has been interpreted, but might even incline us (as per traditional, professional academic commentary) to new understandings of the Bible's contents, themselves.

Chapter 5 is "The Ketuvim in the Coenim: Bible and Apocalyptic in the Films of Joel and Ethan Coen." Film critic A.O. Scott, when reviewing Joel and Ethan Coen's 2009 *A Serious Man*, commented on how this film, unlike their others, directly engaged both Judaica and the Bible. In some ways, Scott is quite correct. None of their films invoke Jewish-American culture or the rabbis on the scale seen in *A Serious Man*, and the Coens rarely to never directly refer to Torah. Yet I would take issue with suggestions that the Coens are sparing or reserved in their use of Bible. They have a particular penchant for the Ketuvim. Alongside *Serious Man*'s use of the narrative of Job (and also Ecclesiastes), the

Psalms appear in *The Big Lebowski* and *O Brother, Where Art Thou*. The book of Daniel has made several cameos (*Big Lebowski, Ladykillers,* and *Barton Fink*) where the Coens use the text of Daniel to establish a general "apocalyptic" tone for the film establishing an early warning of deadly chaos to come. When the Coens turn to Job or the Psalms, they also invoke themes of death and divine judgment (i.e. *Lebowski's* famous funeral home scene or the closing whirlwind of *Serious Man*). I will argue that the Coens use biblical text much in the way they use set/location (*Fargo, No Country for Old Men,* etc.) or cinematography (particularly their reliance on Roger Deakins's trademark light-and-shadow): to create a context of surreality, vacant-yet-dangerous space, and dramatic foreboding. In contrast, then, to Scott, I will argue that biblical literature, particularly the Ketuvim, regularly composes the very "landscape" of the Coen brothers' imagination and vision. The early proto-apocalyptic elements in the Ketuvim, to the Coens, invoke the mystery, absence and risk that, in part, constructs a space for drama to unfold. In turn, the Coen's use reveals the apocalyptic tenor of traditional "wisdom" literature like Job and Ecclesiastes.

Chapter 6 is "'Do Not Forsake Me': Biblical Motifs in Zinnemann's *High Noon*," looks at the use of Bible in US Western movies and literature. Jane Tomkins has argued Westerns are a form of American myth making, exploring identity, gender, and space. Stanley Corkin has argued Westerns reflect Cold War struggles and opportunities. Peter French has asserted that Westerns interpret and subvert Judeo-Christian ethics regarding death and violence. All three scholars identify Zinnemann's *High Noon* as both a landmark in the genre and exemplar of how Westerns "work." *High Noon* uses biblical motifs of the Day of the Lord, "forsakenness," and the personifications of Wisdom and Folly as women to articulate that violence is necessary for true peace, civility, liberty, and honor. Such violence is likened to divine judgment. Understanding this is divine wisdom.

Finally, Chapter 7 is "God's Dice: The Bible in/and Sci-Fi and Fantasy Gaming." This chapter explores the role of biblical images and themes in sci-fi and fantasy role playing games, in both "tabletop" and video game formats. These games, largely emerging during the 1980s remain exceptionally popular today, particularly among US males – both teen and adult. Despite fears of "satanism" and corruption of young minds by evil powers (or spirits), the gaming industry has grown to become a multibillion-dollar annual industry spread into general merchandise, books, television, and film. Various gaming systems invoke several themes, motifs, and characters from mythology in general and the Bible in particular. Overwhelmingly, these symbols draw from apocalyptic literature with key characters such as Satan and key themes such as cosmic war between forces of Good (sometimes "order") and Evil (or chaos). Focusing on Games Workshops *"Warhammer"* franchise, this chapter will explore how these themes provide a "thick" context of cosmic implication for the game but also reflect a real ambivalence. "Good vs. Evil" provides a superficial frame narrative, but the struggle, in the game as in Revelation, often results in authoritarian overreach and fascism. This chapter will argue that biblical text *from Revelation* are chosen precisely because this book, with its motifs of God's wrath, itself struggles with the same tensions.

The third and last part, "Affective Machines: Deleuze, Cultural Studies, and the Next Wave," is the most theoretically dense. I have collected three essays (Chapters 8–10) that intersect with emerging work in both cultural studies and biblical studies on affect and Giles Deleuze's notion of culture/books as assemblage. These essays, again, are ordered so as to proceed from more conventional expectations of "Bible in popular culture" to more theoretically dense work, culminating in post-humanism and new materialism.

In Chapter 8, I open with an essay that examines cultural construction of "Truth" and the commodification – and group co-option – of "nonfiction" or cultural literacy. Chapter 8 is titled "Mysteries of the Bible Documentary: The Bible in Popular Nonfiction Documentary Film." This chapter will examine an array of books and (mostly made-for-TV) documentaries on the Bible. I will examine serious academic resources alongside clearly devotional and faith building documentaries and the somewhat titillating "Lost Bible Discovered" variety of documentary. My focus will be films about the historical Jesus and Noah's ark. Using the techniques of film and documentary studies, this chapter would look at how these documentaries are constructing an experience for the viewer.

Chapter 9 is "'I (Want to) Believe, Lord; Help Me in My Unbelief': Revelation, Raëleans, Mayans, and North American Pop Eschatology." In 1997, 39 members of a UFO cult called "Heaven's Gate" took their own life in their southern California compound. They were convinced an alien spaceship was approaching earth, hiding in the tail of the Hale–Bopp comet. Their shocking act made many scholars aware of the burgeoning world of UFO religions. UFO religions, in many ways, mirror aspects of religious expression found in more mainstream religious communities; given that most UFO religions are located in the United States and Britain, they have a particular tendency to adopt and adapt elements of Judeo-Christian practice. For example, some UFO believers argue that the Bible, itself, is a record of human interaction with alien life (the Raëleans, for example). Other communities (the Urantians) have drafted their own "Bibles," often claiming to have been possessed ("inspired?") by an alien intelligence. The tendency of UFO aficionados to identify "pilgrimage" sites (Roswell, New Mexico) and celebrate a UFO material culture is very resonant with Jewish and Christian devotion to the Bible. This chapter will explore the parallels between some communities of UFO aficionados and some communities of dedicated Bible readers.

And, finally, Chapter 10 is titled "Bespoke Words: The Bible, Fashion, and the Mechanism(s) of Things" and uses Bible and fashion as entry points into work on new materialism and object-oriented ontology. Elizabeth Chin's elegant *My Life with Things: The Consumer Diaries* is late-capitalist and new materialist review of Things and their accumulation and assemblage into complex systems of consumption that fuse subjectivity materiality. Theories of seamless materiality and subjectivity are also critical to Deleuze's idea of "assemblage," and Chin tacks this pattern to her reading of Marx, the politics of anthropology, and her relationship to the material things near and around her. Few materials are nearer or more enveloping than our clothing. Not merely providing warmth and protection, through mechanisms of fashion and the culture that emerges from it, clothing communicates our community, socioeconomic status, and sometimes occupation. Clothing and fashion create the identity we want to project and expose us in ways we don't realize or intend. Fashion and clothing are not just about the garments we put on, but the bodies we dress and the identities we wear (Damhorst, Miller, and Michelman 2000, pp. 12–17). Fashion, though itself just an assemblage of "things," produces emotions like joy, anxiety, desire, disgust, attraction, and alienation. As Brian Massumi might argue, clothing and the fashion industry behind it are (affective) assemblage. They amalgamate an array of materials, practices, and histories, all knit into complex mechanisms of affect, meaning, and ideology. This chapter hopes to tailor these conversations for examination of biblical passages on-and-about clothing and fashion (and the array of scholarly and interpretive communities arising from them). Biblical passages about clothing regulations, body ornament and body display are significant to many confessional readers and to many feminist and queer biblical scholars. As I read biblical text and survey some of its interpretation, I will argue that, like the clothing that we wear, the Bible is an active Thing, creating, through an assemblage of materials, concepts, and affects, social order and subjectivity. Like clothing, Bible is (after Deleuze and Massumi) a machine producing more machines, and biblical criticism is an industry of consumption and display not unlike fashion; in a strange fusion of materiality and agency, Bible and biblical interpretation shroud our body in affective tapestries, weaving themes of concealment and display, stitching and altering the material and social worlds we inhabit.

## Works Cited

Adorno, T.W. (1991). *The Culture Industry; Selected Essays on Mass Culture* (ed. J.M. Bernstein)). London: Routledge.

Aichele, G. (2000). *Culture, Entertainment and the Bible*, Library of the Hebrew Bible/Old Testament Supplement Series, vol. 309. Sheffield: Sheffield Academic Press.

Aichele, G. and Pippin, T. (1997). *The Monstrous and the Unspeakable: The Bible as Fantastic Literature*. New York: Routledge.

Althusser, L. (1969). *For Marx*. London: Allen Lane.

Althusser, L. and Balibar, E. (1968). *Reading Capital*. London: New Left Books.

Bach, A. (ed.) (1994). *The Bible and Popular Culture. Biblical Interpretation* 2 (1).

Bach, A. (ed.) (1996). *Biblical Glamour and Hollywood Glitz*, Semeia Studies, vol. 74. Atlanta, GA: Society of Biblical Literature.

Bach, A. (ed.) (1997). *Women, Seduction and Betrayal in Biblical Narrative*. Cambridge: Cambridge University Press.

Baden, J. and Moss, C. (2017). *Bible Nation: The United States of Hobby-Lobby*. Princeton, NJ: Princeton University Press.

Bakhtin, M. (1994). *Speech, Genres and Other Essays*. Austin, TX: University of Texas Press.

Barthes, R. (1967). The death of the author. In: *Image-Music-Texts* (trans. S. Heath), 142–148. London: Fontana Press.

Beal, T.K. (2005). *Roadside Religion: In Search of the Sacred, Strange and the Substance of Faith*. Boston: Beacon Hill.

Beal, T.K. (2012). *The Rise and Fall of the Bible: The Unexpected History of an Accidental Book*. New York: Mariner Books.

Bennett, T. and Joyce, P. (ed.) (2010). *Material Powers: Cultural Studies, History and the Material Turn*. New York: Routledge.

Berlinerblau, J. (2005). *The Secular Bible: Why Nonbelievers Must Take Religion Seriously*. Cambridge: Cambridge University Press.

Berlinerblau, J. (2008). *Thumpin' It: The Use and Abuse of the Bible in Today's Presidential Politics*. Louisville, KY: Westminster John Knox Press.

Black, F. and Koosed, J.L. (ed.) (2019). *Reading with Feeling: Affect Theory and the Bible*, Semeia Studies, vol. 95. Atlanta, GA: Society of Biblical Literature Press.

Boer, R. (1997). *Novel Histories: The Fiction of Biblical Criticism*. Sheffield: Sheffield Academic Press.

Boer, R. (1999). *Knockin' on Heaven's Door*. New York: Routledge.

Boer, R. (2007). *Rescuing the Bible*. Blackwell Manifestos. London: Blackwell.

Bray, K. and Moore, S.D. (ed.) (2020). *Religion, Emotion, Sensation: Affect Theories and Theologies*. New York: Fordham.

Burnette-Bletsch, R. (ed.) (2016). *The Bible in Motion: A Handbook of the Bible and its Reception in Film*. 2 vols., Handbooks of the Bible and Its Reception. Leiden: De Gruyter.

Butsch, R. (1990). *For Fun and Profit: The Transformation of Leisure to Consumption*. Philadelphia: Temple University Press.

Clanton, D.W. (2006). *The Good, the Bold, and the Beautiful: The Story of Susanna and Its Renaissance Interpretations*, Library of Hebrew Bible/Old Testament Studies, vol. 430. London: T & T Clark.

Clanton, D.W. (2009). *Daring, Disrespectful and Devout: Interpreting the Bible's Women in the Arts and Music*. New York: Continuum.

Clanton, D.W. (ed.) (2012). *The End Will Be Graphic: Apocalyptic in Comic Books and Graphic Novels*, Bible in the Modern World, vol. 43; Apocalypse and Popular Culture, 5. Sheffield: Sheffield Phoenix.

Conway, C.M. (2017). *Sex and Slaughter in the Tent of Jael: A Cultural History of a Biblical Story*. Oxford: Oxford University Press.

Coole, D. and Frost, S. (ed.) (2010). *New Materialisms: Ontology, Agency and Politics*. Durham: Duke University Press.

Copier, L. and Vander Stichele, C. (ed.) (2016). *Close Encounters Between Bible and Film: An Interdisciplinary Engagement*, Semeia Studies, vol. 87. Atlanta, GA: Society of Biblical Literature Press.

Crossley, J. (2014). *Jesus in an Age of Neoliberalism: Quests, Scholarship and Ideology*. New York: Routledge.

Crossley, J. (2018). *Cults, Martyrs & Good Samaritans: Religion in Contemporary English Political Discourse*. London: Pluto.

Damhorst, M.L., Miller, K.A., and Michelman, S.O. (ed.) (2000). *The Meanings of Dress*. New York: Fairchild Publications.

Deleuze, G. and Guattari, F. (1980). *A Thousand Plateaus* (trans. B. Massumi). Minneapolis, MN: University of Minnesota Press.

During, S. (ed.) (1993). *The Cultural Studies Reader*, 2e. New York: Routledge.

During, S. (1996). From the new historicism to cultural studies. In: *Institutions and Cultures: Theory and Practice* (ed. R. Lumsden and R. Patke), 53–83. Amsterdam: Rodopli.

Edwards, K. (2012). *Admen and Eve: The Bible in Contemporary Advertising*, Bible in the Modern World. Sheffield: Sheffield Phoenix.

Edwards, K. (ed.) (2015). *Rethinking Biblical Literacy*. London: T & T Clark.

Elliott, S. and Boer, R. (ed.) (2012). *Ideology Culture and Translation*, Semeia Studies, vol. 69. Atlanta, GA: Society of Biblical Literature Press.

Elvey, A.F. (2005). Matter, freedom and the future: reframing feminist theologies through an ecological materialist lens. *Feminist Theology* 23 (2): 186–204.

Elvey, A.F. (2011). *The Matter of the Text: Material Engagements between Luke and the Five Senses*, The Bible in the Modern World, vol. 37. Sheffield: Sheffield Phoenix.

England, E. and Lyons, W.J. (ed.) (2015). *Reception History and Biblical Studies: Theory and Practice*, Library of Hebrew Bible/Old Testament Studies, vol. 615; Critical Perspectives on the Reception and Influence of the Bible, 6. London: T & T Clark.

Exum, J. C. (ed.) (1998). *The Bible and the Arts. Biblical Interpretation* 6 (3–4).

Exum, J.C. and Moore, S.D. (1998a). Biblical studies/cultural studies. In: *Biblical Studies/Cultural Studies: The Third Sheffield Colloquium*, Journal for the Study of the Old Testament, Supplement Series, vol. 266; Gender, Culture and Theory, 7 (ed. J.C. Exum and S.D. Moore), 20–45. Sheffield: Sheffield Academic Press.

Exum, J.C. and Moore, S.D. (ed.) (1998b). *Biblical Studies/Cultural Studies: The Third Sheffield Colloquium*, Journal for the Study of the Old Testament, Supplement Series, vol. 266; Gender, Culture and Theory, 7. Sheffield: Sheffield Academic Press.

Gilmour, M.J. (2004). *Tangled Up in the Bible: Bob Dylan and Scripture*. New York: Continuum.

Gilmour, M.J. (ed.) (2005). *"Call Me the Seeker": Listening to Religion in Popular Music*. New York: Continuum.

Gilmour, M.J. (2009). *Gods and Guitars: Seeking the Sacred in Post-1960s Popular Music*. Waco, TX: Baylor University Press.

Gramsci, A. (1971). *Selections from the Prison Notebooks* (eds. and trans. Q. Hoare and G. N. Smith). London: Lawrence & Wishart.

Gramsci, A. (1978). *Selections from Cultural Writings* (ed. D. Forgacs and G.N. Smith). London: Lawrence & Wishart.

Gregg, M. and Steigworth, G.J. (ed.) (2009). *The Affect Theory Reader*. Durham, NC: Duke University Press.

Grusin, R. (ed.) (2015). *The Non-Human Turn*. Minneapolis, MN: University of Minneapolis Press.

Hall, S. (1980). Cultural studies: two paradigms. *Media Culture Society* 2: 57–72.

Hall, S. (1982). The rediscovery of 'ideology': return of the repressed in media studies. In: *Culture, Society and the Media* (ed. M. Gurevitch, T. Bennett, J. Curran, and J. Woolacott), 56–90. London: Methuen.

Hoggart, R. (1957). *The Uses of Literacy*. New York: Penguin.

Jameson, F. (1984). Postmodernism, or: the cultural logic of late capitalism. *New Left Review* 146: 59–92.

Jameson, F. (1991). *Postmodernism: Or, the Cultural Logic of Late Capitalism*. Durham, NC: Duke University Press.

Koosed, J. (2011). *Gleaning Ruth: A Biblical Heroine and Her Afterlives*, Studies in Personalities of the Old Testament. Columbia, SC: University of South Carolina Press.

Koosed, J. (ed.) (2014). *The Bible and Posthumanism*, Semeia Studies, vol. 74. Atlanta, GA: Society of Biblical Literature Press.

Koosed, J.L. and Moore, S.D. (ed.) (2014a). From affect to exegesis. *Biblical Interpretation* 22: 4–5.

Koosed, J.L. and Moore, S.D. (ed.) (2014b). Introduction. *Biblical Interpretation* 22 (4–5): 381–387.

Kotrosits, M. (2015). *Rethinking Early Christianity: Affect, Violence and Belonging*. Louisville, KY: Fortress Press.

Kotrosits, M. (2016). *How Things Feel: Affect Theory, Biblical Studies and the (Im) Personal*, Brill Research Perspectives. Biblical Interpretation. Leiden: Brill.

Kotrosits, M. (2020). *The Lives of Objects: Material Culture, Experience and the Real in the History of Early Christianity*, Class 200: New Studies in Religion. Chicago: University of Chicago Press.

Kristeva, J. (1969). *Desire in Language: A Semiotic Approach to Literature and Art*. New York: Columbia University Press.

Kroeber, A.L. and Kluckholm, C. (1952). *Culture: A Critical Review of Concepts and Definitions*. Cambridge, MA: Peabody Museum Press.

Leavis, F.R. (1930). *Mass Civilization and Minority Culture*. Cambridge: Cambridge University Press.

Legaspi, M. (2010). *The Death of Scripture and the Rise of Biblical Studies*, Oxford Studies in Historical Theology. New York: Oxford University Press.

Leneman, H. (2007). *The Performed Bible: The Story of Ruth in Opera and Oratorio*, Bible in the Modern World. Sheffield: Sheffield Phoenix.

Logic, J. (2013). 1967: The birth of the death of the author. *College English* 75 (5): 493–512.

Lyotard, J.-F. (1984). The Postmodern Condition: A Report on Knowledge (trans. G. Bennington and Brian Massumi). In: *Theory and History of Literature*, vol. 10. Minneapolis, MN: University of Minnesota Press.

Moore, S.D. (1996). *God's Gym: Divine Male Bodies of the Bible*. New York: Routledge.

Moore, S.D. (1998a). Between Birmingham and Jerusalem: cultural studies and biblical studies. In: *In Search of the Present: The Bible through Cultural Studies*, Semeia Studies, vol. 82 (ed. S.D. Moore), 20–45. Atlanta, GA: Society of Biblical Literature Press.

Moore, S.D. (ed.) (1998b). *In Search of the Present: The Bible through Cultural Studies.*, Semeia Studies, vol. 82. Atlanta, GA: Society of Biblical Literature Press.

Moore, S.D. (2001). *God's Beauty Parlor and Other Queer Spaces in and around the Bible*, Contraversions: Jews and Other Differences. Stanford, CA: Stanford University Press.

Moore, S.D. (ed.) (2014). *Divinanimality: Animal Theory, Creaturely Theology*. New York: Fordham University Press.

Moore, S.D. (2023). *The Bible after Deleuze: Affects, Assemblages, Bodies without Organs*. New York: Oxford University Press.

Moore, S.D. and Sherwood, Y. (2011). *The Invention of a Biblical Scholar: A Critical Manifesto*. Minneapolis, MN: Fortress.

Munns, J. and Rajan, G. (ed.) (1995). *A Cultural Studies Reader: History, Theory and Practice*. New York: Longman.

Pippin, T. (1996). *Apocalyptic Bodies: The Biblical End of the World in Text and Image*. New York: Routledge.

Radway, J. (2016). In honor of Stuart Hall. *Cultural Studies* 30 (2): 312–321.

Reinhartz, A. (ed.) (2012). *Bible and Cinema: Fifty Key Films*, Routledge Key Guides. New York: Routledge.

Reinhartz, A. (ed.) (2013). *Bible and Cinema: An Introduction*. New York: Routledge.

Sawyer, J.F.A. (ed.) (2006). *The Blackwell Companion to the Bible and Culture*. New York: Blackwell.

Schaefer, D.O. (2015). *Religious Affect: Animality, Evolution, and Power*. Durham, NC: Duke University Press.

Schein, E.H. (1984). Coming to a new awareness of organizational culture. *Sloan Management Review* 25 (2): 3–16.

Schein, E.H. (1990). Organizational culture. *American Psychologist* 45 (2): 109–119.

Sedgewick, E.K. (2003). *Touching Feelings: Affect, Pedagogy, Performativity*. Durham, NC: Duke University Press.

Seesengood, R.P. and Koosed, J.L. (2013). *Jesse's Lineage: The Legendary Lives of David, Jesus and Jesse James*, Library of the Hebrew Bible/Old Testament Studies, vol. 548; Playing the Texts, 14. London: Bloomsbury.

Seesengood, R.P. and Wilson, A. (eds.) (2020a). New materialism and the bible. *Bible and Critical Theory* 17 (2). https://www.bibleandcriticaltheory.com/issues/vol-16-no-2-2020-bible-and-critical-theory/ (accessed 16 October 2023).

Seesengood, R.P. and Wilson, A. (ed.) (2020b). Biblical stuff: the Bible and new materialism. *Bible and Critical Theory* 17 (2): 1–6.

Segovia, F. (1995). Cultural studies and contemporary biblical criticism: ideological criticism as mode of discourse. In: *Reading from This Place* (ed. F.F. Segovia and M.A. Tolbert), 1–17. Minneapolis, MN: Fortress.

Segovia, F. (2000). *Decolonizing Biblical Studies: A View from the Margins*. Maryknoll, NY: Orbis.

Sencindirer, S.Y. (2017). New Materialism. *Oxford Bibliographies*. http://Oxford bibliographies.com/display/document/obo-9780190221911/obo-9780190221911-0016.xml (accessed 17 October 2023).

Sherwood, Y. (2001). *A Biblical Text and Its Afterlives: The Survival of Jonah in Western Culture*. Cambridge: Cambridge University Press.

Stone, K. (2017). *Reading the Hebrew Bible with Animal Studies*. Stanford, CA: Stanford University Press.

Strømmen, H. (2018). *Biblical Animality after Jacques Derrida*, Semeia Studies, vol. 91. Atlanta, GA: Society of Biblical Literature Press.

Surdam, D.G. (2015). *Century of the Leisured Masses: Entertainment and the Transformation of 20th Century America*. New York: Oxford University Press.

Tomkins, S. (1962–1992). *Affect Imagery Consciousness*. 4 vols. London: Tavistock.

Tyler, E.B. (1974). *Primitive Culture*. New York: Gordon.

Wainwright, E. (2010). Introduction. In: *The Bible in/and Popular Culture: A Creative Encounter*, Semeia Studies, vol. 65 (ed. P. Culbertson and E. Wainwright), 1–9. Atlanta, GA: Society of Biblical Literature Press.

Walsh, R. (ed.) (2018). *Bloomsbury Bible and Film Handbook*. New York: Bloomsbury T & T Clark.

Williams, R. (1958). *Culture and Society 1780–1950*. London: Chatto & Windus.

Williams, R. (1996). The future of cultural studies. In: *What Is Cultural Studies? A Reader* (ed. J. Storey), 168–177. London: Arnold.

# Part I

# From CCCS to Late Capitalism

# 2

# Reading Readers

## Modern Evangelicalism's Material (Biblical) Renaissance

This opening chapter, appropriately, will examine the role of the Bible as, itself, an element in US popular culture, noting its role as a political and popular icon. For some, this is an obvious point: the Bible is an item of US culture. For others, the Bible's transcendent and long-standing role as a collection of sacred writings, the inspired word of God, means it sits outside of, if not in opposition to, popular culture. I will, in part, argue that this latter opinion, and also the vigorous resistance to it, is one way the Bible functions as an element of U.S. mass culture and works to mark (sub)cultural identity and affiliation.

In this chapter, I want to look at several questions at once. I will open with a quick review of how the Bible has been viewed in the past 200 years of US popular culture. I won't deeply treat colonial or revolutionary eras; instead I will concentrate on the more modern era after the Civil War. Another argument that I will make is that the Bible and Bible reading have long been prized by Americans, but surprisingly, not equally as much as veneration of the Bible, itself; in many ways, the Bible as icon or symbol outpaces the influence of the Bible's actual ideas, stories, and guidelines. The dissemination of the Bible was also critical to developing notions of Christian identity, and proselytism, in the United States.

My larger argument, however, is going to be this: The Bible's history in US culture has a distinct narrative. In America's earliest history, the Bible was widely assumed to be the bedrock text of American values, identity, and ethics. In the early nineteenth century, American revivalists asserted that the Bible, sincerely read, was the only thing needed (and the only authority suitable) for a Christian thinker. As postbellum America moved into the age of modernity, confidence in a self-interpreting Bible was shaken. In the early twentieth century readers wanted Bibles in contemporary English style with various annotations and study notes, a desire fueled by a growing publishing industry (and US economy) taking advantage of increasing discretionary income arising from a burgeoning economy and heavy immigration – these

*American Standard: The Bible in US Popular Culture*, First Edition. Robert Paul Seesengood.
© 2024 John Wiley & Sons Ltd. Published 2024 by John Wiley & Sons Ltd.

latter also driving increasing frustration and insecurity among citizens encountering an ever-increasing array of diverse peoples. The Bible began to move from book to symbol, and eventually to commodity. As the century progressed, more and more Bibles appeared with "value-added" content and niche marketing. As the twentieth became the twenty-first century, late capitalism and publishing markets affected Bible production. Bibles began, in fact, to be produced in formats that intentionally mimic mass media culture; the American Bible nestles into American mass culture quite comfortably.

This chapter will open with a quick look at one of these contemporary late capitalist mass market Bibles, before turning its attention to a roughly chronological "history" of US thinking about Bibles through a review of bible publishing and marketing, with a brief detour through the larger question of cultural superficiality, marketing, and consumption. We will return, in the conclusion, to our (post)modern Bibles and ask what our current culture, in its context, might be telling us about the mass appeal of the Bible and draw summary conclusions about what we've seen.

## The Bible in Late Capitalism

Scholar and author Timothy Beal, in his book *The Rise and Fall of the Bible: The Unexpected History of an Accidental Book* (2011) describes an airplane encounter with an unusual Bible:

> A twenty-something woman sitting next to me on a plane thumbs distractedly through a fashion-and-lifestyle magazine ... called *Becoming*. On the cover is a Jennifer Aniston look-alike in designer casuals.... Cover lines surround her in bright green and blue type on a purple background: "13 STORIES OF SURVIVAL; THE MUST-HAVE for your wardrobe; LOVE: WHAT IS IT? And How to Find it." ... There are columns about how to lose weight, how to balance work and play, how to find and keep the right man. ... But then I notice other, not-so-standard elements: boxed features and callouts and columns about "Bible Women" and "Bible Stuff to Know," and longer articles with titles like "Matthew," "Romans," and "Revelation." ... What my row-mate is perusing is not just any magazine, or not exactly a magazine. It's a Bible magazine – a "Biblesine," one of a growing line of niche-marketed Bibles in magazine form published by Thomas Nelson.
>
> (Beal 2011, pp. 41–42)

Biblezines have lagged in popularity since Beal's encounter in 2010, but remained a persistent market in the United States, even if their aesthetic is more Instagram than *Teen Beat* (probably due to an overall trend toward social media over glossy print for pop media, in general. Note, for example, the "Alabaster Bible" collection at http://www.alabasterco.com).

In 2014 I was sent a copy of the American Bible Society's publication, *The Illuminated Bible: The Book,* at the time available only in the New Testament, to review for an academic conference panel. Although the text is the complete, unabridged New Testament, *The Illuminated Bible* will not be lightly confused with any other published Bible. Indeed, like the Biblezine described by Beal, it will be more likely confused with a glossy fashion magazine. Like it, *The Book* is published in magazine format, with glossy pages and high-art photos throughout that feature popular figures, moments in contemporary history, and abstract art.[1]

The translation is a casual, contemporary one (Today's English Version). The book lacks any other commentary in the form of notes, introductions, or study

---

1 A quick side note here: The translation lacks any chapter or verse separations (a quality, I must confess, I do find endearing), though the text does have organizational captions, headings in italics which blurb the content of the paragraphs that follow). The cover and spine mimic magazine art; the front cover includes table of contents teasers. "A Good Investment – page 95" sends a curious reader to Luke 14:8–16:8 (yet doesn't clarify which of the parables – the parable of the Great Feast, the cost of being a disciple, worthless salt, the lost sheep, the lost coin, the lost son or the shrewd manager – it intends). The previous page contains both 12:41–48 and 57–59, each of which would apply. "All power comes to an end page 193" sends the reader to a black and white photo of a weeping soldier, accompanied by 2 Cor 1:4 (though, oddly, omitting the reference to God and Jesus that opens the benediction in verse 3). The previous page, however, contains 1 Cor 15 with its declaration of Jesus' triumphant power (15:27) and Paul's citation of Isaiah 25:8's famous challenge to death (15:54–55) in light of resurrection in Jesus. "Questions about marriage" sends us to 1 Cor 8:4–10:8, oddly not 1 Cor 7 (though it is visible on the opposite page). "If Love Gets Cold" sends us to Rev 5:7b-6:9a which has no obvious connection at all that I can see. The page highlights 6:12: "There was a violent earthquake, and the sun became black like course black cloth and the moon turned completely red like blood" (both by different coloration of type and by teaser inset) which doesn't seem, at all, to address cold love. Indeed, it seems far more appropriate for feelings of hot vengeance. The obvious Apocalypse reference (the letter to the Laodoceans 3:14–22 is, again, on the previous page). Finally, "Eyewitness" sends us to a page containing Luke 3:19-5:11, again fairly inexplicable. The prior page, however, discloses Luke's version of Jesus' birth, Jesus' presentation at the Temple, and John the Baptist's ministry (1:80–3:18).

On first examination, I must admit I puzzled over how the various directions I was being led produced any sense of meaning or engagement with the biblical text. I was, I admit, able to puzzle out some significance sometimes. Perhaps a photo of a weeping, exhausted soldier associated with a declaration about power coming to an end is a commentary on global militarism and colonialism's ultimate futility. Others, particularly, "if love gets cold," become sinister by the juxtaposition (wrath and doom associated with fatigue). Yet any sense of meaning I discovered seemed equivalent to what I would expect from virtually any juxtaposition of text and image. Quite frankly, however, the cover blurbs, as they are printed, seem totally random. Closer reading suggests, though, that they may all be off a page.

Clearly, they are all overtly Christian and devotional. This Bible, despite its glam book-for-everyone production quality, is clearly a book aimed at Christian believers. And particularly those searching for a specific type of (evangelical?) spirituality.

aids.[2] The use of "illuminated" in the title is relatively transparent. Of course, it harkens back to the tradition of the "illuminated" or decorated manuscripts, returning us to a manuscript of the Bible that is, once again, an intentional work of art. Like those beautiful manuscripts (or, arguably, also the myriad icons, altars, and frescos depicting Bible scenes) the format of this book, itself, awakens reflection on the Bible as cultural, even fashionable, icon.

*The Book* is filled with glossy, high-art photos alongside simple-English biblical text. Though not every photo is identified, most contain captions, often biblical quotes, that explicitly link the image and the biblical text. Three African American urban youth are juxtaposed with the question of the magi in Matthew 2:1–12 ("where is the baby born to be king of the Jews?..."; p. 10). Another image juxtaposes a woman wearing a *hijab* and holding her child next to the Matthew 1:21 benediction to Mary, "She will have a son, and you will name him Jesus" (p. 9).

Its images suggest that *The Book* is marketed to a broader, spiritually "ecumenical" market, including (either without comment or – by association – positively) images of non-Christians and avowed atheists (Gandhi, Ayaan Hirsi Ali, Muhammad Ali, John Lennon, etc.). Although the book has no images at all of Christian clergy (apart from Martin Luther King, Jr., Mother Teresa, Jim Jones, and Margit Sahlin, pp. 48, 54–55, 212, 232), it includes the Dalai Lama (p. 61). There are numerous photos stressing the urgent demands of global poverty; this, indeed, seems the only "sin" or evil the volume visually calls the reader to act upon (see the "8 ways to change the world" scattered throughout the gospel of Luke).

There are images critical of conspicuous consumption and wealth. A photo of a Chihuahua in a limousine (p. 166) is juxtaposed with Romans 1:23: "They say they are wise but they are fools, instead of worshiping the immortal God, they worship images made to look like mortal birds or animals or reptiles." Romans 14:1–2, "some people's faith allows them to eat anything, but the person who is weak in the faith eats only vegetables," is accompanied by a (somewhat grotesque) image of a cooked goose and a woman's bejeweled hand (p. 179). Wealth and celebrity are condemned in other images (p. 249) that, again, feature "excessive" women. The condemnation of the love of money is placed in a text box (p. 224). Paul's letter to Philemon is punctuated with images of the colonial Congo that emphasize the exploitation of slaves (pp. 228–229). There is an emphasis on global peace: a Jewish and an Arab boy (p. 168) arm in arm alongside "God judges everyone by the same standard." (Incidentally, this is the only overt photo of a Jew in the book.) There is an emphasis on environmental

---

2 No additional commentary is present; the book includes a brief statement about the history and mission of the American Bible Society. No art director, editor, etc. is identified. The New Testament was released in 1992. A second volume (containing the Hebrew Bible – identified as the Old Testament – is in production. Planned for release in 2009, it is delayed.

concerns (p. 172). Often, consumption and environmentalism are linked (p. 215). Celebrity is often critiqued (p. 183) but also embraced (pp. 49, 62, 53).

The emphasis on environmentalism, globalism, and responsible consumption is laudable, yet the volume's format simply oozes with the expendable pop culture it critiques. The stress on environmentalism is undercut by the production, yet again, of another printed Bible (isn't it past time for an app?). As to the critique of wealth, the market niche of *The Book* seems those with expendable income. The format of *The Book* seems at odds with at least part of its own ideology.

At some other moments, *The Book*'s illuminations seem to run at odds with biblical text. The Apocalypse opens with a series of graphic images from a slaughterhouse where the blood, indeed, runs as freely in the images as it does in John's text. Yet the violence in the images is conducted by humans against animals (and, in particular, animals being slaughtered for a purpose – food). Other images accompanying Revelation are of environmental disaster but focus on events and disasters that were perpetrated by human ignorance or greed; disaster becomes the natural result of greed and disinterest. In John's text, however, the destroyer of the earth and its creatures is God and the disasters that confront the earth are of divine origin, framed as Godly justice poured out on misbehaving humans (very literally, e.g. Revelation 16). The images in *The Book* indict humans for the actions God is doing as punishment of humans in the actual words of the biblical text itself. Is this critique of God, Godself, intentional?

When the illustrations turn to global poverty (the only moment when the illustration captions are not biblical text) and environmentalism, there is a clear suggestion that God's true servants are those who care for the poor and for the planet. The abuses of wealth, particularly American consumption, are causes of both global poverty and environmental degradation. Yet, I stress again, this Bible mimics a fashion magazine. The very format of the book is citation of popular culture and gratuitous consumption. This mimicry mocks its ethical critique. Could one find a better icon for conspicuous consumption, orientation toward the ethereal, and lack of substance than a fashion magazine? This Bible seems readily consumable, disposable. I can hardly imagine this text being long-lived with use; I wonder how the binding will sustain. Further, the images are too "of the moment;" it is now out of print. I also doubt that this version of the Bible was often the only Bible anyone owned. It has, in its linking of Bible and popular culture, brought biblical text into the superficial, consumable, transient, and (deliberately) redundant world of popular culture. One may legitimately ask if the Bible benefits from this company.

Although the volume may well have been intended to appeal to people who would not otherwise read a Bible, I suspect, more likely, it was carried and consumed by people who very often read their Bibles, but who worry about openly and publicly reading biblical text. Such an audience, one might argue, would be those most in need of critical reflection on wealth, consumption's evils, environmental concern, and global poverty. This Bible might be one of the few ways to bring biblical text into that world. It may also be intended as a Bible for the notorious seeker – the "spiritual but not religious" person to whom a traditional Bible is a symbol of a type of religiosity they resist. If so, then, at least for some people, the Bible is a symbol more than a book, and the American Bible Society is, in this publishing, acknowledging as much.

But one wonders if we are encountering a slain lamb with the voice of the beast, the inverse of Revelation 13. This volume is marketed toward the precise audience it attempts to critique via the exact means of the systems it rebukes, seemingly repudiating the message it conveys (or, less ambitiously, eradicating the benefits of its message). At the very least, questions of which is signifier and what is signified, in this case, become hopelessly entangled. Although one could argue the format of *The Book* might make the Bible more recognizable or likely to be read by those whose values *The Book* seems to intend to critique, the issue is complicated. Can pop culture – with the embrace of its superficiality and marginal substance, really offer a rebuke of superficiality and marginal substance? Might it not perhaps become a means of co-opting the best counterargument and critique of pop culture, lessening the impact of that critique and reducing its engagement? Should one advocate lessened consumption via a largely disposable document? Will a superfluous, perhaps impulse purchase not undermine arguments against overconsumption? Although the intent is perhaps to bring the Bible into a new market, it takes very little poststructuralist sweat to deconstruct the volume's intention and point out how it seems well at war with its own ideology.

The emphasis on globalism and ecumenicism is also imbalanced. There are no images of Christians at worship. The only image of Jesus is very much, tongue in cheek (p. 211, an image of a Holy Family toy set). As I've already noted, there are only four images of clergy – Martin Luther King, Jr., Mother Teresa, Margit Sahlin, and Jim Jones. In other words, an advocate for racial justice, a poverty advocate, the first woman ordained as a catholic priest (and later deemed heretical), and a straight, white, evangelical mad man. Jews are almost entirely absent. The holocaust is only alluded to by noting a (Christian) man who worked to hide Jews. There are images of Muslims and Hindus and Buddhists. In other words, we find ourselves reading an illustrated New Testament with almost no traditional or conventional images of either Christianity or Judaism, though with images of every other major religious tradition.

Clearly, this book is trying to decentralize this biblical text and its familiar colleagues, to take it out of – perhaps, better, "beyond" – traditional confines. Such is very much in keeping with the American Bible Society's global and ecumenical interests (as we will see shortly in this chapter). Frankly, such is something

I would applaud; Christians and Jews must learn that they do not "own" the Bible. Yet, on the other hand, we have a Bible that has, in its images, completely severed itself from its own conventions and history. In its efforts to capture the immediacy of pop culture, it has cut itself off from its own deep roots of tradition. This absence of context or historicity certainly agrees with *The Book*'s intentional positioning vis-à-vis popular culture; it also plays directly into the very vapidity of popular culture, ironically while casting the Bible as something timeless.

But one fairly asks, "is it? Is the Bible 'timeless?'" Didn't the Bible emerge from a very particular time, place, and context (or, more precisely: very particular times, places, and contexts)? A major cause of confusion to many modern Bible readers in that their own, very particular time and context is so different from the Bible's own, very particular time and context, that parts of the Bible become unintelligible. Isn't the Bible *read* in a very particular (and very different) time, place, and context? Certainly, many modern readers affirm that the Bible is critical to their modern lives, but again: is it really, and, if so, how? Many readers turn to the Bible to seek guidance or insight and find, instead, a mysterious collection of writings referencing strange and far away customs, issues, needs, concerns, and worries; they struggle to find a way to connect this ancient anthology to their (post)modern lives. The Bible, as well, has become not just a sacred text, but an identifying signal. An openly carried Bible projects a sort of identity, as does a worn paperback Bible or a richly bound, expensive Bible. The Bible both lies like a mirror alongside popular culture and is, itself, a product of popular culture. The *Illuminated Bible* raises some fair questions: might the Bible need something more, some "hook," to appeal to modern readers? Once in their hands, do modern US readers know what to do with a Bible? Can it make any sense to someone who lacks years (decades) of training in its interpretation?

## The Bible, New and Improved

Enter an array of "new and improved!" Bibles for sale (or in homes, dorm rooms, office desk-drawers and more), well beyond Biblezines. The Bible is America's perennial best-seller, in part because, being available in an array of translations and formats, a single reader can buy it again and again.

> The Bible business has burgeoned into one of the biggest and fastest-growing fields of publishing, selling many thousands of different Bibles in every imaginable form for many hundreds of millions of dollars a year. Within this brave new world of Christian consumerism, it's getting harder and harder to tell the difference between spreading the word and selling it.
>
> (Beal 2011, pp. 20–21)

The Religion section of a typical big-box bookstore (say, Barnes and Noble) is often shelf upon shelf (or perhaps bookcase upon bookcase) of Bibles. There are dozens of English translations to choose from. To name just a few, one finds: The King James Version, the New King James Version, the Revised Standard Version, the New Revised Standard Version, the New International Version (NIV), Today's English Bible, The American Standard Version, The New American Standard Version, the Good News Bible, Today's English Version, the Jerusalem Publication Society, and many, many more. The Bibles themselves often contain an array of study or reader aids: red letters for the words of Jesus, center column cross-references, topical indices, introductions, study notes, outlines, "background" essays, devotional essays, historical theological essays, and much more. One can find for sale the Teen Study Bible, the NIV Bible for Teen Girls (Growing in Faith, Hope and Love), the NIV Boy's Bible, The Father's Plan: A Bible Study for Dads, God's Wisdom for a Mother's Heart: A Bible for Moms. The Businessman's Topical Bible, The Catholic Study Bible, the Wesley Study Bible, The Holy Bible: Baptist Study Edition, The Prophecy Bible, The African Heritage Study Bible, The Queer Bible, The Women's Bible, The Jewish Annotated New Testament, The Jewish Study Bible, the Amplified Bible, the Oxford Annotated Bible, the "We the People" Bible (endorsed by Donald Trump) and, again, many, many more. On the shelf alongside Bibles are an array of guides, reference works and commentaries. The Bible section of general reader bookstores is often nearly the scale of history or biography (two of America's other great nonfiction reading passions).

As a college professor who has taught undergraduate introductions to the Bible for 20 years, I've lost count of the number of times a student, on the first day of class, has raised her hand to timidly ask, "What type of Bible do we need for this class." Such a question, in its perfectly imperfect wording, captures the disorientation our current moment can produce for the unwary Bible reader. It also poses occasion for two critical questions. First, are the array of books sold as "The Bible" the same book? Certainly, most (at least) have tables of contents with common enough divisors: "Genesis," "2 Corinthians," but there are additional books in/and a variety of sequences. Their wording is different. There are a multitude of Bibles with extra content – explanatory introductions, scholarly essays, footnotes, center-column cross references, and devotionals which certainly shape and color how one understands – or even what – one reads. Like the famed Ship of Theseus, one may ask how many changes or augmentations a Bible can sustain and still, de facto, be the same book.

A second question, perhaps easier to answer, is "how did this happen?" How did we get so many Bibles to choose from? For centuries, most members of religious communities, synagogues, or churches, didn't own their own Bibles but went to a common assembly to hear the Bible read aloud. Indeed, for most of human history, most people have been illiterate. For most of its history, the

Bible was preserved in ancient (dead) languages: Hebrew, Greek, and Latin. Even the literate in the community, without special training, often could not understand the Bible as it was read aloud to them. With the dawn of the printing press (and the famous Gutenberg Bible), when books became mass-producible and, therefore, inexpensive, few homes had more than a single Bible. Now, Bibles are sold by the hundreds and homes (if not individual believers) often have a dozen variations of the Bible. How did we get to our modern moment with such a variety of Bibles? *Why* would anyone own more than one Bible? At least for a US reader and market, some of that answer may lie in a review of the past 200 years of popular thinking about – and use of – the Bible.

## A Self-Evident Book: The Bible and Nineteenth-Century United States

The role of religious freedom in the founding of several of the North American colonies, although sometimes overstated, is also clear (Holmes 2006), and the Bible was an integral part of colonial American life. The first book printed in the colonies was Stephen Daye's *The Whole Booke of Psalmes Faithfully Translated into English Metre* – the famous "Bay Psalter" of 1640, printed in Cambridge, Massachusetts. Early forays into formal education during the colonial period were, as we will see later, largely to ensure a population literate enough to read their Bibles. When the nineteenth century began, reading the Bible was seen as imperative to a life of faith and integrity. Bibles were prized, and many regarded it as self-evident; any sincere reader, reading a quality translation, would discover God's word. Bibles were also integral to growing missionary movements, and the Bible became a marker of both faith and American identity. By the century's end, however, confidence in a self-interpreting Bible was under serious challenge, even as the Bible's deep connection to cultural and national identity were solidifying.

Public discourse in the United States of the nineteenth century was a mixture of political idealism, pragmatism, and of Christian revivalism. By the century's end, the revivalist energies of the antebellum years and emerging Victorian sentimentalism were both enhanced by the trauma and losses of the American Civil War. Although many saw the war's bloodshed and loss in apocalyptic terms, both before and after the war, others felt a growing sense of American millenarian, utopian destiny. The Bible spoke to both.

The nineteenth century brought serious challenges to the traditional veneration of Christian faith. The years immediately prior to and after the Civil War were also years of denominational schism with splits over doctrinal quibbles, but, notably, also divided along the lines of Civil War loyalties and abolition. Charles Darwin had published a method of understanding human origins that did not require the presence of a creator. European biblical scholarship was increasingly turning to questions of "higher criticism" uncovering an array of historical inaccuracies in the Bible (for a closer review of these tensions, particularly surrounding intersecting with popular Christian views of the apostle Paul, see Seesengood 2011). The nature, reliability, and merit of the Bible became a national conversation, and scholars were making increasingly sophisticated and rational arguments against the literal truth of the Bible and traditional understanding of its authorship. The Bible found new critics, but also vigorous defenders. In the earliest decades of the nineteenth century, the Bible was a device for colonial expansion abroad and a wave of domestic revival movements.

Christian "missions," understood as expansive proselytism into newly "discovered" or settled colonies by Europeans of the Americas, Africa, and Asia, began in earnest in the late sixteenth and early seventeenth centuries and reached their nadir, among protestants, in the nineteenth century (for expansion, see Seesengood 2011). Initially, Christian missions in the Americas were engaged primarily by the Roman Catholic Church, particularly the churches in Spain and Portugal. By the nineteenth century, Christian missions were largely protestant and arising from anglophone nations. These missions were organized by industrious, para-church societies that raised and administered funds and maintained exacting records and that carefully vetted and trained missionaries. Over the course of the century, leading Christian theory argued that the most effective means of world evangelism was to foster indigenous means of Christian expression. These mission campaigns were supported by a growing number of (ambitious) organized "Bible societies" (such as the American Bible Society, publisher of *The Bible Illuminated*).

The history of "modern" protestant missions, and particularly the history behind the founding of nineteenth-century Bible societies in the United States and United Kingdom, could rightly begin with the work of William Carey and his "Inquiry into the Obligation of Christians to use the Means for Conversion of the Heathens" (Carey 1792. For more detailed discussion, see Seesengood 2011). Carey used Isaiah 54 as foundational text, and the character of Paul, especially his "missionary journeys" described in the Acts of the Apostles, as paradigm for a new model of the emigrant, foreign missionary, a figure who left home to settle in foreign lands in order to teach Christianity and convert indigenous peoples (see Bosch 1991; Tucker 1983; and Neill 1991). Carey was also author of a key tract arguing "Christian evidences" that included "unassailable" arguments for the Bible's infallibility appended to later copies of his sermon. Similar arguments had been written by William Paley in tracts circulated in 1791. The truth of Christianity and the inspiration of the Bible were demonstrated by (not resulting in) the Bible's infallibility (a position Carey argues using 2 Timothy and Hebrews). These arguments not only legitimated Christian evangelism and dissemination of the Bible, they made both of these tasks morally obligatory.

Over the next 150 years, as US, British, and French political and economic colonialism expanded, new opportunities presented themselves for missionary activity in the colonial territories, with focus on China, India, southeast Asia, Africa, and remote South America. Along with this expansion in missionary work came dissemination of the Bible, often translated into indigenous languages by missionaries, and the rise of US and British Bible societies to foster and finance this work. Christian mission (and missionaries) framed itself as a living-out of the narratives of the Acts of the Apostles, particularly of the biography and missionary work of the Apostle Paul. Critical examples would be the mission outreach of Adoniram Judson (see Thornburn 1906, p. 149), Hudson Taylor (see Tucker 1983, p. 73), or Thomas Charles (see Canton 1904; Febvre and Martin 1997). Charles, very notably, from his work as a Bible seller in Wales, became an evangelist for the production of Bibles in indigenous languages, an advocacy that directly led to the founding of the British and Foreign Bible Society (BFBS) in 1804 (see Seesengood 2011). Dissemination of the Bible among "the colonies" and elsewhere was, in and of itself, understood as a form of missionary endeavor, reflecting a widespread confidence among many protestants that simple Bible reading, almost alone, would lead to conversion and Christianization. The root of this confidence was, of course, 2 Tim 3:16.

Within decades of the British and Foreign Bible Society, similar organizations were founded throughout the English-speaking world. Among a few examples are the Pennsylvania Bible Society (1808), the American Bible Society (1816), the Edinburgh and Glasgow Societies (merging quickly into the Scottish Bible Society in 1825), the Australian Bible Society (1817), the Bible Society of New South Wales (also 1817), and societies in Colombia (1809) and New Zealand (1846). These would merge to form the United Bible Societies, which still operates and publishes some of the standard scholarly editions of the Bible in its original Hebrew and Greek (Seesengood 2011).

Bible societies functioned with a mission statement and rationale rooted in Protestantism's particular readings of the Bible. Such protestant orientations resulted in controversies among some Bible societies and between Bible societies and the catholic establishment. The Scottish Bible Society formed because the BFBS began to circulate Bibles with the Apocrypha (additional Old Testament books found in Roman Catholic canons, but not protestant). The tensions were felt on both sides of the catholic/protestant divide. Pope Gregory XIV issued an encyclical in 1844 (*Inter Praecipuas*) that condemned the widespread dissemination of the vernacular Bible. American protestants saw this as implicit acknowledgement by the Catholic Church that catholic doctrines were not biblical nor resonant with ideals of *sola Scriptura* that undergirded most protestant (not merely Lutheran antecedent) ideology.

Inherent in those claims of "Scripture only" as basis for authority, however, is an implicit confidence that the Bible *can* be read without any "human" teaching or doctrine – or culture – shaping the reader, that the pure and unfettered word of scripture, read sincerely and with a humble and open heart to God, is not only intelligible, but even possible. Beyond a few references to "the Law and the Prophets," the Bible, as a collection of disparate writings, nowhere lists its own contents, nowhere lists which books should or should not be included within its boundaries of authority; the very idea of a fixed "canon" is an imposed doctrine (and the diversity of "canons" and orders to the Bible – the Syriac canon, the catholic canon, the standard protestant canon, the orthodox canon, the Tanach, etc. demonstrate that canon is not an obvious, nor a-theological, listing of books). Even the words of the Bible invoked controversy, as evidenced by the complex issues surrounding the translation of the Christian initiatory ritual of baptism. The Greek word *baptizomai* can be translated as either "washed" or "immersed." The difference is notable, given, for example the allegiance of some protestant denominations such as Baptists, who insist on an exclusive, and soteriologically critical, interpretation (see, on this controversy and its effect on Bible societies and missions, Seesengood 2011).

Other "human" political and national interests affected missionary work, often enabling it. The nineteenth century was an era of Anglophone colonization, and one aspect of colonization is intellectual and cultural hegemony. For example, British control of India resulted in the transformation of the official, legal language to English, along with the construction of British-style schools, civic processes, courts, and industry. Along with secular, civil transformation, colonialism also introduced religious transformations. Often, these were imposed as a set: English literacy was often produced by training students to read the Bible, a goal of literacy entangled with both economic and political engagement. A key participant in this process of religious colonization were the missionary programs of large societies such as the para-church groups, the American Bible Society and the British Bible Society.[3] Bible societies began at roughly the same time anglophone colonization was reaching its zenith.

In the 1900s, with US cultural and (capitalist) economic shifts and expansions, the pressures and needs of (economic) colonization and the (hegemonic) expansion of Christianity alongside US and British nationalism, attenuated various arguments about the historical reliability of the various biblical books. Changes in nineteenth-century politics and science brought the Bible new challenges. The growth of Christian missions spread the Bible, but also revealed the challenges inherent in claims about a simple, self-evident Bible. Finally, the

---

3 On the connection between early missions and colonization, see Bosch 1991, 226–229, 302–336. On the fusion of economic, political, and religious interests vis-à-vis the dissemination of the Bible, see Sugirtharajah 2001, pp. 140–174.

same cultural changes that spread the Bible also began to intertwine with political, economic, and national identities.

## The Rise of the "Value-Added" Bible: The American Bible in the Age of Modernism

During the twentieth century, in the United States, pressures upon the idea of a fully (self) sufficient Bible grew. The idea that a collection of serious readers could agree as to what the Bible actually *said* (let alone what that *meant*) was imperiled. Bible readers needed as much help and guidance as could be given.

For example: a central problem to assertions that the Bible contains all Truth and speaks to our every modern concern is that, really, if one is honest, the Bible doesn't contain all knowledge, and the issues that arose from modernity made that even more pronounced. There are very many fields, very important to modern human life, which are not directly mentioned in the Bible, let alone fully explicated: human genetics, nuclear weaponry, climate change, abortion, and more. Much of what the Bible does say is unclear. To read a Bible historically requires one to know a great deal about ancient history, norms, language, memes, and values, and twentieth-century education much more rarely devoted much attention to ancient history and languages. Even more, modernist modes of Bible reading, sleuthing an author's intended meaning, requires one to know something about precisely where, when, and by whom the Bible was written (a much greater challenge than novice readers might imagine).

As we've seen, during the nineteenth century, there were very strong cultural, affective, and nationalistic motivations merging into an existing stream of American veneration for the Bible. As these forces converged, Bible advocacy and Bible reading became more than religious practice. Love of the Bible, and loyalty to the Bible alone, and in particular the public expression of this love and loyalty, took on increasing social importance through the late nineteenth and into the early twentieth century. One manifestation was birth and the rise of fundamentalism in the early twentieth century.

"The word 'fundamentalist' itself was not used in print until 1 July 1920, when it was defined by Curtis Lee Laws, editor of *The Watchman Examiner*, a national Baptist weekly." (Davis 2008, p. 176). Fundamentalism is "militant rejection of modernity in the name of religion;" it is an attitude, not a specific doctrine (Davis 2008, p. 176). Historically, though, Christian fundamentalism did have elements of common doctrine including literal inspiration of the Bible and biblical inerrancy; opposition to "higher criticism" and defense of Mosaic authorship of Torah; insistence on biblical miracles as actual events; the virgin birth of Jesus; the actuality of the resurrection of Jesus; salvation by faith only; opposition to Mormonism, Jehovah's Witnesses (called "New Dawn"), and Roman Catholics. All these positions were outlined in the 90 essays – each written by a different expert in religion, science, history, or sociology; most all with advanced graduate degrees from leading institutions – that comprise the 12 volumes of *The Fundamentals* (1910–1915), a pamphlet series (turned four-volume book) published by oil tycoons Lyman and Milton Stewart and distributed widely to scholars, clergy, and interested laity. It is common to see US fundamentalism as primarily a religious response to modern science. The articles do not betray much interest in Darwin at first; only one or two articles address the issue of evolution head on, and one of these, written by a Christian geologist, is speaking more toward cosmogony and the Big-Bang. Many of the original contributors were theistic Darwinists, as were the Stewart brothers (Davis 2008, p. 188). Fundamentalism, and this is a key point, was less a reaction to challenges regarding the nature and reality of God, and much more a vigorous defense of the veracity of the Bible. *The Fundamentals* certainly found a readership and became a hugely popular collection. Its large success paralleled the publishing success of Moody Press and its ever-popular Scofield Bibles (more about each of these to come).

Through Moody Press, Dwight Moody and his Illinois-based Moody Bible Institute, published and disseminated hundreds of tracts – usually assertions of biblical superiority over modernity – in the 1920s. Moody was following a path blazed by the Stewarts. He in turn would be inspirational to Billy Graham whose post-World War II publishing wing dominated American religious literature (Boyer 2008, p. 19). With respect to Bible publishing, however, perhaps the earliest severe jolt to the US industry was Cyrus Scofield's 1909 annotated Bible published by Moody Press. Scofield, an evangelical and early charismatic, was a devotee of the Scot John Nelson Darby's new methods of Holy Spirit led reading of biblical text. Darby believed recent visions and revelations from God had given the secret for interpreting the Apocalypse of John. Jesus was soon to return and call all the faithful to heaven (the Rapture) leaving behind the unregenerate. Next, the earth would endure a period of purging terrors, rehabilitative in intent, called the Tribulation. In God's absence, a terrible tyrant (the Anti-Christ) would rule. Jesus would eventually return, set things right, defeat the Anti-Christ, and rule for a 1000-year millennium.

Darby insisted all this was clearly spelled out in scripture. Readers might be forgiven, however, for asking where. Darby would counter that the idea develops via a series of verses, many read in ways dismissive of immediate context, in ways uninitiated readers would consider haphazard, random, or out of original context. A reader led by the Holy Spirit could, however, see otherwise disconnected verses as part of a unified reading, very literally building a new Bible, patchwork, from parts of the old. Darby insisted that the Holy Spirit was now revealing, unveiling, a mystery long held in scripture – a hidden code. Later disciples though had trouble sorting out all the exegetical and hermeneutical complexities. Scofield's Bible, with its center-column cross-referencing and introductory notes, enabled average or unschooled readers to follow the train of Darby's argument. To say the Scofield Bible was a success in Bible sales in America – particularly in the western states – is a radical understatement (Boyer 2008, p. 29). Scofield's Bible is the first, successful "value added" Bible marketed and sold in America. The early twentieth century, perhaps inspired by Scofield's success, but definitely encouraged by the explosion in Christian book printing, saw an array of new Bible translations (Boyer 2008, pp. 24–26).

Religious book sales bloomed in the twentieth century, publishing an array of literary genres: fiction, devotional literature, "life guide" self-help books (on diet, home stewardship, etc.), religious history, doctrine, biographies, biblical commentaries and more. Responding to popular interest, the Religious Book Club (RBC) offered select books by subscription. A monthly catalog arrived which featured a recommended selection; the selection shipped automatically to readers, who also had the option of declining or of selecting other or additional titles from a catalog list. All titles were judiciously picked not only for doctrinal purity, but also for market interest. Books that were too wordy or scholarly were rejected (and were such poor sales) as were those the market deemed too "worldly" or doctrinally suspect. To facilitate sales (and reach the widest possible market), selections of the month were decidedly "middle-brow, demi-intellectual, safe selections of literature" (Hedstrom 2013, pp. 221–222). "RBC readers clearly wanted books that reconciled faith and modern science, religious pluralism and protestant superiority, but they only wanted books that achieved this reconciliation in particular – middle brow – ways" (Hedstrom 2013, p. 227).

In the United States, readers had "an unprecedented array of genres delivering the Word made print" (Cohen 2008, p. 3). As Cohen notes "textual hegemony never meant interpretive uniformity; if *sola scriptura* is Protestantism's birthright, hermeneutical discord, even among members of the same ecclesiastical body, qualifies as its afterbirth" (Cohen 2008, p. 7). Of course, many denied this, arguing that sincere, informed, and genuine people – the legendary "Men of Goodwill" – would concur on the Bible's plain meaning. As Cohen continues:

> [T]he use of a single edition grounded the nearly universal assumption that scripture's wisdom lay on the surface, not in arcane figures or encryptions. ... From the Revolution to the Civil War, common sense philosophy guided theological exploration, assuring Americans that applying right reason to the literal words would bring the truth to light. Possessing the same text encouraged a widespread feeling that the Bible's meaning was essentially transparent – or at least should have been.
>
> (Cohen 2008, p. 8)

This naïve belief in a reader-ready, doctrine free Bible in part, as I've argued, fueled the expansion of several missionary oriented Bible Societies. (Boyer 2008, pp. 14–15) but also encouraged domestic Bible publication, dissemination, ... and sales. The now famous origin story of the Gideon Bible – two Christian businessmen on the road who met in a tavern, encouraged one another, and vowed to form a society where Bibles were disseminated free of charge to hotels, hospitals, and on street corners – gave rise to later, similar practice by Mormons and Buddhists (Boyer 2008, p. 17). By the twenty-first century, Gideon Bibles can be found in most US hotels and are regularly given away on street corners.

## The American Bible in Late Capitalism

In post-World War II United States, the publication of the Bible has exploded. Millions of Americans, in continuation of the assertions of the Fundamentalists, insist that the Bible is critical to their faith and lives, even as they seem increasingly less aware of the contents of the Bible. They may be forgiven, perhaps; the array of study Bibles and their "value-added" content could destabilize any confidence that reading the Bible without specialized training or guidance is a dubious proposition. What has emerged, however, is a "late capitalist" Bible – a Bible published largely for appeal to a distinct consumer niche and demographic, a reason for buying and rebuying the Bible according to a reader's choice and self-assessed identity group or needs. In other words, the paradigmatic US Bible has become, paradigmatically, a commodification of the Bible and a merger of Bible readers and capitalism itself.

Always a best-seller, the Bible now markets itself to an increasing array of niche markets. On the one hand, we find Bible's with integrated study notes and devotional matter, normally marketed to niche groups: parents, children, men, women, academics, and (with Oxford's *Jewish Annotated New Testament*) even across the borders of religious communities themselves. As Beal's opening example depicts, we also find Bible's that merge biblical narrative and graphic image(s). The Bible is appearing more and more not only on the internet and as Biblezines but also in cinema and as comic book. When the Bible is merged with, or translated into, these different, graphic, visual media, the images associated with biblical text function as commentary and interpretation and also to embed affect. Images that are striking, arousing, disgusting, enraging, frightening, or confusing translate those affects directly into the biblical text that accompanies them. The visual Bible is an enlarged Bible.

Despite frequent laments about the displacement of the Bible in our culture and broad biblical illiteracy, it seems to be doing as well as really any book could in our modern publishing context. Clearly, as Beal noted (Beal 2011, pp. 20–21), if the Bible isn't being read, it isn't because no one can find a copy. The Bible market of the US book trade, despite (because of?) the ubiquity of the Bible, has never been sated.

> The Bible business has burgeoned into one of the biggest and fastest-growing fields of publishing, selling many thousands of different Bibles in every imaginable form for many hundreds of millions of dollars a year. Within this brave new world of Christian consumerism, it's getting harder and harder to tell the difference between spreading the word and selling it. ... In today's consumer culture, we are what we buy, wear, and carry. We identify ourselves by our patterns of consumer choices, by the market niches we buy into. It's gone beyond that post-Cartesian proof of existence, "I shop, therefore I am." Today it's closer to "I shop for what I am." The culture industry makes and markets identities. I want to be outdoorsy, so I buy a lot of Gore-Tex. ... My big New Year's resolution might be to become an organized person. So the first thing I do is go to the home store and buy a bunch of plastic boxes. ... I want a more God-centered life. I want to be "in the Word." ... So what do I do? Buy a Bible.
>
> (Beal 2011, pp. 20–21, 35)

The Bible remains fundamentally prominent, but something fundamental is changing about the way people engage with the Bible. The Bible is becoming a popular consumer item that appeals to, and creates, its buyer's social and demographic identity.

Certainly, one might argue that the Bible has long been a book looked at more than read, more (source of) icon, image, or religious symbol than religious text, a cipher for politics and identity, a book more iconic, more looked at, than read. Further, there are serious questions to be raised about the Bible's role in current discourse, and how modern readers perhaps over-stressed the Bible's value. The Bible seems a book whose devoted reception has exceeded its contents' actual influence on popular thinking. The Bible has become both a symbol of identity, and an accessory. The publication of Biblezines, or the *Bible Illustrated*, are marking more of a trend than may be realized at first glance.

What strikes me, in reflecting on this last point, is how this evocation of the superficial, indeed the very celebration of the superficial and fashionable, constructs, in a way, a type of depth. Yet another way of imagining a *Bible illuminated* is to move beyond thinking of a decorated Bible and imagine a Bible exposed to light, seen for what it actually is. It was difficult for me to read *The Bible Illuminated* without thinking of Mark C. Taylor's 1998 *Hiding*. Taylor's work is an exploration of poststructuralism and postmodern culture and its intersections with theology. *Hiding* takes up some of the themes of Taylor's earlier work, *Disfiguring*. Both were influenced by Derrida's *Glas* in format and Jameson's *Postmodernism* in argument. Taylor's main theme is the exploration of superficiality, with a particular focus on consumption, skin/flesh, and transience and how these themes form a postmodern engagement with God. His central chapter, titled "De-signing," like the *Bible Illuminated* incorporates design elements of a high-fashion magazine.

Taylor opens with a theoretical survey of fashion that demonstrates the substance inherent in the superficial before he turns to applying the same critique to the tensions inherent in separation of signifier and signified. He writes:

> Fashion is profound in its superficiality. The profundity of fashion does not involve depth but reflects the infinite complexity of a play of surfaces and knows no end. In the absence of a depth that grounds, fashion remains fraught with ambiguity – irreducible ambiguity. This ambiguity which borders on the enigmatic, is what renders fashion simultaneously attractive and repulsive. On the one hand, to label something fashionable is to embrace it as smart, sophisticated, elegant, current and timely. On the other hand, to characterize something as fashionable is to dismiss it as trendy, trivial, inconsequential, insignificant, and fleeting. (pp. 167–168)

Or, as Yukio Mishima notes:

> Why must it be that men always seek out the depths, the abyss? Why must thought, like the plumb line, concern itself exclusively with vertical descent? Why was it not feasible for thought to change direction and climb vertically up, ever up, toward the surface? Why should the area of the skin, which guarantees a human being's existence in space, be most despised and left to the tender mercies of the senses? ... If the law of thought is that it should search out profundity, whether it extends upwards or downwards, then it seemed excessively illogical to me that men should not discover depths of a kind in the "surface." (1970, p. 167)

Taking this as an ambitious call to arms, Taylor (1998) first notes that "fashion is directly related to the feminine and indirectly associated with the artificial, the frivolous, fickle, sensual, and most important, less functional" (p. 174). His analysis uncovers a host of assumptions about fashion and the fashionable. For example, prior cultural critique has contrasted women's fashion with men's. "Whereas women's fashion is artificial, frivolous, idiosyncratic, sensuous and useless, men's fashion is [seen as] natural, serious, universal, reasonable, and functional" (p. 183). Citing Adolf Loos, Taylor writes:

> Fashion is most civilized ... when it is least obvious: "to be dressed correctly ... is a question of being dressed *in such a way that one stands out the least*." That which stands out least is either common or universal.

Refined fashion is neither idiosyncratic nor ostentatious but standard-ized or uniform. (1998, p. 183)

We will return to the theme of Bibles and/as fashion in a later chapter, but, for now: In the history of fashion, pursuit of the most fashionable is linked to dis-play of wealth, and restrictions on fashion mark social and civic responsibility and function to create social taxonomy.

To return to Tim Beal, Beal argues that the Bible, alongside its status as sacred text, useful for doctrine and moral instruction, the Bible has become, like fashion, a cultural sign, a cipher of identity. Beal refers to this as a "cultural icon" (Beal 2011, p. 5) and cites, as an example, the cultural role of the Ten Commandments in the U.S. social politics. Decorative or display copies of the Decalogue, found in some American civic spaces and in countless rural roadside signs and tourist attractions, are often designed in such a way that they either heavily abbreviate the actual words of Exodus or they cannot be read at all. It is the *symbol* of the decalogue, not the actual wording, that is the point. The Ten Commandments, then, actually function in American popular culture as a political and social identity marker, a symbol. A nation's flag functions practically in its declaration of sovereign control (particularly useful at sea or on a battlefield), but it also functions symbolically as a marker of social identities and loyalties. So, also, a Bible. In addition to its role as a book containing a record of founding stories, myths, and doctrines, the Bible is, itself, iconic. The Ten Commandments function as synecdoche for the Bible as a whole and well illustrate the Bible's role as a cultural icon.

> A cultural icon is different from a traditional icon. A traditional icon is a particular material object that is believed to mediate a transcendent real-ity, and its power to do so is created and maintained by various rituals people practice in relation to it. An example might be a Bible used to swear in a new president, or a handwritten Torah scroll presented to a congregation in a synagogue. A *cultural* icon is not so concrete. It is not tied to a particular material object, visual image, or ritual practice. Its outlines are a little vague, hard to define sharply. It's a condensation of what people who identify with it believe in and value. It says something about the culture in which it holds iconic power.
>
> (Beal 2011, p. 5)

## Are Bibles *Read* or Just Looked at?

Alongside late twentieth century growth in Bible marketing and sales (and I note, growth in sales of *annotated* and *study* Bibles in particular) is a growing sense among many scholars and clergy of a general sense of popular unfamiliarity with the Bible's actual contents – its stories, ideas, precepts, and even characters. This pessimism toward popular biblical literacy is not, one must admit, without some justification.

Stephen Prothero has noted the high regard for religion, religiosity and the Bible has found in American culture (Prothero 2007). But Prothero has also noted the high levels of ignorance among many Americans vis-à-vis what the Bible actually says (Prothero 2007, pp. 35–38). Beal observes some similar facts:

- Less than half of all adult Americans can name the first book of the Bible.
- More than 80% of born-again or evangelical Christians believe that "God helps those who help themselves" is a Bible verse.
- More than half of graduating high school seniors guess that Sodom and Gomorrah were husband and wife, and 1 in 10 adults believes that Joan of Arc was Noah's wife.
- Almost two-thirds of Americans can't name at least five of the Ten Commandments. (Beal 2011, p. 31)

Prothero ascribes the disconnection between American popular insistence upon the value of religious (biblical) values, and the rather remarkable popular ignorance of both, to a lack of formal education in religion in the traditional American education system. In Europe, for example, veneration for religion and the Bible are much less than in the United States, but general knowledge of both is also higher, and many European education systems often include modules on religion and the Bible (though usually from a secular perspective Prothero 2007, pp. 22–24, 53–55). Prothero usefully traces the role of religion in American education to provide a historical perspective on how we arrived where we are (pp. 60–122). Yet, changes in educational approach and curriculum do not account for the significant disparity between professed allegiance to the Bible and practical ignorance of its contents. A far simpler explanation could account for all the data Prothero (like Beal) observes: Americans culturally venerate the Bible, but they don't actually *read* one much, and, when they do, they tend to read parts of it over-and-over while ignoring others, and they likely read notes – or even more likely commentaries or devotional books *about* the Bible – much more, and much more closely. Perhaps even among the devout or educated readership, the Bible is revered more than directly engaged, read *about* more often than read *from*. Multiple translations, study aids, notes, guides, and commentaries become ways to produce, in effect, multiple Bibles for market but also perhaps to over-write the actual content of the Bible. Certainly, it would account for how *so many* US communities are *so convinced* that they read the Bible, yet that *no one else* is doing so. They are, functionally, reading different Bibles, written, in some cases by the market's invisible hand.

To be fair, lamentation of broad biblical illiteracy is not new. It is a lament, in fact, somewhat tropic. "Insiders," adherents to Judeo-Christian faith, are often very convinced that "outsiders," including people of no particular faith along-side those outside familiar denominations, are illiterate of the Bible. This trope is particularly common among protestants who, for an array of theological and historical reasons, foreground the believer's personal encounter with the Bible. Biblical literacy needs some clearer definition (see further Edwards 2015). Also, as Beal notes, at one level, biblical illiteracy

> is simply a subset of book literacy in general, which is clearly in decline. A recent report by the National Endowment for the Arts indicates that, between 1992 and 2002, the number of adults who read at least one liter-ary book in the course of a year dropped by 14 percent. The number of adults who read a book of any kind also dropped, by seven percent, and judging from the data on younger readers, the future of bibliographic culture is not bright: among adults eighteen to twenty-four years old, the decline in literary reading was 55 percent greater than it was among the general adult population.
>
> (Beal 2011, p. 33)

Edwards is certainly correct that the Bible retains a significant place in cultural literacy vis-à-vis book readership in general (how many, for example, would include or notice even a cursory reference to *Middlemarch* in a political speech). But, then again, one might reply to her by noting most people don't *believe* they have read or know the contents of George Eliot. The Bible is quite different.

## Our Bibles, Ourselves

One might, then, return to the *Bible Illuminated* and ask precisely what its turn toward the fashionable – indeed, its imitation of fashion literature – renders deeply superficial about the Bible. What do *The Book*'s new clothes conceal and what do they reveal? What, for example, is significant in its turn toward fash-ionable non-compliance with the standard "uniform" of the Bible, adorned with an array of annotative accessories.

My office is filled with Bibles. I have two shelves of them, in various English, French, German, and Spanish translations. Some have study notes; some do not. Some contain deuterocanonical books, some don't. Some are hardbound; some are paperback. Some are in (reconstructed) Greek, some Hebrew, some Latin. These Bibles I read, I mark with notes, I lay splayed atop one another and stack in working piles to the side of my desk. Next to that desk, though, sits the large, brown, leather-bound Bible my mother once read, her last Bible, its gilt-edged pages filled with her pencil-marked notes from the Bible-reading that gave her comfort during her cancer treatment. Its worn leather marks the memory of the hands that first held me. It sits by my desk next to a photo of my wife. I do not mark in it; I rarely read it, but seeing it, sharing my space with it, comforts me in ways beyond its words.

Is the Bible more powerful when it functions as a symbol rich with so many affects and memories, or when it is read? Is a mass Bible ever able to become a rich source of meaning to a single individual? Is a Bible that both can and will be read by masses consigned to being fashionable and mass in its appeal and message? How does late capitalism's notion that "mass culture" is, in effect, a culture of fragmentation into multiple niche identities, selected and consumed by preference, complicating this entire conversation?

Undoubtedly, this turn toward the fashionable in Bibles like *The Illuminated Bible* will result in a Bible that some people will take up and read, particularly some who would most likely avoid reading a Bible like my mother's. That seems to be the very point. The Bible has been translated into some print version of Twitter. But more is happening here, I think, than that. The *Bible Illuminated,* by its very superficiality, provokes questions about the depth and usefulness of biblical text, even Bible ownership and propagation, mirrors US nineteenth and twentieth century transformations. One might also notice: precisely as Bibles are becoming ubiquitous due to free (or subsidized) dissemination, there is a rising opinion shift that results in much broader markets for Bibles. As the book become freely available, there is suddenly a need for everyone to *purchase* a new, unique copy.

In its high-fashion (feminine?) garb, the biblical text camps it up for a rich, carnivalesque, romp that raises, as all good carnivalesque-cum-fashion-week-cum-musical-review-cum-Bravo-network icons will, questions about what is "traditional" or "appropriate" or "deep," and why and who benefits by these conditions. The *Bible Illuminated* invites, very unintentionally, I think, by its absence of substance, deep questions about the Bible's role as US icon, about whether or not increasing the ubiquity and accessibility of the Bible ultimately renders it meaningless, or, we may wonder instead, what possible meanings there were in the gilded pages of Moroccan leather-bound Bibles of yore. Were those "traditional" Bibles any more tied to church tradition or their own historical depth, any more consistent in their forms and contents? If they were, what did that consistency say? What is signified behind the icon of the Bible, traditional or non? What has happened to the Bible as it has become ubiquitous – the goal of both its authors, its texts, and many of its readers? What, in the end, is revealed when the Bible is illuminated, not by the light of candles or stained glass, but by rude and hard runway lights. *The Book,* despite the confidence raised in its unassuming, innocuous title of common noun and definite article, in the ultra-casual-contemporary way the title itself translates its ancient name, doesn't really answer these questions. But it is, I admit, often pretty to look at while one thinks about it.

## Works Cited

Beal, T.K. (2011). *The Rise and Fall of the Bible: The Unexpected History of an Accidental Book*. New York: Houghton Mifflin Harcourt.

Bosch, D.J. (1991). *Transforming Mission: Paradigm Shifts in Theology of Mission*, Society of Missiology Series. New York: Orbis.

Boyer, P.S. (2008). From tracts to mass-market paperbacks: spreading the word via the printed page in America from the early national era to the present. In: *Religion & the Culture of Print in Modern America* (ed. C.L. Cohen and P.S. Boyer), 14–38. Madison, WI: University of Wisconsin Press.

Canton, W. (1904). *A History of the British and Foreign Bible Society*. London: John Murray.

Carey, W. (1792). *An Inquiry into the Obligations of Christians to Use Means for the Conversion of the Heathens*. London: Hodder and Stoughton (repr. 1891).

Cohen, C.L. (2008). Religion, print culture, and the Bible before 1876. In: *Religion & the Culture of Print in Modern America* (ed. C.L. Cohen and P.S. Boyer), 3–13. Madison, WI: University of Wisconsin Press.

Davis, E.B. (2008). Fundamentalist cartoons, modernist pamphlets, and the religious image of science in the scopes era. In: *Religion & the Culture of Print in Modern America* (ed. C.L. Cohen and P.S. Boyer), 175–198. Madison, WI: University of Wisconsin Press.

Edwards, K. (ed.) (2015). *Rethinking Biblical Literacy*. New York: Bloomsbury Academic Press.

Febvre, L. and Martin, H.-J. (1997). *The Coming of the Book*. London: Verso.

Hedstrom, M. (2013). *The Rise of Liberal Religion: Book Culture and American Spirituality in the Twentieth Century*. New York: Oxford University Press.

Holmes, D.D. (2006). *The Faiths of the Founding Fathers*. New York: Oxford University Press.

Mishima, Y. (1970). *Sun and Steel by Yokio Mishima: His Personal Testament on Art, Action, and Ritual Death* (trans. John Bester. New York: Kodasha USA.

Neill, S. (1991). *A History of Christian Missions*, Penguin History of the Church, 2e. New York: Penguin Books.

Pattemore, S.W. (2010). Green bibles, justice and translation. *The Bible Translator* 61 (4): 217–226.

Prothero, S. (2007). *Religious Literacy: What Every American Needs to Know°–°And Doesn't*. San Francisco: HarperSanFrancisco.

Seesengood, R.P. (2011). 'Wrestling with the 'Macedonian call': Paul, Pauline scholarship and nineteenth-century colonial missions. In: *The Colonized Apostle: Paul through Postcolonial Eyes* (ed. C.D. Stanley), 189–205. Minneapolis, MN: Fortress Press.

Sugirtharajah, R.S. (2001). Textual peddlers: distributing salvation°–°colporteurs and their portable bibles. In: *The Bible and the Third World: Precolonial, Colonial and Postcolonial Encounters*, 140–174. Cambridge: Cambridge University Press.

Taylor, M.C. (1998). *Hiding*. Chicago: University of Chicago Press.

Thornburn, J. (1906). *The Christian Conquest of India*. Cleveland: J. H. Lamb.

Tucker, R. (1983). *From Jerusalem to Irian Jaya*. Grand Rapids, MI: Zondervan.

# 3

# Graphic Bibles

## The Word Becomes (Affecting) Image

Contemporary scholarship has explored several genres of graphic representation of the Bible, and there is an increasing body of literature examining the Bible's appearance in comic-book format, which is appropriate given the number of occasions when the Bible makes serious cross over into the graphic novel genre.[1] One engaging, and perhaps paradigmatic, Bible-comic is Robert Crumb's *The Book of Genesis Illustrated* (Crumb 2009). Crumb's work is famous for its graphic sexuality, its crude and distinct use of line and shading to create "weight" and its generally visceral content. Crumb's script is the complete, unabridged text of Genesis. Reviews (and Crumb's own description of the work) stress that he has followed the text with absolute fidelity, omitting and adding nothing. He, of course, is hardly the only person to make such assertions.

In this chapter, I will use Crumb's *Genesis* to interrogate those claims, exploring how Crumb "translates" biblical text by adaptation into a new medium. I would like to concentrate on two particular (sets of) questions, all assuming a model of cultural studies informed by the work of Hoggart, Hall, and others (esp. Hoggart 1958; Hall 1977, 1980, 1981; see During 1993) and informed by Gramsci and Althusser (esp. Gramsci 1985; Althusser 1969; Althusser and Balibar 1968). First, I would like to examine how Crumb's images both create and reflect popular notions of gender, ethnicity, and cultural (sub)alterity; I will concentrate here upon his depictions of women. Second, I am interested in exploring how Crumb's images intersect, perpetuate, and, at times, challenge what Robert Alter has called the "reticence" of biblical narrative. These two

---

1 Note for example, Clark 2010; Balinisteanu 2012; Locke 2012; Parham 2005; Oropeza 2005; Price 2012; Lewis and Kraemer 2010. On illustrated Bibles, see Pavlac 1993; Beal 2010; Dupertuis 2012. On comics as aspects of Christian (often evangelical) general pop culture and evangelistic tools, particularly the (infamous) Chick Tracts, see Haines 1982; Carmody 2008; Metz 1981; Clark 2009; Philips 2013.

*American Standard: The Bible in US Popular Culture*, First Edition. Robert Paul Seesengood.
© 2024 John Wiley & Sons Ltd. Published 2024 by John Wiley & Sons Ltd.

questions, foregrounded by the study of how Crumb "translates" biblical text into a new genre, demonstrate the reality of a form of "epicriticism" always-already present in the engagement of biblical text by its readers. Finally, as I conclude, I'd like to at least indicate a new direction for reading the Bible and/as graphic image: the implications of the affective force of illustration juxtaposed alongside the reticent, unadorned biblical text.

## Graphic Bibles

Graphic novels are emerging as critical and sophisticated modes of writing. Illustrated narrative is a very old art form, arguably one of the first visual arts depending upon the interpretation of ancient cave paintings. Graphic illustration of literary and sacred texts were standard through most of western history introducing literature to the illiterate. By the twentieth century, comic art expanded to original themes but was regarded as children's literature, most likely because of its resonance to readers with limited literacy. In the 1950s, several adult series were launched focused largely on horror and science fiction. In the late 1960s and 1970s, comic art began to expand into original literature aimed at adults.[2]

Biblical scholarship on graphic novels has been limited until relatively recently but has proliferated. This increase comes, in part, with a growing number of serious adaptations of the Bible into graphic novel/comic book format (one thinks, for example, of not only Crumb, but also of Chester Brown's serialized adaptation of the gospels of Mark and Matthew in the pulp magazines *Yummy Fur* and *Underwater* and Brandon Powell Smith's *The Brick Bible*) and other works that gloss (offer midrash on?) biblical characters (such as Brown's *Mary Wept over the Feet of Jesus*, Craig Thompson's *Blankets*, or Tom Gauld's *Goliath*). With the rise of cultural studies approaches in literary criticism, and the attendant dissolution of the binary division of "high" and "low" literature, in English departments, a development concurrent with the change in graphic literature to adult audiences, comic books became legitimate fodder for literary critics in the 1980s. This criticism expanded through the 1990s. Early biblical criticism on graphic and illustrated art began in the 1990s with a rise in cultural criticism, particularly film (see, e.g. Freedman 2011; Meskin 2011. cf. Cook 2012).

Comic books and graphic novels, by definition, use visual art to communicate alongside written text. Graphic novels/comic books communicate their content via dual sets of signs. The written narrative must be regarded alongside the visual images that are subject to many of the same theoretical approaches

---

2 For brief history of comics and scholarly turn toward graphic literature, see Freedman 2011.

applicable to art criticism and film critique (Meskin 2011). To "interpret" a comic book requires the unification of literary criticism (examining such things as plot, the narrative voice, characters, settings), art criticism (art history, visual references, form, shape, color, line, shadow, expression, etc.), and often genre, all of which can also be examined through a variety of ideological and methodological lenses (feminist critique, psychoanalytic, postcolonialism, social-scientific critiques, poststructuralism, etc. See Freedman 2011; Meskin 2011).

In 2009, Robert Crumb published his much-anticipated graphic rendition of Genesis. The relative disinterest among biblical scholars[3] does not coincide with the extreme interest this volume awoke among fans of graphic and illustrated novels in general and Robert Crumb, in particular.[4] Crumb's long career as an illustrator is itself colored by his own remarkable biography.[5] Born in Philadelphia, Pennsylvania, Crumb had his most successful commercial (and, many might argue, artistic) collaboration was with the comic writer Harvey Pekar, particularly in Pekar's critically acclaimed series *American Splendor* (for a representative anthology, see Pekar 2003). *American Splendor* was an autobiographical review of the life of Pekar with particular focus on his at-times-down-at-heels life as a civil servant in Cincinnati, infatuated with collecting rare-press jazz records (Pekar was also a notable jazz critic), negotiating a series of ordinary romantic and personal relationships, struggling financially, and his constant quest for a broader audience for his literary work. Pekar's style included direct address to the reader and heavy narration. Pekar is, in many ways, an "everyman intellectual," an autodidact widely read in political theory and philosophy, art criticism, serious literature and history.[6]

Crumb's other work is, at times, sporadic and notable for major themes of graphic sexuality and crude humor. Crumb self-describes as a "sex addict," quite frank about his numerous adulterous affairs (many producing children), his near obsessive masturbation, and his near-constant sexual fantasy; Crumb is also remarkably self-aware of how these impulses toward sexual expression arise from complex and confusing responses to various levels of dysfunction and social misadjustment and various forms of abuse arising from within his

---

3 Most reviews or notice were of the type of Byassee 2010 and Anderson 2010 – both rather popular and brief in their treatment. Both also play upon the theme of "graphic" bibles and "R-Rating." More substantial are Pauley 2011 and Petersen 2010, pp. 120, 125–126, though the latter reading is brief.

4 For a sampling of the popular excitement note the major reviews of Johnson 2009, Hajdu 2009, Luscombe 2009, Colton 2009, Mouly 2009, Baker 2009, and Spitznagel 2009.

5 An excellent review of Crumb's life is available in the 1994 documentary *Crumb* (dir. Terry Zigoff; Sony Pictures).

6 Defining himself as an "illustrator," Crumb is also famous for his iconic images "keep on trucking" and Fritz the cat, each produced in the 1960s.

family of origin, particularly surrounding his mother. He is an avowed atheist and regards his own Jewish identity with significant nuance and open secularity.

Crumb's artistic style is distinct. His illustration uses crude, blocky figures and heavy lines. His image framing is often rather basic; he prefers full figure and "midfield" composition. Crumb's use of line boldly directs the reader's eye. He uses these heavy lines, and also deep shading and shadow, to create characters that lift from the page. In addition, his work is often heavily detailed. He has a particularly precise eye for architectural and landscape detail; much of his work draws from photographs or real-life figures. When drawing human figures, Crumb focuses upon facial lines and hair, drawing out a visceral and at times crude representation of his figures. Their faces are lined and worn, yet highly expressive – particularly in his representation of eyes – and readily communicate anger, surprise, or joy capturing the exact nuance of expression to illustrate a character's inner thoughts and feelings.

Crumb's work has been exhibited in major galleries and has garnered significant critical attention; Crumb is one of the few illustrators of graphic literature and comics who has "crossed over" into the main-stream art world; in many ways, his work is responsible for drawing both critical attention to comic books as a literary genre and for inspiring other graphic artists to move in their work from simple illustration of children's literature to the production of stand-alone, adult-oriented comic books as a new genre of serious literary production.

## Robert Crumb on Genesis

Despite the famous adage, in this case, the cover of *The Book of Genesis Illustrated by Robert Crumb* certainly suggests the work's contents.[7] The central image is that of God (an old man with flowing hair and beard and white clothes), casting Adam and Eve from the Garden of Eden. A Rubenesque and rather busty Eve is looking back tearfully as she clasps the hand of her husband, sullen and carrying a farming tool. They are dressed in animal hides that barely cover their bodies. They step from lush grasses bestrewn with flowers and shaded by trees onto an arid, rock-strewn path with distant and rugged looking mountains beyond. They are surrounded by flies. The image suggests a turn from or loss of innocence, a fitting allegory for a cartoon depiction of Genesis that will both de-center a nostalgia over the purity found in biblical text even as it distorts a child-like innocence inherent in comic art. This is not a work for children.

---

7 In many ways, *The Book of Genesis Illustrated* is a very difficult book to reference or cite. It does not contain verse designations for the various chapters of Genesis. It also does not have page numbers of any type.

Indeed, the cover asserts as much. Noting that "All 50 chapters" will be covered in a work that is "the first book of the Bible graphically Depicted" we learn that "graphic" is something of a double-entendre; we are assured that in this comic there will be "Nothing Left Out!" and other warnings suggest that "Adult Supervision Recommended for Minors." Would that every Bible bore such cautions. The rear cover stresses the comprehensiveness of the work, surveying the stories included (all the major stories of Genesis), assuring us also of comprehensive treatment of "all the 'begots'" and the "table of nations" and depicting God, again, surrounded by the images of the Patriarchs (Abraham, Isaac and Jacob), the Matriarchs (Sarah, Rachel, and Rebekah – though not Leah), Joseph and Pharoah, Noah, Adam and Eve, and the Serpent.

Crumb's preface lays out his agenda and approach in language that borders upon the confessional and will awaken, for some of us, memories of academic honor codes or oaths:

> I, R. Crumb, the illustrator of this book, have, to the best of my ability, faithfully reproduced every word of the original text, which I derived from several sources, including the King James Version, but mostly from Robert Alter's recent translation, *The Five Books of Moses* (2004).
>
> (preface)

Quickly appended to this declaration of textual fidelity is Crumb's admission that "I ventured to do a little interpretation of my own, if I thought the words could be made clearer, but I refrained from indulging too often in such 'creativity,' and sometimes let it stand in its convoluted vagueness rather than monkey around with such a venerable text." Antiquity and the inherent quality of the narrative, not divine inspiration or biblical authority, is the source of Crumb's respect for Genesis. He notes that

> Every other comic book version of the Bible ... contains passages of completely made-up narrative and dialogue, in an attempt to streamline and 'modernize' the old scriptures, and still, these various comic book Bibles all claim to adhere to the belief that the Bible is 'the word of God,' or 'inspired by God,' whereas I, ironically, do NOT believe the Bible is the 'word of God.' I believe it is the words of men.
>
> (preface)

Crumb goes on to articulate a process of biblical composition, codification, and redaction, where the Bible reaches its final form (at least of the Torah) during the Exilic and Persian eras, an historical reconstruction that is entirely resonant with the arguments of historical-critical scholars. Crumb indicates he used personal assistance with Hebrew phrases and spellings and based many of his images on photos of modern Bedouins from Morocco. Crumb clearly did additional reading in scholarly and rabbinic commentary, though he does not use much annotation. The conclusion of his book contains a brief chapter-by-chapter commentary (omitting chapters 4, 5, 7, 14, 15, 18, 22, and 33–37). He cites Robert Alter in the preface (and in notes to chapter 24) and Savina Teubal (*Sarah the Priestess* 1984 in his notes to chapters 12, 21, and 31. He is probably also referring to her work in his notes on chapters 13, 16, 17, 24–26, and 38). Crumb references the *Epic of Gilgamesh,* the *Ennuma Elish,* and Lilith traditions in his notes to chapters 3 and 8, though he does not name them. He cites "the Midrash" that Terah (Abram's father) was a seller of idols (chapter 11), and he also alludes to traditions of "crossroad" deities in his notes on chapter 32. Crumb is also aware of Wellhausen's source critical arguments particularly on the varied creation accounts (chapter 2), archaeological and literary data on ancient Hebrew polytheism (chapters 6 and 31), nineteenth-century racial and ethnic interpretations of various genealogies (chapters 9, 10, and 11). He does not include a bibliography.

Several of Crumb's images and series of images merit review and reveal elements of biblical text potentially over-looked by general reading. A general survey of his images from the prologue of Genesis 1–11 demonstrates this point. The transition between the two creation accounts in Chapter 1:1–2:4 and Chapter 2:4b-3:24 is stark and clear; the exuberance and innocence of the sexual expression of the first couple are delicately drawn. Crumb's depiction of the serpent clarifies the etiology of the serpent's curse in chapter 3. His sensitive rendering of facial expression as the primal couple consume the forbidden fruit is sublime. His depiction of the cherubim reflects general ancient near eastern iconography. Crumb depicts the murder of Abel in chapter 4 with a brutality that matches the sparseness inherent in the biblical text. His review of the generations in chapter 5 organizes this material in blocks that help readers to understand that, according to biblical text, Noah was alive at the time of Adam's death (a similar effect is achieved in chapter 11 when one realizes that the biblical narrative, again, allows for a brief overlap in the life span of Noah and Abram). The Nephilim in Genesis 6 draws on the Epic of Gilgamesh; a scene that seems to depict Gilgamesh and Enkidu slaying Humbaba illustrates 6:5. The worship of Moloch, with its reputed human sacrifice is depicted in chapter 6, as is the tradition of Abram's father, Terah, as a seller of idols in chapter 11. The variations of the flood narratives are slightly obscured, though the transition of expression in chapter 9, as God makes a new covenant are remarkable. Chapters 10 and 11 are a tour-de-force of Crumb's visual research into ancient near eastern art, iconography, and language. (He even captures, accurately, Accadian and Babylonian cuneiform and Middle Egyptian hieroglyphs. He returns to the hieroglyphs in 42 and 44 as a script for Joseph speaking in Egyptian.) Crumb is graphic in his depiction of Noah's drunkenness, Abram's sex with Hagar and

Sarah, the destruction of Sodom, Lot's sex with his daughters, Jacob's sex with his wives Leah and Rachel, Onan's masturbation, and Judah's sex with Tamar. All these stories, normally skipped in children's versions of Genesis, clearly speak to Crumb's intent to "graphically depict" the entire, exact text of Genesis. The juxtaposition, sometimes startling, of comic book art and graphic sexuality (a collision as discomfiting as Art Spiegelman's retelling of the Holocaust with cartoon cats and mice) communicates more clearly than any essay could how earthy sexual and graphic biblical text can be. Genesis and its stories are beloved in synagogue and church and are frequently taught to children. Crumb's illustrations force a reflection on just how "child friendly" these stories actually are.

Savina Teubal (1984) argues Genesis – indeed, the whole of the Torah – was an edited compendium of ancient Hebrew literature that was, by design, suppressing an earlier strata of myth and literature that reveals an epoch of matriarchic society and the primacy of female deities. Teubal argues that this transformation from matriarchy to patriarchy and its attendant shifts in religion occurred, at various times, across the entire ancient near east. Crumb is clearly taken with this thesis. Though he may well have done reading in addition to Alter and Teubal (and, indeed, I think he did), much of his data on ancient near eastern mythology, ritual and biblical source criticism could easily be mediated via these two sources, alone. The absence of specific argument or additional citation suggest this is the case.

Though Crumb keeps any direct engagement with Teubal confined to the endnotes, his images are certainly influenced by a strong feminist eye. Biblical text is notoriously andro-centric, and Crumb is certainly loyal to his text. Yet women as drawn by Crumb often display characteristically strong features, convicted expressions, and powerful activity. Crumb also opts to include women, silent, as observers in male-oriented scenes in ways that make them active participants in the drama of the frame. Unlike biblical text, women appear (though, one must admit, often silently) on nearly every page of Crumb's comic. This is not to say, however, that Crumb's treatment is unambivalently feminist. Crumb frequently depicts women – often nude – as victims of violence and even human sacrifice. His female characters are uniformly sexualized with exaggerated breasts, prominent buttocks, and often exposing significant flesh (particularly plunging neck lines and bared thighs). In a sense, this is very much in keeping with traditional depiction of women in graphic literature – a literature that, despite its recent turns toward "adult" audiences and literary nuance – still tends to preserve a somewhat adolescent infatuation with the female body (Balinisteanu 2012).

For Crumb, women figures are central and women characters become much more vivid. Yet their strength is predicated upon their sexuality and, one presumes, their ability to procreate. In many ways, this latter, inspired in Crumb by Teubal, resonates with the actual text of Genesis where women are most notable for their fertility and most powerful via their sexuality as they inhabit a text fecund with creation and earthiness. Popular culture both reflects and constructs popular ideas and conventions[8]; Crumb's Genesis both reflects and produces scholarly "meanings" and interpretation.

## "Translation" of Word into Image

In a broad review on the significance of illustration and adaptation of biblical text, David Petersen asks:

> Are artists "illustrating" the Bible text, or is there a more profound interpretation at work? Or are they using biblical literature as an occasion to make a point about some issue that does not inhere in the biblical text? Put simply, what do artists "do" with a biblical text?
>
> (Petersen 2010, p. 121)

I would answer that the depiction of biblical text is a form of interpretation of biblical text. Characters are drawn with expressions indicating feelings and inner dialog. The ascription of these feelings is an interpretive move. The location of characters "in frame" for various scenes shapes the way a scene is understood, which is a form of interpretation. At times Crumb's images explicitly interpret; his scene of a "frisky" encounter between Isaac and Rebekah set in king Melech's garden resolves a famous textual and lexical chestnut in Genesis 26.

Despite real concerns about over-application (see Clark 2010), many techniques from film theory can be applied to the interpretation of graphic novels and comic art. One perennial problem in adaptation of a literary work to graphic medium (normally film) is the limitation of scale and the effectiveness of expression. Novels, simply put, tend to wander. Contemporary novels often reveal the inner thoughts and ideas of characters. Novels have complex plots with interrelated subplots that advance the thesis of the work or add nuance to its arguments. Film cannot capture these nuances. Without the rather wooden device of voice-over, film cannot easily narrate a character's inner thoughts. This inner dialog and emotion must be communicated via dialog, soundtrack, acting, cinematography, lighting, props, and sets, and more.

Crumb faces similar limitations in illustrating a literary work. Narration and some inner dialog can be articulated via floating text boxes typical for comic art. Crumb must articulate many elements of meaning by alternate means.[9] He may

---

8 This idea is fundamental in Birmingham School approaches to cultural studies. See Exum and Moore 1998 and Moore 2000 for defense. For examination and examples related to religion, Bible, and comics, see Balinisteanu 2012; Wertham 1954; Clark 2009.

9 An issue not specific to his own project. See Carmody 2008 and Mundhenk 2002.

communicate via framing, background, expression, character inclusion and position and more. Each of these elements are interpretations, arising from interpretive decisions made by Crumb as he "translates" the text of Genesis into a graphic novel format. In essence, then, in his "illustration" of Genesis, Crumb is creating an entirely new literary work that is the juxtaposition of the text of Genesis and his illustration-interpretation. Crumb's work reveals that there is no way to simply illustrate biblical text or to produce a graphic novel of Genesis that is "just" Genesis. Every attempt is the production of a new work.

One significant moment of this intersection is, again to borrow from film criticism, in Crumb's use of perspective, shot plotting, and framing as a means of constructing the viewer's gaze. A good example of this is Crumb's depiction of the women of Genesis. Crumb uses his liberty as illustrator to include women in many frames, even when the women are silent. In giving them presence, he also gives them voice. Yet Crumb's drawings are highly sexual. Women, again and again, are naked. They thrust their (very rounded) buttocks toward the reader/viewer or kneel before male characters. All the female characters have large breasts and are drawn to appeal to a puerile, adolescent taste. Their clothing often reveals their bodies, particularly their breasts. The gaze in this text is a highly sexualized, highly objectifying eye. Influenced by Teubal, Crumb incorporates women in ways that resonate with her thesis. Dominant and powerful women are exposed, but are exposed in ways that cannot fail to note the potential and power in female reproduction and motherhood. Crumb's images perform a celebration-but-sublimation of Teubal in much the same way that Teubal argues Genesis itself sublimates-but-depends-upon ancient pre-biblical matriarchies.

In his own survey and review of Crumb, Petersen suggests:

> Crumb's *The Book of Genesis*, though deploying a contemporary artistic idiom – the comic – forces the reader to engage the entire biblical text. The reader must confront all the scenes in Genesis, not just those deemed important, whether for artistic interpretation or for critical study. Further, Crumb has done his best to place the text in its ancient context, both by offering a vaguely Semitic profile to his cast of characters and by introducing what he takes to be the scenery of the ancient Near East. ... The ... reader is receiving "one more" commentary. Only with Crumb's *The Book of Genesis* does one actually confront biblical text.
> (Petersen 2010, p. 126)

"Illustration" as well as "graphic" take on dual meanings when discussing Crumb's work. The text is displayed in its full, exposed sense. Like many of its female characters, the words of Genesis – even the curious, the diseased, the private words – are stripped, exposed, subject to gaze; Genesis under Crumb's hand is laid out for examination – scandalous, entertaining, or clinical. It is brutal in its nakedness – a nakedness effected by illustration. The reader of *The Book of Genesis Illustrated* is, indeed, receiving, simultaneously, text and commentary. The commentary, arising from the juxtaposition of Crumb's illustration and the language of Genesis, inhere (to use Petersen's word) and integrate commentary and text in a way analogous to the relationship between genome and epigenome: Crumb's illustrations, the accrual of centuries of scholarship and tradition, activate or suppress elements of text. This dynamic is particularly vibrant in Genesis, a work of literature whose very (genetic?) structure creates reader-commentators. Agreeing with Petersen, though, one is left to wonder how one can "actually confront biblical text," via Crumb or via any other critic. Like an epigenome, reading (and prior readers) alters the genetic structure of a text, "turning on" certain possibilities, suppressing others, adding some potentialities of meaning while eliding or eliminating many more.

## The Reticence of Biblical Image

Crumb's collaboration with Robert Alter is as fertile at awakening insight as his use of Teubel. The literary critic Robert Alter (*The Art of Biblical Narrative*, 1993) has done extensive analysis of biblical literature as literature. One component he has brought centrally to the attention of critics is what he calls the "reticence of biblical literature." He works, for example, with the *Aggidah* (the famous story of the offering of Isaac by Abraham in Genesis 22), noting how much the inner reaction, emotion, and feeling of all the characters are suppressed, in part, by the text. We are almost never told what people "think" or "feel." We, as readers, must infer this by our engagement with, and interpretation of, the dramatic action of the text. The horror of the narrative, matched with this reticence, builds deep ambivalence and tension in the reader. Eric Auerbach has done similar work with Homer, writing about the reunion scene between Odysseus and Penelope. Noting the scene, again, does not have an omniscient narrator who reveals inner thoughts and emotion (these must, again, be discovered by the reader's interaction with the dramatic narrative), Auerbach describes the scene, somewhat famously, as one "fraught with background." In general, ancient literature doesn't reveal much about feeling, inner thought, character motivation – character depth is constructed solely by narrative and drama and interaction. This, in general, heightens the complexity of characterization and reader investment.

Crumb's "illustration" of Genesis, as a "translation" of the text of Genesis into the genre of graphic novel, in many ways augments the reticent text. The absence of direct access to the inner lives or motives of characters is compensated, in part, by the visual nature of the work. Like film or theater, Crumb can construct scenes or guide the viewer-reader's gaze in ways that express and create affect. Even as he is bound by a reticent narrator, Crumb's illustration is not only interpretation of Genesis, but the translation of Genesis into a new genre. In some ways, the reticence of biblical narrative is matched by the reticence of graphic narration. Crumb's *Genesis Illustrated* is a juxtaposition of biblical text, film, and graphic literature – all of which struggle with explicit articulation of inner emotion, focusing upon narration and depiction as means of communication of inner self. The result of this union, however, is highly provocative and evocative of meaning. On the one hand, the evocative power of the reticent text is curtailed by the provision, by Crumb, of visual cues that restrict potential interpretations. Yet, on the other hand, Crumb's illustrations serve as an illumination of the manuscript, filling in some reticence but also producing others.

## Conclusion

Tim Beal notes an interesting parallel between the growth – the "bloom" – of Bible publishing and plant reproduction. Fruit tree production tends to decline as a tree ages. In the tree's last years, however, there is a sudden bloom of both flowers and fruits. It is not uncommon to see dramatic increases in production and productivity in the final two or three seasons of a flowering plant. Far from being a sign of renewed vigor, these bumper crops are actually "distress crops;" A plant, shortly before dying, will devote the last of its resources to fruit production (in an effort to perpetuate itself). Beal suggests that one might argue the sudden rapid growth in Bible production is harbinger of the end of a certain view and status of the Bible. The Bible, in the "twilight of print culture" certainly seems to be less the common text it once was. One cannot assume the type of biblical literacy once considered normal. Certainly, print culture is shifting, and may well be in decline. But, one asks fairly, are books? Is the Bible?

Beal is not the only one to look at reproductive biology as a metaphor for the spread of Bibles. In his 1998 article, Hugh Pyper considers the Bible as a "selfish meme." His essay draws from the genetics work by Richard Dawkins. Dawkins famously refocuses the process of reproduction and life from the level of organism to the level of DNA. Complex organisms do not use DNA to reproduce, Dawkins argues, so much as DNA has managed to construct complex organisms as the machinery for their own perpetuation. Genes are "selfish"; they create life (and urges within life forms) as a means of their own survival. Pyper takes this idea and considers the Bible. What if, he asks, the Bible is actually a document that has created religious and cultural systems in order to perpetuate itself.

Somewhat tongue-in-cheek, he wonders if Bibles have independent agency. Certainly, the question has limits. But it also awakens real thought on whether or not Bibles in Judaism, Christianity, and scholarly and cultural biblicism, the Bible as a text-system, has a (for lack of a better word) autonomous power.

We can certainly note (with some amusement) the irony in using Darwin (or Dawkins, for that matter) to speak to the spread of evangelicalism's Bible. But we might also do more. Putting our two ideas together, perhaps the recent proliferation of Bibles, and *illustrated* Bibles particularly, is not a distress crop, but a mutation: the rise of a new species to see that the Bible continues. Beal nicely notes the traumas of the present moment toward print; digitalization and internet are changing the way we understand "texts" and their authority. When animals encounter new environments, they often die. But they also change. Beal argues, faced with fundamental environmental changes, the Bible is initiating a distress crop in order to see that something within it survives. But in rapid reproduction, one encounters the chance, always, for mutation and change. Following Pyper, perhaps these suddenly "new" Bibles are the Bible's attempt to persist, to find a way, to find the correct strategy, the right DNA strand, to survive. We can't escape noticing that this moment is not just the blossoming of digital technologies, it is also a moment for the sudden, stratospheric ascension of late capitalism. So, given the changes imposed upon the Bible by digitization and late capitalism, mediated by Althusser's views on the real "agency" of systems, but also of things, maybe the current moment is the Bible acting out its own preservation in our climate of global, total capitalism. In our present moment of cinema and internet, spare text, alone, no longer has the affective force required for its own preservation. What is needed is a new fusion of graphic and textual that can compress an array of affective signals and messages, interpretations, and ideas, into a single frame.

Crumb offers his work as an illustration, without addition, of the text of Genesis. Criticism of graphic novels must critically address the literary aspects of the novel, but must also be attuned to the way that images collaborate with that narrative to produce the aggregate "meaning" of the final, composite product. Crumb's illustration of Genesis is an interpretation, a "translation" of the book of Genesis into an entirely new genre. This translation brings with it an always-already alteration of the text of Genesis. There is no way to illustrate a text without, simultaneously, interpreting it.

One example of this principle on Crumb's work can be seen in his presentation of female characters. Relying on Teubal, Crumb's illustrations presume a textual history behind Genesis that charts the rise-and-fall-and-eventual suppression of women's religion and matriarchy. As a result, his images frequently foreground women. Yet his images just as frequently sexualize women. Crumb's images implicitly re-perform the process of textual transmission and alteration that he sees behind Genesis. The result is an altogether new work, a re-written

Genesis, that sparks renewed attention to textual and graphic resonances as new and fecund, affective species, ripe for interpretation.

## Works Cited

Alter, R. (1993). *The Art of Biblical Narrative*. New York: Norton.

Alter, R. (2004). *The Five Books of Moses*. New York: Basic Books.

Althusser, L. (1969). *For Marx*. London: Allen Lane.

Althusser, L. and Balibar, E. (1968). *Reading Capital*. London: New Left Books.

Anderson, G.A. (2010). The Bible, rated R. *First Things* (200): 13–15.

Baker, K. (2009). Comics star R. Crumb gets serious with Genesis. *San Francisco Chronicle* (30 October). https://www.sfgate.com/entertainment/article/comics-star-r-crumb-gets-serious-with-genesis-3282719.php (accessed 18 October 2023).

Balinisteanu, T. (2012). Goddess cults in techno-worlds: tank girl and Borg queen. *Journal of Feminist Studies in Religion* 28 (1): 5–24.

Beal, T.K. (2010). The end of the word as we know it: the cultural iconicity of the bible in the twilight of print culture. *Postscripts* 6 (1–3): 165–184.

Byassee, J. (2010). R-rated scripture. *The Christian Century* 127 (1): 11.

Carmody, T.J. (2008). Converting comic books into graphic novels and digital cartoons. In: *Understanding Evangelical Media* (ed. Q.J. Schultze and R. Woods), 186–197. Downers Grove, IL: IVP Academic.

Clark, E. (2009). Of Catholics, commies, and the anti-christ: mapping American social borders through cold war comic books. *Journal of Religion and Popular Culture* 21 (3): https://www.utpjournals.press/doi/abs/10.3138/jrpc.21.3.003 (accessed 15 October 2023).

Clark, T.R. (2010). Prophetic voices in graphic novels: the 'comic and tragic vision' of apocalyptic rhetoric in *Kingdom Come* and *Watchmen*. In: *The Bible in/and Popular Culture: A Creative Encounter*, Semeia Studies, vol. 65 (ed. P. Culbertson and E.M. Wainwright), 141–156. Atlanta, GA: Society of Biblical Literature Press.

Colton, D. (2009). Illustrator R. Crumb is drawn to God with his latest project. *USA Today* (19 October).

Cook, R.T. (2012). Why comics are not films: metacomics and medium-specific conventions. In: *The Art of Comics: A Philosophical Approach* (ed. A. Meskin and R.T. Cook), 165–187. New York: Wiley.

Crumb, R. (2009). *The Book of Genesis Illustrated*. New York: Norton.

Dupertuis, R.R. (2012). Translating the Bible into pictures. In: *Text, Image and Otherness in Children's Bibles* (ed. C. Vander Stichele and H.S. Pyper), 271–289. Atlanta, GA: Society of Biblical Literature Press.

During, S. (1993). Introduction. In: *The Cultural Studies Reader*, 2e (ed. S. During), 1–30. New York: Routledge.

Exum, J.C. and Moore, S.D. (1998). *Biblical Studies/Cultural Studies*, Journal for the Study of the New Testament Supplement Series, vol. 266. Sheffield: Sheffield Academic Press.

Freedman, A. (2011). Comics, graphic novels, graphic narrative: a review. *Literature Compass* 8 (1): 28–46.

Gramsci, A. (1985). *Selections from the Cultural Writings* (ed. D. Forgacs and D. Nowell-Smith). London: Lawrence & Wishart.

Haines, A.B. (1982). 'Christian' comic books. *Christian Century* 99 (2): 47–48.

Hajdu, D. (2009). God gets graphic. *New York Times* (22 October).

Hall, S. (1977). Culture, the media and the 'Ideological Effect'. In: *Mass Communication and Society* (ed. J. Curran, M. Gurevitch, and J. Woollacott), 315–348. London: Edward Arnold.

Hall, S. (1980). Cultural studies and the centre: some problematics and problems. In: *Culture, Media, Language: Working Papers in Cultural Studies, 1972–79* (ed. S. Hall, D. Hobson, A. Love, and P. Willis), 15–47. London: Hutchinson.

Hall, S. (1981). Two paradigms in cultural studies. In: *Culture, Ideology and Social Process* (ed. T. Bennett, S. Boyd-Bowman, C. Mercer, and J. Woollacott), 19–37. London: Batsford.

Hoggart, R. (1958). *The Uses of Literacy*. Harmondsworth: Penguin.

Johnson, R.2009). The creation of R. Crumb's 'Genesis. *Los Angeles Times* (29 October).

Lewis, D.A. and Kraemer, C.H. (2010). *Graven Images: Religion in Comic Books and Graphic Novels*. London/New York: Continuum.

Locke, S. (2012). Spirit(ualitie)s of science in words and pictures: syncretising science and religion in the cosmologies of two comic books. *Journal of Contemporary Religion* 27 (3): 383–401.

Luscombe, B. (2009). Genesis: the world according to R. Crumb. *Time Magazine* (1 November).

Meskin, A. (2011). The philosophy of comics. *Philosophy Compass* 6 (12): 854–864.

Metz, G. (1981). Jack Chick's anti-Catholic Alberto comic book is exposed as a fraud. *Christianity Today* 25 (5): 50–53.

Moore, S.D. (2000). *In Search of the Present: The Bible through Cultural Studies*, Semeia Studies, vol. 82. Atlanta, GA: Society of Biblical Literature Press.

Mouly, F. (2009). Comic strip by R. Crumb: the book of Genesis. *New Yorker* (8 June, 15 June).

Mundhenk, N.A. (2002). Translating bible comics. *Bible Translator* 53 (4): 402–413.

Oropeza, B.J. (2005). *The Gospel According to Superheroes: Religion and Pop Culture*. New York: Peter Lang.

Parham, T. (2005). Superheroes in crisis: postmodern deconstruction and reconstruction in comic books and graphic novels. In: *The Gospel According to Super-Heroes* (ed. B.J. Oropeza), 197–214. New York: Peter Lang.

Pauley, G.E. (2011). Seeing Abraham and Isaac. *Perspectives* 26 (3): 318.

Pavlac, R. (1993). Bang! Zow! Christian comic books join the fight for teens: Thomas Nelson, marvel team on glossy project. *Christianity Today* 37 (8): 318.

Pekar, H. (2003). *American Splendor*. New York: Ballantine (Repr. *American Splendor: The Life and Times of Harvey Pekar*. New York: Doubleday, 1986 and *More American Splendor: The Life and Times of Harvey Pekar*. New York: Doubleday, 1987.

Petersen, D.L. (2010). The bible in public view. In: *Foster Biblical Scholar-Ship: Essays in Honor of Kent Harold Richards* (ed. F. Ritchel and C.W. Miller), 117–133. Atlanta, GA: Society of Biblical Literature Press.

Philips, A.G. (2013). Vampires, werewolves, and other assorted creatures: the apocryphal bestiary of chick publications. *Journal of Religion and Popular Culture* 24 (2): https://www.utpjournals.press/doi/abs/10.3138/jrpc.24.2.277 (accessed 15 October 2023).

Price, R.M. (2012). The seven-sealed comic book: the book of Revelation in the graphic novel *Kingdom Come*. *Journal of Unification Studies* 13: 215–233.

Pyper, H. (1998). The selfish text: the Bible and memetics. In: *Biblical Studies/ Cultural Studies*, Journal for the Study of the New Testament Supplement Series, vol. 266; Gender, Culture, Theory, 7 (ed. J.C. Exum and S.D. Moore), 71–90. Sheffield Academic Press.

Spitznagel, E. (2009). Robert Crumb thinks God might actually be crazy. *Vanity Fair* (22 October).

Teubal, S. (1984). *Sarah the Priestess*. Athens, OH: Swallow Press.

Wertham, F. (1954). The curse of the comic books: the value patterns and effects of comic books. *Religious Education* 49 (6): 394–406.

# 4

# "Eat This Book"

## The Bible and the American Diet

This chapter will explore the notions of "biblical eating," an increasingly complex matrix of issues and concerns with a particular eye toward Bible and popular culture. In this chapter, I want to delve into "culture" using the work of Conrad Ostwalt and Michael de Certeau. Food and diet are, fundamentally, popular and mass culture. As we will see, scholarship on the intersection between Bible and American diet has addressed the origins and transformation of the food production companies of Kellogg's and Welch's, the changing definition of kosher and kosher demarcation, the recent rise of "biblical vegetarianism," the Bible's role in contemporary discussions over the environment and animal rights, modern weight loss-via-Bible-guidance movements (Weigh Down Watchers, etc.), and contemporary evangelical "reclamation" of biblical kosher regulations. This chapter explores several of these food-Bible intersections and will ask what these modern engagements reveal about the structure, content, and practicality of biblical instructions regarding food. I will also use the work of Roland Boer (who, in turn, uses Marx and Levi-Strauss) to argue that food consumption, particularly "biblically" influenced food consumption is intrinsically tied to a host of ethnic, cultural, and class-status constructions. As such, despite their ubiquity and seeming innocence, food and diet are powerfully political actions. Jewish and Christian forms of diet control emerge as significant moments of a late capitalist approach to identity construction via production and consumption.

## The Bible and Cultural Studies

"What has Athens to do with Jerusalem?" Tertullian

*We wake in the morning at 7:00, our little boy climbing into our bed as our alarm goes off. We talk and slowly stir. She takes him to his room to get him dressed. I tend to the dogs downstairs. We reunite in the kitchen. I feed the dogs kibble as she prepares*

*American Standard: The Bible in US Popular Culture*, First Edition. Robert Paul Seesengood.
© 2024 John Wiley & Sons Ltd. Published 2024 by John Wiley & Sons Ltd.

*an egg and some toast for the boy. I put a kettle on the stove for coffee. I shower and dress while she serves him and fixes some bread and cheese for herself. I return and feed him apple slices while we play silly word games; she showers and dresses. I put some olive oil in a heated skillet and put a sliced bagel in the toaster. I crack an egg into the skillet breaking the yoke to fry it firmly. The radio is on with the morning news. My son is telling me a story about his coloring book of superhero characters. I turn the egg and pepper it; I put a slice of cheddar cheese on it. He is playing with the dogs, feeding them from the kitchen table; I tell him to stop. I pull the egg and cheese out of the skillet and put them on the bagel for my breakfast. He drinks his milk and eats a few cheerios; I sit next to him and eat my breakfast and drink my coffee. He rises to begin to play while I pack my bag for the day – loading up my papers, some books, my computer. I prepare a lunch of walnuts, cheese, pears, and bread, and I leave for campus and my office. She will stay home today, to tend to the boy and to write.*

Perhaps the two most notable changes in humanities scholarship in the last 50 years are significant shifts in the "texts" under review and a proliferation of the methods and ideologies employed by the reviewers: what are we reading, and why/how are we reading it? Biblical studies, as is its (canonical) want, has lagged somewhat in these transformations but certainly seems to be catching its wind for the chase. As we have noted, publisher's catalogs, journal articles, conference (sub)sections, and new course offerings on Bible and various aspects of popular/ mass culture are expanding exponentially. Even concerns about ideological orientation – modernism, postmodernism, postcolonialism, various approaches to subjectivity such as gender and sexuality, queer analysis, the posthuman, and more – seem to be becoming normal fare, as if a grudging acceptance, based upon some grim sense of *stare decisis* if nothing more, is settling across the field.

As we saw in Chapter 1, the recent turn toward popular culture by biblical scholars is not without history and precedent. The rise of cultural studies as a formal discipline, as a methodological and systematic examination of popular and mass culture, spread through the humanities during the late 1960s.

Recalling Chapter 1, we note that Hoggart et al. were largely responding to major pedagogic and cultural shifts arising from the economic and technological growth that followed World War II. Improved manufacturing reduced the gap between highly and semiskilled workers, leaving more people with more money and more leisure. Technology expanded into entertainment with the growth of television and film and the cheapening of print. The gaps between wealthy and poor (in Britain and the United States) narrowed. More people went to college using veteran benefits and applying military training to peacetime uses. Colleges and universities enjoyed unprecedented enrollments, yet many students seemed to lack "cultural knowledge" of previous generations.

As Chapter 1 argued, in the 1930s, F. R. Leavis (1930) argued (persuasively, at the time) that education should consist of cultivating "proper" leisure and exposure to the mainstays of western literature, art, music, etc., avoiding crass "mass" culture. In many ways this distinction marks a long-standing, Victorian separation between "vulgar" and "cultivated," rooted in economic and class differences. Hoggart's (1957) *Uses of Literacy* challenged some of these ideas. Hoggart analyzed how "working-class" Britons read and use their literacy. He challenged much of the idea and content of "high" culture, celebrating working-class values, even as he also challenged "mass culture." Raymond Williams's (1983) *Culture and Society* took the argument further, arguing that differences between "high" and "low" culture are social norms designed to perpetuate and protect class divisions and distinction. As economic and political systems such as those in the United States came of age, formal distinction between social classes (the red line of "gentry" and "peasant") grew at least semipermeable and opaque. The result is a growing social anxiety over class and status. It became increasingly essential to demonstrate one is not "common" or "vulgar."

In its origins, cultural studies, as manifested by the work of Richard Hoggart, Raymond Williams, Stuart Hall, and the Centre for Contemporary Cultural Studies (CCCS) at the University of Birmingham was largely resting on the work of Gramsci and Althusser and rooted in Marxist assumptions of production, consumption, and class and social hierarchy (During 1993). As Chapter 1 details, Hoggart founded the Birmingham CCCS in the early 1960s. The CCCS was later led through the 1960s and 1970s by Stuart Hall. In these years, general Marxist assumptions were dominant, and the CCCS was exploring how these social divisions were reflected in ideas of "culture" and how "culture" worked to create and perpetuate these distinctions. Some notable examples are the two works on a popular television news program, *Nationwide*. These studies explored how this "news" program actually created cultural and social values that perpetuated social divisions and advanced ideas central to maintaining "productivity" by workers. As we saw, Gramsci argued subdominant social groups, the "subaltern," participate willingly in the construction of systems that keep them oppressed, perpetuating, for example, systems of racism, gender control, religious persecution, etc. Louis Althusser, again met in Chapter 1, argued that social structures called "institutions" (religion, family, the military, education) are constructed to perpetuate the social group on the whole. This of necessity means that they will perpetuate forms of social domination. The CCCS was interested in exposing these structures. (This history and its connection to early work on the Bible and popular culture has been presented in a variety of places, as Chapter 1 noted briefly; see Moore 1998; Boer 1999.)

Despite such a high-modernist childhood, as cultural studies has blossomed among the humanities, it has found, through its passionate trysts with continental philosophy and literary theory, ready incentive to settle down and convert to postmodernity. Forgetting what lies behind, regarding it, it would seem, as rubbish, cultural studies has embraced the all-surpassing joy of late capitalism and poststructuralism. A key temptation has been the heady draw of Kristeva-influenced ideas of intertextuality – where evocative moments of commonality between text without regard to any real citation, allusion, or intention – seductively tempts scholars to dip into a whole array of analytical potential. Even those who would stop short of Kristeva's (1980) call for the obituary of the author recognize the limits of arguments for intentionality and concede, if only at the level of functionalist analysis, productive potential in intertextuality's poststructuralist approach.

Work in cultural studies has also, from its inception, foregrounded exposure, critique, and interrogation of systems of gender, social, economic, and intellectual hierarchy; it has been, if nothing else, suspicious of the construction and propagation of a whole array of meta-narratives. Leaning in toward the postmodern from the beginning, as new understandings of the "post" in postmodernity have gained in consensus, cultural studies seems both the source and the natural end of postmodernity. To begin, we could note Frederick Jameson's (1991) postmodernity as an intentional focus upon production, consumption, selection, and the celebration of superficiality and transition; Jameson's ideas find their complete expression in the examination of mass culture. Stephen Moore and Yvonne Sherwood, in tandem with other voices such as J. Z. Smith, have argued that the current interest in religion or Bible in/and/as mass culture is not only the next obvious wave in the field, but is the best articulation of all these various methodological energies churning together (Moore and Sherwood 2011; Smith's presidential address 2009).

As Exum and Moore (and others) have noted (1998) as cultural studies has proliferated among biblical scholars, it has not always brought sharp theoretical focus along with it. Perhaps, though, this is also a manifestation of a Jamesonian notion of postmodernism – the celebration of superficiality. These changes are certainly also facilitated by new technologies. To turn to cultural studies, then, is to turn toward questions of the postmodern, itself. If Jameson was right, and it seems more and more that he was, popular or mass culture is both the crucible and the mold for the postmodern – it is the alpha and omega, the beginning and the end of late capitalism and its focus on superficiality. Cultural studies is perhaps not just *a* method of postmodern reading, but *the* method.

## Defining "Culture" and the "Culture of Everyday Life"

"Culture is first of all a practical science of the singular." Michael de Certeau (2011, Vol. 2, p. 256)

*As I arrive on campus, my first visit, after leaving my coat and bag in my office, is to the department mailroom and the coffee pot. I return to my office, reviewing my mail – electronic and physical. I log onto the internet listservs on news, higher education, and recent scholarship. I write some emails. I record student grades. I finish my coffee. I leave for my classes. My first is a seminar on creation mythology. We discuss, for today, some readings on the interpretation of myth. We discuss, from our reading, a theory that argues hunter-gatherer communities of humans told myths of humans related to nature, in nature, as partners with animals and natural beings. With the transition to agriculture, humans became settled and their mythology changed. These mythic systems revolved around Sky God and Earth Goddess. The two merge in soil and rain to produce a fecund mud of creation; the gods unite and reflect the rhythms of agriculture. Myth and ritual reproduce this union. The gods become a household, and mythic traditions arise about a long-ago paradise where human and divine lived side by side in nature. Now the divine has receded.*

*In my next class, we are reading Herodotus in Greek. We read a portion of his account of the Persian Wars, where Xerxes pushes southward toward Athens, leaving ruin and potential famine in his wake. My next class, my last for the day, is a seminar on Scripture and Cultural studies. We discuss Althusser and Gramsci. After class, I eat my lunch in my office while I watch John Oliver on my computer. During office hours, I grade. I pause for a walk around campus and return to a cup of hot tea. I sip it, wishing I had something sweet, while I play, and lose, a game of chess against the computer. I review and revise some college documents. I see a due date for an internal report is pending; at least, today, I have no administrative meetings in my afternoon. I answer more email. Tired, and vaguely annoyed by the last email I read, I surf around on social media for a while before I realize it's time to admit the truth: I'm done here today. I pack to leave for home. I check my mail again, rinse my coffee cup and return it, and speak casually for a moment with a colleague in the hallway before leaving the building into the twilight.*

What are we studying when we study Bible and culture? Are we studying the Bible, via its appearance in culture, or are we studying culture, using Bible as a tethering theme? The field of biblical studies has engaged cultural studies for a host of reasons, perhaps one for each scholar. Biblical scholars engaging cultural studies have also tended away from classic CCCS theories and assumptions, adopting an array of methodologies and ideologies – again, perhaps as many different ones as there are different scholars. Much of this work has been provocative. Even when lacking clear theory, the juxtaposition of mass-culture analysis and the celebration of superficiality, even when merely implicit as the result of methodological eclecticism, such work resonates with memes of postmodernity. Like postmodernity itself, the lack of coherent program has been regarded as liberating by some, as confusion by others. The best scholarship has raised questions about the Bible's role in cultural and economic (normally postcolonial) structures, about the Bible's participation in systems of ideology and identity, about the location and privilege of biblical scholarship (and the limits of each).

Perhaps, however, some central questions should still be addressed. Biblical scholars have been slow to engage conversations about what, precisely, "culture" might actually mean or constitute, let alone "mass culture," a term that strains against its own seams in a world where the internet both fosters ubiquity and erases coherence, where everything is both global and atomistic at once. One hesitates to recall here the ubiquity of culture, *all* culture, as we have defined it.

Peeping over the disciplinary walls of biblical studies into the library cubical of nearby anthropologists reveals the complexity of this question even more. Modern anthropologists would define "culture" as a variety of technologies and techniques fostered and fused together by human groups and not merely "products" of art, entertainment, or habitation (see the classic works by Malinowski 1931 or Geertz 1973). "Culture" is both everything around us and the ideologies that these items both foster and reflect. "Culture" is the essence of daily life. Indeed, from such a model, the very question of the Bible in-or-and popular culture is deeply problematized. "Bible" and "biblical" ways of being cannot be set against pop culture; they are inseparably pop culture, as well. In a sense, to discuss the Bible and popular culture is to already privilege Bible as something against or superior to or distinct from broader culture. This assumption, as the term "culture" is being used among contemporary social scientists, is senseless.

Our stunned biblicist, letting go the cubicle top and sinking back to her chair, realizes after a few moments of thought that such definitions of "culture" and the problem of privileging biblical text has real implications for setting apart "religion" itself. Durkheim and his progeny have defined the "religious" as the engagement of the "sacred," the opposition to the "secular." Yet this binary seems increasingly tenuous. In his 2003 *Secular Steeples: Popular Culture and Religious Imagination*, Conrad Ostwalt makes just this argument. As he is summarized by Terry Clark:

> Ostwalt focuses upon the "functional authority of religion" rejecting the notion of a dichotomy between sacred and secular forces in society, which have traditionally been understood as locked in an endless struggle for superiority ... Ostwalt argues that the social location of religious authority naturally shifts over time. There is an ebb and flow within society concerning which individuals, groups, or institutions wield authority to speak on religious matters and to influence behavior and values. This does not reflect a diminishment of religious sensibility or value per se over a given period of time. If religious behavior and/or sensibility is a "fundamentally human characteristic" as Ostwalt suggests, then "the religious impulse will not disappear with secularization."
>
> (2010, p. 142)

For Ostwalt, the very separation of the sacred and the profane – of religion and "culture" – is impossible. Ostwalt is a functionalist in his definition of religion. What happens when the secular "encroaches" into religion (or vice versa) is actually a transitional flux. The "sacred" flows in and out of the religious and the secular, leaving some religious forms (texts, places, values) desiccated while secular structures suddenly become deeply significant (in the technical sense of that term). "In such an environment, new cultural forms, including literary forms, will be created to take the place of those texts that become marginalized, practically speaking, because they have become devoid of sacred value" (p. 143). To the extent to which Ostwalt is correct, what we are actually observing in the examination of "Bible in popular culture" is a new, hybridizing, evolution of both "Bible" and "popular culture."

Realizing that religion and the Bible are not separable from culture awakens still more inquiry about what boundaries, if any, can be meaningfully placed around "culture" at all. "Culture" is not merely art, entertainment, social structures, or artifacts. It is the entire array of techniques and technologies for living that surround us, all immersed in – fostering, reflecting, adjusting, perpetuating, generating – ideology, subjectivity, social group and class, economic location, and more. The logical extension of this idea is the exploration of culture within the means of daily, practical life.

Michel de Certeau's landmark *The Practice of Everyday Life* explores this idea in acute detail. His work, arising directly from (indeed, many say as the logical apex of) Hoggart's CCCS approach to cultural studies, argues that the fullest examination of "mass culture" must engage with the ins and outs of daily life, noting that "culture" is defined primarily as those items in use to supply physical needs and answer pressing questions. Our modern world occludes our pursuit of primary needs to a large degree. We do not, as a whole, spend our time crafting tools for agriculture or hunting. We do not, on the whole, spend substantial amounts of our daily time finding and preparing food. Or do we? These problems still remain and still occupy much of our attention. One could argue (and Certeau does) that the resulting sense of "leisure" time and the transformation of our systems of work and social organization are exactly why popular culture speaks so readily to status, and social hierarchy. One must have leisure to pursue popular entertainment or "culture." To have leisure is to be removed from the necessity of (subaltern) work to provide daily essentials; it is, in effect, to have a "staff" (direct or indirect, seen or unseen) tending to one's biological needs. Certeau describes his agenda:

> The purpose of this work is to make explicit the systems of operational combination which also comprise a "culture," and to bring to light the models of action characteristic of uses whose status as the dominated element in society (a status that does not mean that they are either passive or docile) is concealed by the euphemistic term "consumers." Everyday life invents itself by poaching in countless ways upon the property of others.
>
> (p. xi)

Certeau followed his first volume on the culture of "everyday life" with a volume treating food, specifically.

This linkage of culture (as most broadly defined) and the examination of hierarchy does return meaning to questions exploring "religion" and the Bible in/as popular culture. Religion, and the Bible, presume to construct systems of meaning and validation of ideology. To study their location or immersion in popular culture – whether as protest or as prompter – is to study both. The theologian Kathryn Tanner, basing her comments on these immersive and holistic definitions of culture, has urged against "assumptions about culture as a summary of human universals." (1997, pp. 159, 165–166). Theology (and, frankly, any form of humanistic inquiry) should attend to a "primary interest in the particular" (pp. 159, 167).

Following Tanner, I would argue that the study of the Bible in/and/as popular culture should be equally concerned about the mechanisms of daily life as it is with the appearance of Jesus on *Family Guy* or similar moments. The most fundamental space for the intersection of daily life, ideology, status, class and, therefore, the crossroads of "culture," is diet.

## The Biblical Scholarship on/and the American Diet

*So, do not worry, saying "what shall we eat?" or "what shall we drink?"* Matthew 6:31.

*I return home for the day. I leave my office in the basement of the chapel and take the short walk to my Volvo station wagon, our only car. I drive to my house, at the moment, a restored three-story Victorian brownstone on a lovely street near a park and a playground, just along the western boundary of the city's historic district. My city was once beautiful and prosperous; it was a center of rail shipping for food, coal, and textiles to the markets of Philadelphia. It isn't any longer. We have off-street parking (a luxury here). I garage the car and enter the house through the kitchen.*

*My wife and my son are there. The dogs greet me. My son scrambles down from the kitchen table to see me. I can hardly put down my bag. My wife is beginning dinner. The kitchen is an array of cutting boards, boiling pots. She is mincing garlic. She is listening to the news on the radio; NPR again. I come into the house and take my son with me upstairs. We put my bag in the office and go together into my bedroom where I change out of my suit and tie and into jeans as he jumps on the bed. I hang my clothes, my shoes, my tie carefully back in the closet. I put on warm socks. We go back downstairs together. He has not stopped talking since I arrived.*

*I begin chopping shitake and cap mushrooms. Garlic in olive oil and butter is already simmering in a copper pot on the stove. She is chopping peppers; water is steaming in another pot. Our little boy climbs back into his chair at the kitchen table with his comic books. My wife and I talk. She tells me about her writing for the day. We teach in the same department; I tell her about the irritating email and other matters. We talk about students. We talk about our son (who keeps interrupting us with questions about Batman or to tell us about his morning cartoons). I feed the dogs who wiggle and dance around us like honeybees. She is making a salad of greens, pears, and feta cheese, all under balsamic vinegar.*

Like cultural studies in general, food studies – work that examines food and diet with their socioeconomic, ethical, environmental, and cultural aftereffects – are emerging as a clear interest of both the academy and American popular culture. Television programming now includes an array of programs focused on food and cooking. Bookstore shelves burst with not only cookbooks but books on food consumption and diet guidelines. Michael Pollan, Peter Singer, Jim Mason, and others have raised critical questions about the ethics of our food selections, noting how the American diet results in challenges to environmental preservation, the ethical treatment of animals, and equitable and humane employment of other human beings (Singer and Mason 2007; Pollan 2007). Obesity and scarcity, both forms of malnutrition, are becoming a major public health concern.

These phenomena have not gone without scholarly review. A burgeoning number of studies have explored our collective angst over diet and food production. Generally collected under the rubric of "Food Studies" this work explores a variety of questions ranging from ethics to medical advisement, to environmental studies, to the sociopolitical implications of food (see, in general Counihan and Van Esterick 2013; Alba 2013; Belasco 2006). This work, grouped more for common interest and scholarly focus than for particular methodologies or ideology, holds interest for scholars of the Bible.

Certainly, the Judeo-Christian Bible and the religious communities that interact with it have long had an interest in food. Within the Hebrew Bible there are restrictions on diet; food production and dietary choices are brought within the realm of religious ritual. Food is a metaphor for abundance and God's presence (Ps 23; 136:25; Exod 16:12, etc.). The redemption of God's people is metaphorically described as a communal banquet (e.g. Mal 3:10). Food plays a central symbolic role in rituals such as Passover (e.g. Exod 12). The provision of manna is a symbol for God's protective presence (Exod 16). Famously, the Hebrew Bible establishes the rules of *kashrut* forbidding certain foods and bringing the daily meal table into ritual space (Lev 11:1–47; Deut 14:1–19; Exod 23:19). The gospels record miracle stories of Jesus where food is, as in Hebrew Bible, symbolic of God's presence (Mark 6:30–44; Luke 9:10–17; Matthew 14:13–21; John 6:1–15). The gospel of John presents Jesus describing himself as the "bread of life" (John 6:35). One of the most central rituals in Christianity surrounds the consumption of food and wine (Mark 14:12–25; Luke 22:7–38; Matthew 26:17–29; 1 Cor 11:23–35). Commensality was a critical issue in the early community of Jesus's followers, as gentile and Jew encountered one another in worship; Paul's letters address and reflect this debate (Rom 14; 1 Cor 8).

Unlike Judaism, Christianity (with a very few notable exceptions among sectarian groups like the Jehovah's Witnesses) has not produced a systematic program of food regulation, despite the proscriptions in Acts 15 against the eating of animals killed by strangulation and against the consumption of blood. This is not to say, however, that Christianity has neglected food. Diet restriction is a regular component of many Christians engagement with both Lent and Easter. In the Middle Ages, food restriction and diet were key components of the construction and expression of popular piety, particularly among adolescent girls.

Certeau, drawing from Levi-Strauss, has argued that food is an inherently political action. What we eat defines our place in a host of socioeconomic and political communities. In the United States today the choice to become vegetarian is laden with political and identity overtones in many regions. What we eat marks our social status. How we prepare our food marks social status. Where we eat and with whom we eat, as well, mark social status. Since the work of Claude Levi-Strauss, sociologists and anthropologists have recognized that food production and description are integrally linked to our social identity, setting the boundaries of ethnicity and integrally connected to religious ritual and myth. Religion often enforces food boundaries. Mythology and ritual are connected to food.

## Biblical Eating

*He said to me, O mortal, eat what is offered to you; eat this book, and go, speak to the house of Israel. So I opened my mouth, and he gave me the book to eat. He said to me, Mortal, eat this book that I give you and fill your stomach with it. Then I ate it; and in my mouth it was as sweet as honey. Ezekiel 3:1–3*

*She uncovers the pot of boiling water and puts in some bulgur. She has also prepared a second salad of roasted sweet potatoes and steamed broccoli, all covered in a light apple vinegar, which she has put into the refrigerator to cool. She has dressed and prepared some brussels sprouts as well. I put them into the pan with the garlic and mushrooms. We talk the whole time. The radio is still on. My little boy wants me to read him a story; I do. She finishes braising the brussels sprouts and adds diced tomatoes and peppers, then covers the pan and begins working on a small plate for the little boy (some tofu cubes, rice cakes, a few vegetables, cut-up kiwi and apple, some cheese). I am very hungry. I have been eating from the various pots since I arrived home, "tasting" them. She begins putting unneeded pans in the sink. I set the table, turn off the radio, and turn on some music in the dining room (Monteverdi's Orfeo). She tosses the bulgur and brussels sprouts together into a glass bowl and adds more feta. I take the boy upstairs to wash for dinner.*

*When I return, she has set his place at the table. I put him in his chair and start him eating. She and I fill our plates in the kitchen, then sit opposite one another at the table – a large walnut refectory table with transom legs and four high, straight chairs. We eat and continue talking.*

That food and food consumption can be linked to various forms of Judeo-Christian expression is patently obvious to anyone who has dealt with inviting a minister, priest, or a rabbi over for dinner (in our house, we have sometimes had all three). Yet many might be surprised that food and food production are linked with the expression of spiritual and ethnic identity within many communities of American protestants, particularly in the way they have engaged New Testament interpretation. Beginning in the late nineteenth century, this interest in diet by American protestants continues into the twenty-first.

In his *Whitebread Protestants: Food and Religion in American Culture*, Daniel Sacks examines the complex ways that American protestants linked food and diet to their own expression of spirituality (Sacks 2002). In addition to expressing their religious values, this linkage also performed aspects of American Protestantism's self-construction of their own socioeconomic and ethnic status.

For example, Sacks opens with a review of nineteenth- and early twentieth-century protestant debates regarding communion practices (Sacks 2002). The two central issues were: the necessity of a common cup for communion and the use of fermented, alcoholic wine. American protestants put great stock in reliance upon biblical authority and example. In the gospels, when Jesus dines with his disciples for the final time, he passes around a communal cup of fermented wine declaring it to be his blood and calling for his disciples to repeat the ritual practice after his death as a memorial. As new science arose regarding hygiene and the spread of infectious disease, citing the rise of many disease outbreaks in American urban centers (the influenza epidemic of 1918 for example) many American protestants became leery of sharing a common cup and began a practice of distributing the wine at communion in separate, single-serving size, hygienic cups. This practice was seen by some as a mere expedient but by others as a violation of biblical norms. Many American protestants in the early twentieth century were also deeply involved in campaigns against general alcohol consumption. Citing the decline of American cities by the abuse of alcohol by the new immigrant poor, many American protestants began to argue that consumption of alcohol, even in moderation, was an evil; rituals of worship should not perpetuate the practice. The prominent chemist Richard Welch developed a technique for production of grape juice that would not ferment. Biblical exegetes began to problematize translations of "fruit of the vine" as found in Matthew, Mark, and Luke, leading to arguments that Jesus did not, in his lifetime, consume alcohol (Sacks 2002). Despite the objections of some that nonfermented wine was a violation of biblical precedent, the practice quickly became the norm. Though the arguments emerge as liturgical and biblical,

Sacks points out rather clearly that they were also, at base, arguments rooted in political activity and assumptions about the state of the poor and were reflecting fears of immigration. Christian temperance writers, again and again, painted the problem of public consumption of alcohol via images of poor immigrant families under attack. Concerns over hygiene in communion arose amid a general clamor about new immigrant classes, associated in popular wisdom with the spread of disease.

Concerned about methods to combat gluttony or drunkenness, an array of Christian protestant groups espoused "Christian eating" reforms (Sacks 2002). During the late nineteenth and early twentieth centuries, American manufacturing and industrial growth was exponential. While increasing disparity of wealth resulted in a marked increase in the rural and urban poor, it also produced significant wealth, and, so, significant increase in consumption, among established (generally protestant) American families. With enhanced production and transportation technologies, Americans were able to use their discretionary wealth to buy an array of food products.

Responding to this sudden increase, many American protestants began to decry excessively rich diets. Too much, or too rich, food was understood as gluttony. Exegesis of Luke 12:13–21 was taken as defense of a host of dietary reforms. Reformers turned to 1 Corinthians 8:1–13 not merely to examine Communion protocols, but drawing-out principles of equitable food distribution and antigluttony agendas. These were, in turn, appended to readings of James 1:9-7 and 2:1–17 to call for reforms in diet based on economic liberation. Frequently conjoined with Acts 15:20 and various dietary laws outlined in Leviticus (such as Leviticus 3:17), many exegetes began to argue that excessive consumption of meat was particularly immoral. The convergence of these various lines, many also merging with Christian Temperance movements, resulted in wholesale dietary reform among many American protestants that have had lasting impact on American food consumption. For example, W. K. Kellogg developed his corn-based breakfast cereal to promote Christian temperance and to offer a vegetarian option for a robust breakfast (on Kellogg, see Wilson 2014).

These nineteenth- and early twentieth-century movements continue in modern forms of American protestant and evangelical Christian food practices. Consider, for example, the "Weigh Down Watchers" (WDM). Founded as "Weigh Down Ministries" (under the supervision of the Remnant Fellowship Church, which also manages WDM publications) in 1986 by Gwen Shamblin, this organization has grown from a small, congregationally based community of (mostly women) evangelicals to a community expanding beyond the Remnant Fellowship circle of 100 churches worldwide, publishing materials through Doubleday and with a website (http://www.weighdown.com) providing online encouragement and an array of support products such as food journals, dietary aids, and more. The organization, following the pattern of the popular Weight

Watchers encourages proper nutrition and dietary control via a system of coded "cards" or foods that allow easy, intuitive assessment of food portions, caloric information, and dietary balance. What sets the group apart from traditional Weight Watchers is an intentionally spiritual focus. Describing the group's mission and raison d'être, the website reports:

> We have been created with two empty, needing-to-be-fed holes in our body. One is the stomach, and the other is the heart. ... The stomach is a literal hole in our body which is to be fed with the proper amount of food. As for the heart, I am speaking figuratively of our deep-down feelings. To satisfy these deep-down feelings, needs, or desires of the heart, we may often turn to food and overload our stomach with more than it needs. ... Trying to feed a hurting, needy heart with food or anything on this earth (alcohol, tobacco, antidepressants, sexual lusts, money, the praise of other people, etc.) is a common error. The person who attempts to feed a longing heart with food will stay on the path to overweight. Those who pursue an overindulgence of alcohol or tobacco or power will also reap the consequences of those pursuits. There is nothing inherently evil about food, alcohol, tobacco, money, credit cards, etc. However, it is wrong to become a slave to any of these things or to let them master you. (https://www.weighdown.com/how-weigh-down-works/weigh-down-approach/, para. 2, 3, 4)

WDM does not consider itself a "diet program" but a spiritual mentoring program that focuses on food.

Or consider the movement generically known as "biblical eating" – a mixture of evangelical (often charismatic) Christian thinking and current whole foods, organic, "natural" dietary supplements. The center of this movement is difficult to locate, but the industry is certainly robust. Annual sales for the US market for Christian diet and health publications have been estimated to exceed $1 billion annually (Radermacher 2017, pp. 208–211). Most of this market are websites, books, and (pay to attend) seminars such as those by Ernest Coldhew of Illinois (but now writing and speaking in the greater Philadelphia area). Coldhew is a follower of Ernest Holmes's United Church of Religious Science (founded in the early twentieth century. See http://scienceofmindarchives.com) and claims that his insights for biblical whole foods came as a result of a glossologic revelation that occurred during worship; in ecstatic devotion, he began to repeat Acts 15:29 in a variety of languages (interview with the author, 2016). He took this as a sign of the "Lord's Anointing" being put upon him, calling him to a "ministry of food" to a malnourished America. Coldhew insists that the proper diet for Christians is lacto-ovo vegetarianism and that this diet is clearly taught in scripture. Eating of meats is forbidden after the destruction of the Jersualem Temple in the year 70 CE. Coldhew argues that the only acceptable meat eaten in the bible was meat slaughtered via sacrifice to God (a position affirmed, he says, in Acts 15). Romans 14 allows the consumption of meat only under these circumstances. Sacrifice of animals to God, Coldhew argues, was permissible only in the Jerusalem Temple. Now that this building is destroyed, vegetarianism is the only biblical option. For the past 15 years, Coldhew has carried out his ministry of nutrition, combining a recommended program of a whole-foods diet heavy in microbiotics and a regime of prayer and anointing to heal a variety of ailments from fibromyalgia to Crohn's disease to (he claims) attention-deficit/hyperactivity disorder in children and various forms of cancer in adults. Coldhew has focused his ministry on the rural and urban poor, preferring to work with individuals (whether believers or not) who cannot afford health care. Jesus, he argues, ministered to the poor; so shall he.

Or, finally, consider the Christian Whole Foods movement. Evangelical literature has sparked a very popular movement espousing both whole foods and vegetarianism called the "Daniel's Diet." Begun by Phillip Bridgeman (2009), this popular diet mimics the diet of Daniel and his friends in Babylon. It centralizes vegetarianism with an emphasis on non-genetically modified (GM) foods, unprocessed ingredients, eschewal of pesticides, and a focus upon vegetables. (See http://www.danielsdiet.com.) Among other groups, also motivated by concerns of GM foods, processed sugars, and various chemical additives, the Christian evangelical Max Torres began the company "Food for Life" (http://www.foodforlife.com/about_us/our-story). Emblazoning their (non GM, pesticide-free, no refined sugars, organic, whole grain) baked products with references to Ezekiel 4:9 ("Take also unto thee wheat, and barley, and beans, and lentils and millet, and spelt and put them in one vessel..."), the company produces bread and pasta products using a mixture of organically grown wheat, barley, beans, lentils, millet, and spelt. The company website urges a return to "Godly eating" that respects the creation of God in all its forms and celebrates its intention to "nourish and build up the Body of Christ" (without comment on either the slogan's juxtaposition of multiple biblical verses or the mixed and inappropriate use of the metaphor from 1 Cor 12:27). They also reference 1 Cor 6:13 ("Food is meant for the stomach and the stomach for food – and God will destroy both one and the other. The body is not meant for immorality, but for the Lord, and the Lord for the Body"), which they apparently interpret as a mandate against obesity and improper diet. What they have produced in their sprouted grain loaf is a bread that has the lowest glycemic index and load of any bread, a literal godsend to diabetics, whatever their theological bent, who are looking for convenient lunch. There are also an array of organizations and groups calling for a pesticide-free, organic, and gluten-free bread for eucharist services (see, for example: https://medium.com/the-good-news-satire/opinion-a-whole-wheat-organic-option-of-holy-bread-should-no-must-be-provided-during-b65dbbe7dc05); the body of Christ, they argue, should be responsibly and sustainably produced and edible without harm by all.

One could, of course, note that several of these examples are marketing strategies. Certainly, the evangelical Christian market is a burgeoning one that many manufacturers and advertisers lust after in their hearts. Assuming something beyond cynicism, we could well note that in light of Jameson's views of mass culture and postmodernity, "market driven" is suddenly also significantly tied to ideology. And, indeed, these are highly commercial activities that have been, no doubt, very profitable (and profitable by intention). Yet they also all position themselves prophetically and clearly make a call for both themselves and their consumers to self-identify as something broader than "mere" consumers; indeed, the impulse here is to construct a religiopolitical identity by and -through consumption (in nearly every sense of the word), again, after the logic of Jameson's late capitalist superficial depth.

What emerges from this survey is an awareness of a persistent practice by American protestants of ethnic and socioeconomic identity being expressed via dietary regulation rooted in religiosity and Bible. Indeed, the pressures of subjectivity are clearly affecting the practice of biblical interpretation itself. American protestants are not primarily forming dietary practice as a result of dogma and biblical criticism; instead, they are reworking biblical readings to articulate a rationale for dietary proscription that is arising from distinct urges to articulate socioeconomic, political, and ethnic identities.

## The Bible, Pop Culture, Food, and Consumption

*[And the angel] said to me, "Take and eat [the scroll]. It will turn your stomach sour, but it in your mouth it will be sweet as honey." I took the little scroll from the angel's hand and ate it. It tasted as sweet as honey in my mouth, but when I had eaten it, my stomach turned sour. Then I was told "You must prophesy again about many peoples, nations, languages and kings."* Revelation 10:9–11

*Conversation flows through dinner. We talk about work and the news. We talk about family. Our son tells us a story about bugs coming from cracks in the ceiling and a giant who makes friends with them. He sits next to my wife who augments his plate with bites from her own. I collect the plates and wash the dishes as the conversation flows from table to sink. The little boy plays with the dogs. He helps me to let them out and then to water and feed them. It is time for his bath. I take him to the tub, then to a story, then to his pajamas, toothbrush, more stories, finally, to bed.*

*I return downstairs to find my wife with computer and papers spread upon the ottoman. The television is on, its flickering images serving as signifier for the modern hearth and comforting connection to the world beyond our home. The sound is low and its images are largely unheeded. She is watching a cooking contest where amateur cooks are given weekly challenges and judged by popular chefs. I take my books and sit next to her. I read. I have a notepad nearby where I jot a few ideas; I will be home tomorrow writing, and she will teach. I feel vaguely guilty about not grading student papers. The vague guilt passes quickly enough. We do not talk much – occasional remarks planned-but-forgotten earlier, some new thought sparked by our reading or by the quiet television or its images. We both pause to watch the critical elimination round of the program.*

In 1998, the journal *Semeia* published a theme issue on "Food and Drink" in the Bible. The volume was a collection of essays that rather blandly reflect the volume's title. In his response essay for the volume, Daniel Boyarin, among other criticisms, took the volume to task for failing the essential mandate of *Semeia*, which is to promote and explore the fruitfulness of new methods of biblical exegesis. Little seemed to connect the various essays in the volume apart from a general interest in food; the essays were united by subject, but lacked methodological theme. Boyarin observes:

> I have before me three truly fine but utterly conventional papers that puzzle me completely as to what might be considered experimental about them and therefore lead me to query their place in *Semeia* or perhaps even the continued relevance of that rubric. ... In what sense do we find here "experimental" – as the mandate for *Semeia* requires – or even particularly theoretically informed scholarship? ... I found these papers, in themselves, illuminating, but all the more compellingly raising for me, therefore, the question of theory or experimentality as an issue for thematization.
>
> (1999, pp. 223, 225)

Several of the essays Boyarin reviews position themselves as "intertextual," arguing that their methodology is arising from a review of parallel ancient texts and practices alluded to or cited by the Bible. Boyarin rightly questions this understanding of "inter-textuality." He writes:

> I find it distressing to see "intertextual" being used ... as a synonym for "cognate" or "parallel" or "context" with no value-added over those "old fashioned" terms. Notwithstanding its usage in recent work in biblical studies, "intertextuality" was not coined as a fancy way of naming the investigation of lexicographical or semantic parallelism with a view to further specifying meanings, a type of research that could have been and indeed was done regularly a century ago. ... "Intertextuality" ... refers to anonymous codes, the ruptures and registers of language itself.
>
> (1999, pp. 224, 225)

In many ways, Boyarin's critique is accurate. To be sure, the editors do not highlight a single methodology. Further, an abundance of biblical scholarship could be cited, which is using a very loose form of "intertextuality" as theoretical lens, often offering little by way of critical analysis of biblical-mass culture interengagement. However, with the value of hindsight, it is apparent that the *Semeia* volume did, in fact, anticipate an emerging trend in humanities scholarship – food studies. And certainly, he is correct in the authors' misuse of "intertextual" *when they say they intend to be intertextual*, but, given Barthes and Kristeva's sense of the word – where "meaning" arises from the juxtaposition of seemingly unrelated things, in this case diet and the Bible, but which have some intuitive connection in the reader, in this case the scholars themselves – what the essays actually *perform* is, I would argue, a type of cultural studies and intertextuality. Their problem is that they do not foreground, or even seem aware of, what holds their readings, and even the collection itself, together. What "Food and Drink in the Bible" lacked was a strong and clearly articulated theoretical rationale. Or, perhaps better: the problem is not so much that an intertextuality isn't *there*, but it's more that such engagement isn't fully expressed – a troublesome issue because, in this case, it also really isn't sufficient.

One potential rationale could be found in the work of Roland Boer. In his 1999 monograph *Knockin' on Heaven's Door*, Boer explores the intersection of Bible and popular culture. His final chapter, "Graves of Craving," imagines a conversation in a local McDonalds restaurant between Karl Marx, Claude Levi-Strauss, and a biblical scholar (himself) reading Exodus 16 and Numbers 11. From Biblical text, Boer observes how these chapters use food to identify the immigrant and ethnic status of Jews on exodus from Egypt. The biblical diet in Exodus functions to construct an ethnicity and ideology – even in grumbling, the Israelites identify themselves as distinct from their Egyptian captors via food, lamenting the "fleshpots of Egypt" as they chew through manna. The commensality produces identity. These food practices in biblical text also engage critique of the technologies of (food) production in interesting ways (God, in other words, provides the manna; humans collect and fashion it). Boer explores, simultaneously, the sociocultural implications of McDonalds, examining its modes of production, social status, "traveler" orientation, and more. He weaves both conversations together by invoking the work of Levi-Strauss and Marx.

Boer's essay includes some general observations about food and its potential to mark socioeconomic status, its relationship to ritual, and its broader connection to systems of production and consumption. Boer observes:

> [A]ny viable left politics needs to consider seriously the mass patronage of places like McDonald's. For in many areas there is a distinct class divide that manifests itself in the choice of places to eat: the clothes,

appearance, and age of those in McDonald's and, for example, a more expensive restaurant, mark a difference between youth and elderly over against the more well-heeled young and middle aged, between relative poverty and wealth, between places where the patrons live, and so on.

(1999, p. 148)

As Boer notes, food marks socioeconomic status. When these concerns are united with those of the study of "everyday life" (as found in Certeau who is, by the way, cited in turn by Boer as an influential figure for Boer's own methodology), then some particularly interesting and fruitful lines of analysis emerge. Food is the essence of the political and of popular culture.

Within Judaism, food clearly marks boundaries between community insiders and outsiders. These boundaries, indeed, are the precise moments for tension between Gentile and Jew among Jesus's earliest followers. Yet these same energies are present in a variety of American religious groups. American protestants would argue their views are more biblically based than sociocultural. Indeed, many American protestants construct an identity that is at odds with popular culture. This is not the case.

Food and diet foreground systems of production and consumption in the starkest possible terms. Once humans began to organize into collectives with definable social roles after the dawn of agriculture, human societies began to have more and more individuals further and further removed from the mechanisms of food production. This social organization has tended toward systems of hierarchy. Nineteenth-, twentieth-, and now twenty-first-century Christian protestant infatuation with food consumption are political actions, themselves related to systems of social structure and, accordingly, production and consumption.

I would suggest, then, that the rising phenomenon of the intersection between diet and spirituality is very much a field where biblical scholars have an interest. The phenomenon not only offers moments for exploration (and perhaps critique) of popular biblical interpretation. It also offers a glimpse of the interengagement of biblical text and popular culture; it offers a moment for reflection on the integration of religiosity into/as an aspect of popular culture itself.

I would further suggest that, when biblicists turn toward the examination of dietary and food systems among American protestants or any other group, they will do so most productively when then have an organizing theoretical frame – or at least motive – ideally one beyond simple reliance upon unexamined "intertextuality" or simple concurrence or "parallel." One of the more fruitful methods would be those informed by cultural studies analysis, particularly that of Michael de Certeau.

Examination of food traditions among American protestants and evangelicals seems particularly productive here. Evangelicals and protestants, on the whole, are a community who do not see themselves – and are not widely seen by outsiders – as having religiously mandated dietary restrictions. Yet, within their American expression, these "white bread protestants" are among the most energetic and active at developing food regulation and dietary control in the name of faith. Further, American evangelical and protestant communities foreground their use of biblical text to fashion their life choices. Exegesis is the basis of culture. Yet we can see, as well, that in several cases social pressures and culture produce exegetical energies. These manifest in food regulations that not only perform a given reading of biblical text but also manifest a host of cultural identity markers where communities are defined and performed by their consumption.

In our current moment of late capitalism, questions about social status, community definition, and production-consumption matrices have not gone away. They are arguably even more central. Contemporary American protestant and evangelical food programs are plugging into this same system for community description and definition.

*She switches around through other programming options after the episode ends. We do not like to watch violence; we do not have cable (just streaming). Not wanting something heavy or to start something new right now, the options are few. We find some old situation comedies we've seen before. I am too tired to read any longer, and I am hungry. I go to the kitchen and select my favorite pot. I pour in a tablespoon of vegetable oil and put it on a burner on the stove. As it heats, I pour a glass of milk and slice a few bites of cheese from a block of sharp cheddar. When the oil is hot, I add some popcorn and put on the lid as I take out one of the large glass bowls from the pantry. The dogs hear the corn pop and come running. I put the popped corn in the bowl and sprinkle on some salt. I have burned a few kernels. I turn to get a small plate for the cheese. The dogs are sitting, watching me expectantly. I throw the dogs each a few kernels which they catch in the air. I take my plate, my cup, and my popcorn back to the living room. My wife eats it with me; she flicks through the corn seeking the burned kernels – her favorites. We talk a bit more.*

*We watch the evening news as far as the weather report for tomorrow. We talk briefly about what remains to be done tomorrow. I collect the dishes and take them to the sink; I let the dogs out one last time; I close them into the mudroom off the kitchen where they kennel for the night, turn down the heat, turn off the lights, and go to brush my teeth. I change for bed. My wife arrives from her own ablutions. I lie abed, thinking about the day, wondering about the next. The taste in my mouth is sweet as I drift asleep.*

## Works Cited

Alba, K. (2013). *Routledge International Handbook of Food Studies*. New York: Routledge.
Belasco, W.J. (2006). *Meals to Come: A History of the Future of Food*. Berkeley, CA: University of California Press.

Boer, R. (1999). *Knockin' on Heaven's Door*. New York: Routledge.

Boyarin, D. (1999). A question of theory or experimentality? In: *Food and Drink in the Biblical World*, Semeia Studies, vol. 86 (ed. A. Brenner and J.W. Van Heuter), 223–225. Atlanta, GA: Society of Biblical Literature Press.

Bridgeman, P. (2009). *Daniel's Diet: The 10-Day Detox and Weight Loss Plan*. Mona Vale, NSW: Ark House Press.

de Certeau, M. (2011). *Practice of Everyday Life*, 3e. Berkeley: University of California Press.

Clark, T. (2010). Prophetic voices in graphic novels: the 'comic and tragic vision' of apocalyptic rhetoric in *Kingdom Come* and *Watchmen*. In: *The Bible in/and Popular Culture: A Creative Encounter*, Semeia Studies, vol. 65 (ed. P. Culbertson and E.M. Wainwright), 141–156. Atlanta, GA: Society of Biblical Literature Press.

Counihan, C. and Van Esterick, P. (ed.) (2013). *Food & Culture: A Reader*, 3e. New York: Routledge.

During, S. (ed.) (1993). *The Cultural Studies Reader*, 2e. New York: Routledge.

Exum, J.C. and Moore, S.D. (1998). Biblical studies/cultural studies. In: *Biblical Studies/Cultural Studies: The Third Sheffield Colloquium*, Journal for the Study of the Old Testament, Supplement Series, vol. 266; Gender, Culture and Theory, 7 (ed. J.C. Exum and S.D. Moore), 20–45. Sheffield: Sheffield Academic Press.

Geertz, C. (1973). *Interpretation of Cultures*. New York: Basic Books.

Hoggart, R. (1957). *The Uses of Literacy*. New York: Penguin.

Jameson, F. (1991). *Postmodernism: Or, the Cultural Logic of Late Capitalism*. Durham, NC: Duke University Press.

Kristeva, J. (1980). Word, dialogue and novel. In: *Desire in Language: A Semiotic Approach to Literature and Art* (ed. L.S. Roudiez), 64–91. New York: Columbia University Press.

Leavis, F.R. (1930). *Mass Civilization and Minority Culture*. Cambridge: Cambridge University Press.

Malinowski, B. (1931). Culture. In: *The Encyclopedia of the Social Sciences* (ed. E.R.A. Seligman), 621–646. New York: Macmillan.

Moore, S.D. (1998). Between Birmingham and Jerusalem: cultural studies and biblical studies. In: *In Search of the Present: The Bible through Cultural Studies*, Semeia Studies, vol. 82 (ed. S.D. Moore), 20–45. Atlanta, GA: Society of Biblical Literature Press.

Moore, S.D. and Sherwood, Y. (2011). *The Invention of a Biblical Scholar: A Critical Manifesto*. Minneapolis, MN: Fortress.

Oswalt, C. (2003). *Secular Steeples: Popular Culture and Religious Imagination*. New York: T & T Clark.

Pollan, M. (2007). *The Omnivore's Dilemma: A Natural History of Four Meals*. New York: Penguin.

Radermacher, M. (2017). *Devotional Fitness: An Analysis of Christian Dieting and Fitness Programs*, Popular Culture, Religion & Society. A Social-Scientific Approach, vol. 2. New York: Springer.

Sacks, D. (2002). *Whitebread Protestants: Food and Religion in American Culture*. New York: Palgrave McMillan.

Singer, P. and Mason, J. (2007). *The Ethics of What We Eat: Why Our Food Choices Matter*. Philadelphia: Rodale Books.

Smith, J.Z. (2009). Religion and Bible. *Journal of Biblical Literature* 128 (1): 5–27.

Tanner, K. (1997). *Theories of Culture: A New Agenda for Theology*. Lexington, KY: Fortress Press.

Williams, R. (1983). *Culture and Society: 1780–1950*, 2e. New York: Columbia University Press.

Wilson, B.C. (2014). *Dr. John Harvey Kellogg and the Religion of Biologic Living*. Bloomington, IN: Indiana University Press.

**Part II**

**The Intertextual Bible**

# 5

## The Ketuvim in the Coenim

Bible and Apocalyptic in the Films of Joel and Ethan Coen

The three essays in Part II of the book, "The Intertextual Bible," are written to demonstrate an intertextual focus in Bible and cultural studies. I have chosen to focus on the Bible in entertainment media. Two chapters explore cinema; the third looks at role playing games (both tabletop and video games). In current US scholarship, a huge portion of work on Bible and cultural studies (the majority?) deals with the Bible in film and media. I would also argue that intertextual approaches are the most common methodologies they employ, though not necessarily explicitly, or even knowingly. Indeed, many biblical scholars misuse the word "intertextual" when they use it at all (or, perhaps more accurately, use it so reductively that it becomes a sort of misuse). For many, "intertextual" refers to a book or writing – a literal text – cited in-or-by another book or writing, most commonly the use of Hebrew Bible in nascent Christian writings.

I am using "intertextual," as discussed in Chapter 1's introduction, in a Kristevan sense (Kristeva 1980; note also Alfaro 1996), mediated to US biblical studies scholarship via Fernando Segovia (Segovia 1995). The cultural products I've chosen all "quote" or invoke Bible explicitly, though they need not have. An intertextual reading focuses on the scholar/reader as lynchpin or hinge between two "texts." The insight, or "meaning," produced is what arises upon/after reflection on the two textual encounters. An intertextual reading can expose latent implication, nuance, or (mis)perception in either "text" or in the reader. At other times, such as the examples in this section, a reading might reveal how one text has influenced, or been interpreted, by another, exposing how a text functions as a cultural cipher, signifier, or influence (as well as how one text lends its influence or affect to another).

This latter approach, very much in keeping with Segovia's agenda, is also, I believe, one of the more common in anglophone scholarship on the Bible and cultural studies. Scholars unearth or detail an occurrence of citing or alluding to Bible. This citation is then analyzed, occasionally for its potential to reveal

*American Standard: The Bible in US Popular Culture*, First Edition. Robert Paul Seesengood.
© 2024 John Wiley & Sons Ltd. Published 2024 by John Wiley & Sons Ltd.

underattended nuance inherent or implied in the biblical text, but more often as a form of history of interpretation or reception criticism. As I have argued elsewhere (Seesengood 2022), reception criticism and cultural studies approaches are related but not identical. Cultural studies is a (very useful) species of the reception critical genus. The three essays in this section take up these questions, beginning with Bible and film (for premier see the stellar work of Burnette-Bletsch 2016; Reinhartz 2022; and Walsh 2018).

## What's in *Your* Bible?

What makes a book a "Bible" or a movie a "Bible film?" Both questions are deceptively complex. Many of us *think* we know how to define a Bible, but most Bible readers engage the book as a part of a community with a clear history and set of expectations. An array of communities – most of them religious communities – read the Bible, often with great seriousness, regarding it as a sacred text for learning about God and guiding one's life. When readers from different communities encounter one another, however, they often note fundamental differences in the books they read.

To begin, as we noted in Chapter 2, there are numerous variations on the Bible as published – numerous translations, study editions, guided readers, "hyperlink" chain reference systems, study notes and annotation, and more. These clearly affect how one reads and engages with a Bible; critical words for a community's doctrine or practice are downplayed or even missing from another's. A more fundamental issue, however, is what canon (or list of approved books) is represented in one's Bible. The number and order of the books in a Bible can be quite different. The Bible largely used by protestants has 66 books, split into two "testaments" (an Old and a New). Roman Catholics have the two testament division, but also include the Apocrypha and extensions to the books of Esther and Daniel. Orthodox Christians have yet another canon list. A number of Christians are quite happy reading a Bible containing only the New Testament (perhaps accompanied by the Psalms or Proverbs).

Jews, of course, have only one "Testament," though for obvious reasons would blanch a bit at designating it as the "Old" one. Many Jews, when not simply saying "Bible" or "Torah," would use "Tanach" – so named as an acronym of its three parts: "Torah" (law), *Navi'im* (Prophets), and the *Ketuvim* (the "Writings") – however, also orders its books quite differently. The distinction of order and grouping would seem, perhaps, insignificant, and in some cases it is. The "Prophets" contain books both by, but also featuring, Hebrew prophets, combining in one section what Christians often designate as "History" and the "Major" and "Minor" prophets. Other changes, however, are perhaps noteworthy. The Ketuvim contains the books many Christians would designate as "Wisdom" writings (Song of Songs, Psalms, Proverbs, Ecclesiastes, Job), and other books such as Esther and Ruth, but also 1 and 2 Chronicles and, a surprise to many novice students, the book of Daniel. The Ketuvim in the Hebrew Bible contains later books and writings. Chronicles is clearly a review (and revision) of Israelite history and identity as told from a much later post-post exilic community (Kelso 2007). Daniel, as its polyglot text displays (with portions written in Hebrew, Aramaic, and Greek) was under composition at quite a late point in Jewish history; far from being a record of a Jew living under Babylonian rule announcing his mystical prediction of future events, Daniel is seen by many Jewish readers (and most critical, academic scholars) as a book that reached its final form and content during the Maccabean revolt (Collins 1994; Hartman and Di Lella 1977). The placement of Daniel among the Ketuvim, and not the Navi'im, is more than just a difference in order, it reflects a very different sense of the book's context, contents, and significance, differences so great they culminate, de facto, in two different books altogether.

What constitutes a "Bible film" is equally troublesome at times to resolve. Like defining a Bible, the "center" of the continuum is easily noted – a Bible film should be a movie that tells the stories of Bible characters. The margins, however, become rather blurry. Would films such as *Ben Hur* or *The Robe,* (or, indeed, the *Life of Brian*) – where the movie's plot is set in Bible times and lands, and characters encounter (briefly) biblical characters – be "Bible movies" even if their protagonists and plots are not biblical? What about Cecil DeMille's *The Ten Commandments*, which has greatly expanded upon biblical text, giving the character of Moses and elaborate coming-of-age narrative (roughly half the film) as a backstory? Indeed, alteration of the Bible narrative is inevitable as the movie is adapted into a new storytelling format; *can* one make a movie that does not alter Bible?

Far from being a trivial philosophical debate or pedantry these questions reflect a central tension: who decides what is a complete and proper Bible or an "authentic" adaptation of one? When has an interpretation or a presentation of the Bible ceased to be a presentation of *Bible* (not to mention become so "erroneous" as to constitute blasphemy; Sherwood 2012). In the United States, thankfully falling askance of these questions rarely has life-or-death implications or results in formal trials and devastating consequence (though this has certainly happened in the history of biblical interpretation). It is, however, quite clear that the norm for US understandings of what is a "Bible" and how it ought to be read is a protestant model. To read from radically outside that frame, to read and interpret the Bible as a Jew, becomes a moment of cultural protest integral to questions about community, identity, and assimilation and it is a moment of reading that risks broader cultural discipline of a variety of forms.

## The Coenim

Joel and Ethan Coen are perhaps the most decorated duo in the history of the American cinema. They have been nominated over a dozen times for Academy Awards (the Oscars), winning twice (Best Original Screenplay for *Fargo*; Best Adapted Screenplay for *No Country for Old Men*). They received the Cannes Palme d'Or for *Barton Fink*. Their movies have combined for 48 Oscar nominations (with seven wins); they have directed seven Academy Award performances by their actors (with two wins). Siblings (Joel is the elder by three years) they grew up outside Minneapolis, Minnesota; Joel went on to study film at New York University (and briefly at the University of Texas, Austin), and Ethan studied philosophy at Princeton. The two collaborated on their first feature film, *Blood Simple*, in 1984.

The Coens write, direct, and produce their movies with joint credit, famously refusing to identify which brother wrote or directed a given scene or element (in general, note Redmon 2015). The Coens (meticulously) edit their own films, as well (often under the pseudonym of Roderick Jaynes). They are famous for their precision and attention to detail with verbally lush scripts, precise mise-en-scène, pinpoint costuming, elegant cinematography and lighting (they often collaborated with the legendary cinematographer Roger Deegan), and carefully curated soundtracks of American roots music. Their scripts show a mastery of pacing and characterization, their direction displays keen sense of timing. A typical Coen enters into an established film genre and simply revels in it, whether that genre is "true crime" (*Fargo* – a movie that famously claimed to be based on true events, despite being utter fiction), Western (*True Grit* or *No Country for Old Men*), Detective Noir (*Blood Simple, Miller's Crossing*), Screwball Comedy (*Burn After Reading, Intolerable Cruelty*), or even movies about the making of movies (*Barton Fink, Hail Caesar!*).

Film critic A. O. Scott (2009), when reviewing Joel and Ethan Coen's *A Serious Man*, suggested that this Coen film uniquely engaged both Judaica and the Bible. In some ways, Scott is quite correct. None of their films invoke Jewish-American culture or the rabbis on the scale seen in *A Serious Man*, and the Coens rarely to never refer to Torah. Yet I would take issue with a suggestion that the Coens are sparing or reserved in their use of Bible (on the Coens and Bible, in general, also note Lindvall 2016 and Walsh 2019).

Scott, of course, was writing prior to the release of *Hail Caesar!* whose central concept is the making of a Golden Era "Sand and Sandals" epic, akin to *The Robe* and the Hollywood culture of cynicism, disbelief, and irreligiosity among the cast and production team for a movie aimed at a pious audience (on this movie and its various ironies, see Hicks-Keeton and Concannon 2019). Their 2017 *Ballad of Buster Scruggs*, a collection of short films set in the classic

American West, contained the short "Meal Ticket," a movie depicting the dark life and grim end of a traveling quadruple amputee novelty actor (Harry Melling) at the hand of his caregiver (Liam Neeson). Melling's character, billed as the "Wingless Thrush," repeats dramatic monologues to ever-dwindling audiences in frontier towns. Among his speeches is a reading of Genesis 5 and its account of the murder of Abel by Cain, a story whose grisly "am I my brother's keeper" darkly foreshadows the short's squirm-worthy end.

The Coens, however, have a particular penchant for the *Ketuvim*. Alongside *Serious Man*'s use of the narrative of Job (and also Ecclesiastes), the Psalms appear in *The Big Lebowski* and *O Brother, Where Art Thou*. An epigram taken from Proverbs begins *True Grit*. Daniel is invoked in *No Country for Old Men* and, as we will see, *Barton Fink* and *Ladykillers*. In this chapter, I intend to survey *Barton Fink* and *Ladykillers*. In each film, Daniel is explicitly quoted and the themes of Daniel permeate these films, establishing a critical "mode" of storytelling. The Coens are, in part, telling their stories with, by, and through biblical text. The Coens use biblical text much in the way they use set/location, costumes, lighting, or cinematography, often in the same scenes. With these two films as paradigm, I would argue that biblical literature, particularly the *Ketuvim*, and even more particularly, Daniel, regularly composes the very "landscape" of the Coen brothers' imagination and narrative thesis. Finally, the Coens demonstrate the difficulty in defining a "Bible Movie," even as they exemplify a non-Christian way of reading and relating to the Bible.

## *Barton Fink* (1991)

The use of Daniel in *Barton Fink* has been noted, most significantly in Matt Stefon's 2008 *Journal of Religion and Film* essay (Stefon 2008) The movie, set in 1941, explores the world of the golden age of the American film industry. *Barton Fink* opens with shots of the backstage action of a Broadway play. The opening montage is a series of curtain pulleys, ropes, backstage machinery, and bored stagehands, all establish concerns with the mechanisms of art and fate. The title character, Barton Fink (John Turturro), is a New York (Jewish) playwright obsessed with his vision to capture the angst and poetry of the "common man." After a critically successful opening of his play (lauded by critics in "The Herald"), Fink is given an offer to go to California to write screenplays. Eschewing the "crassness" of Hollywood, he takes a room in the run-down Hotel Earle. The Earle is a nebulous world-between-worlds, a space between time(s). Roger Deakin's distinct camera work and lighting, a general weighty atmosphere of Caravaggio-like heavy colors, dark shadows, and piercing light, captures the Earle's dark-cornered opulence. Long, establishing shots of seemingly endless hallways and corridors produce a sense of expansiveness, labyrinthine continuation, and isolation (a common trope in the Coen's cinematic landscapes). Strange winds hum through the hallways. The lobby of the Earle is heavily planted with tropical and exotic greenery; the wallpapers are patterned in various vegetative prints, hanging artificial gardens. In the heat and humidity, the grand wallpaper is slowly sweating itself from the walls. Ringing a bell at the desk summons Chet (Steve Buscemi) who emerges from a trap door in the floor (recalling the ascent from "hell" typical of classical theater); Chet opens a huge registry for Fink to sign invoking a sinister affect.

Celebrated in New York, Fink stumbles as script writer, unable to understand the basic genres of B film scripts and completely naive to the production needs and procedures of filmmaking. Fink is assigned a "wrestling picture" by the studio head, Lipnick. Fink has never seen any popular films and has absolutely no knowledge of "wrassling." Lipnick talks quickly in fragmented, apparently random observations. If Lipnick is wildly vague in his requests, he is palpably clear in his demands. Seeking that "Barton Fink feeling," he curtly dismisses Fink with the ominous announcement that "we're all expecting great things."

Fink, alone in his dingy room in the Earle, is stuck with the opening. He becomes distracted by the sound of weeping and laughter from the next room. In frustration, he calls to complain. Almost immediately, the occupant, Charlie Meadows (John Goodman), pays Fink a visit. Meadows turns out to be jovial and good humored about the matter, insisting on a drink and conversation to apologize. Meadows says he is a traveling insurance salesman. When he learns that Fink is a writer "for the pictures," he is impressed and complimentary. Fink begins to explain his vision, affirming the "hopes and dreams of the common man are as real as those of any king" and declaring his desire to create a new dramatic form for them. Meadows attempts to express his own thoughts on the matter, but is repeatedly interrupted by Fink who will later opine the struggles of "the life of the mind," something he says Meadows would not understand.

The next day, Fink is sent to meet his producer, Ben Geisler (Tony Shaloub). Learning that Fink has no idea what to write and alarmed at Lipnick's personal interest in the project, Geisler advises Fink to meet with another writer and get some help. As fortune would have it, Fink almost immediately meets and befriends W. P. "Bill" Mayhew, a notable novelist (whom Fink deeply admires), now also a screenplay author. Mayhew pines for his long-lost Mississippi, often waxing nostalgic. Mayhew, roughly based on William Faulkner, is a drunk who, like Fink, can no longer write. He has a secretary and lover, Audrey Taylor. Officially, Mayhew says he will not write since he won't compromise. As the movie continues, however, we have repeated hints that Mayhew, as well, is stymied by the demanding pace and fragmented nature of film writing. Mayhew's only substantial gift to Fink is an autographed copy of his greatest novel,

*Nebuchadnezzar.* Mayhew inscribes it: "may this little entertainment divert you in your sojourn among the philistines."

Fink returns to his script no better for the "help." Fink's relationship with both Charlie and Audrey deepens. Charlie arrives, exhausted from his sales trips ("I'm only trying to offer piece of mind") to inquire about how "the life of the mind" is progressing for Fink. Fink is even less able to write. Fink returns to his producer and is shown dailies of a new wrestling picture being shot by the studio. Fink is certainly unprepared for the disjointed and fragmented nature of an active film shoot. As he watches take after repetitive take, all without context or narrative, he is both confused and horrified. Desperate over his writer's block, Fink calls Audrey and asks for help; hoping to steal Mayhew's ideas for wrestling pictures, he discovers that Audrey is actually author of all Mayhew's scripts and perhaps even his great novels. She manages to calm Fink and the two have sex. The next morning, Fink awakens to find her murdered. Charlie quickly comes to the rescue, disposing of the body. Fink rushes to a meeting with Lipnick who is, again, as mercurial as he is ridiculous. He again asserts he is expecting "great things," yet Fink has no idea about what. Charlie revisits a distraught Fink and tells Fink that he must leave for a few days and asks Fink to watch over a mysterious package. Hesitant, but obligated, Fink agrees.

Alone, desperate, and completely miserable, Fink turns to the Bible. Shot one of this pivotal scene is from the perspective of Fink's desk, looking up at his distraught face. In shot two, the camera is positioned from well above, looking down on Fink (divinely?) as he rifles the desk and finds a Gideon's Bible. Returning to a close shot of Fink's face, he flips through the pages for inspiration. As he reads, the camera alternates between his perspective as reader and the book's perspective on Fink. His first turn is toward Daniel 2:26 ("art thou able to make known to me the dream which I have seen and the interpretation thereof"). Atop the page, the reading guides identify the passage as "the king's dream." Scanning down, he finds Daniel 2:30, which is actually an adaptation of the text of Daniel 2:5: "And the king, Nebuchadnezzar, answered and said to the Chaldeans, I recall not my dream; if ye will not make known to me my dream, and its interpretation ye shall be cut in pieces, and your tents shall be made a dunghill." The scene is silent except for a dog barking in the distance (recalling Ps 22:16 or Jer 15:1–3?). Fink turns next to Genesis 1 where he finds his own script as the first two verses: "Fade in on a tenement building in Manhattan's Lower East Side. Faint traffic noise is audible; As is the cry of fishmongers. And God said, 'Let there be light.'" The phone rings.

Two detectives wish to speak to Fink. Fink, on the way to the lobby, has a conversation with the aged elevator operator, Pete. Fink asks if Pete has read the Bible. Pete asks back, "the Holy Bible?" Fink: "Yeah." Pete: "Yeah. I think so. Anyway, I've heard about it." The detectives reveal that his friend Charlie is actually a notorious serial killer "mad man Mundt." Mundt kills and decapitates his victims. The police ask questions about a mysterious female body found without a head. Fink is overwrought. Without warning, one of the detectives asks if Fink is a Jew, then they leave after making a vague anti-Jewish insult. Fink returns to his room and examines the roughly head-shaped box left by Charlie. Sitting at the typewriter, he is suddenly inspired to write. His opening now is "Fade in. A young Hassid opens a door..." Fink lurches through the manuscript. Finishing his script for "The Burly Man" in a blur, he rushes out to the USO for a dance and a drink, announcing to the drunken sailors as he points to his own head "I am a creator. This is my uniform. This is how I serve the common man."

On return to the Earle, Fink again finds the police. Mayhew is also dead and beheaded. As the police conduct the interview, strange sounds are heard from the hallway; Mundt is back and has set the hotel ablaze. Mundt appears and rushes the police, shouting "Look upon me. I will show you the life of the mind. I will show you the life of the mind" and kills them both. He allows Fink to go free after intimating that he has killed not only Mayhew and Audrey but Fink's family in New York. He has done so because, he says, Fink would not listen. Mundt enters his own room, presumably to die in the blazing Hotel Earle. Fink salvages his script and takes it to Lipnick who hates it. Despite Fink's pleas that he was only "trying to show you something beautiful," Lipnick insists that he will never allow the script to be seen and that he will keep Fink under contract, suppressing anything he might write. The prophet Fink is, Cassandra-like, never to be heard.

Stefon very aptly notes the strong connection between Dan 7:15 (where Daniel is "terrified" by the "visions in his head," which are made clear by both the Son of Man and Gabriel) and Barton Fink's moment of literary catharsis. Further, Stefon observes, "The boundary between vision and reality is in fact broken when Barton takes the advice ... [from] Charlie ... 'Make me your wrestler ... Then you'll lick that screenplay.'" (Stefon 2008, p. 14). Stefon quickly dismisses Palmer's assertion that Charlie is Fink's Golem (p. 15), yet I wonder if too quickly; such an interpretation provides an excellent link with Fink's obsession with creation and bringing to life the "common man". He is equally quick in dismissing the blazing Earle as Fink's descent into Hell (p. 15), seeing the conflagration as another reference to Daniel (the fiery furnace). Here I think he may be too quick, though Stefon is clearly correct that Charlie, metaphorically and actually, "saves" Fink.

Neither Stefon nor Palmer has explored the real potential that Charlie may not even exist but is a manifestation of Fink's own mad, broken vision, and psychotic fantasy. Charlie describes himself as the embodiment of the "life of the mind." The Earle is clearly a metaphor for the psyche, particularly the private rooms. We see Charlie only in this environment, and he seems to be almost conjured by the incantations of writing and Fink's typewriter. As Charlie and Fink confront one another in the hallway of the burning Earle, the juxtaposition of their images (similar costumes, postures, and congruent shot framing) suggests identification. Charlie is both product and resolution of madness arising from broken and fragmented vision.

Stefon is certainly correct that the tone and mood of *Barton Fink* is apocalyptic and eschatological. Each scene hastens decline and ruin, culminating in murder, dismemberment, and fire. The invocation of Daniel and his role as seer also invokes Daniel's dark and apocalyptic visions. Fink, like Daniel, is a captive taken into a foreign land and forced to articulate the vision of his new king. Turning to the Bible for inspiration, he presciently turns to Daniel, also a displaced, exiled "diviner." Yet, rather than finding inspiration or comfort, Fink finds only ominous warnings of dismemberment and his own trivial prose. Daniel also establishes Fink's alienation even as it is a warning of the coming apocalypse of fire he will endure. "One like a son of man" will come in violence and make Fink's visions all too clear.

## *Ladykillers* (2004)

Stefon's excellent essay on *Barton Fink* does not note that the Coens again return to Daniel in their 2004 *Ladykillers*, and these two films, in many ways, form a diptych, much as *Ladykillers* also returns to many of the character types and setting of *O Brother, Where Art Thou?* The film is set in a small town in northwestern Mississippi, very near the river. This small town is invaded by Professor G. H. Dorr (Tom Hanks) who arrives, claiming to be a professor of classics from the University of Mississippi, Hattiesburg, on sabbatical and seeking to study Renaissance music. He takes a room for rent from Marva Munson, an elderly widow and devout Christian, and introduces her to a collection of four other men identified as his fellow musicians. They intend to rehearse Renaissance music, using period instruments, in Mrs. Munson's root cellar.

In reality, Dr. Dorr is intent on an elaborate scheme to tunnel from Mrs. Munson's root cellar toward the storehouse and vault of the nearby Bandit Queen, a riverboat gambling establishment (whose counting houses are on shore, beneath ground). His cohorts are his partners in crime. Though beginning well, things rapidly go awry and several (comic) setbacks occur. For example, a large rock is encountered, which prompts an elaborate scheme by Dorr to send Mrs. Munson with a friend to a gospel concert in Memphis while his gang attempts to blow through the stone. The pyrotechnics expert, Garth Pancake, ineptly blows off his own right forefinger. Despite these and other dilemmas (and several near-miss moments of Mrs. Munson discovering their plot), the gang manages to steal a million dollars from the Bandit Queen, described by Dorr as the "Sodom of the Mississippi Delta." At the moment of their success, however, they are discovered by Mrs. Munson. Despite attempts to once again confuse her or allay her misgivings, Mrs. Munson remains firm, insisting that she will go to the authorities unless the thieves return the money and attend church with her. Horrified at the possibility he will be forced to "engage in divine worship," Dr. Dorr convinces his gang that they simply have no choice but to kill Mrs. Munson.

Mrs. Munson's husband, Othar, is a surprisingly active presence in the film, particularly given that he is dead long before the events of the film unfold. Othar's portrait hangs in Mrs. Munson's living room. The painting's eyes and expressions vary, expressing his (dis)pleasure from beyond the grave. In addition, Mrs. Munson's beloved cat, Pickles, acts in ways that seem sentient. It is unclear if he is or is not an agent of providential care or perhaps even mediating between the living and the dead. One by one, Dorr's gang's attempts at murder (comically) fail and each would-be-murderer is, himself, slain. Pickles is instrumental in foiling the most dangerous plot on Munson's life. The dead body of each gang member is dropped from the city's gothic bridge over the Mississippi and onto a passing garbage barge below. By morning, the gang is all dead, their bodies sent to the nearby garbage dump. Mrs. Munson, finding them gone, assumes they have run away and attempts to return the money. Not taken seriously by the authorities, she is told to keep the money. She decides to give it to Bob Jones University (a school to which she is devoted). In the final scene of the movie, Pickles, himself, drops the last physical remnant of the gang – Pancake's severed and lost finger – from the bridge onto a passing trash barge. The closing music begins, "Let the light from the lighthouse, shine on me."

The characterization, setting, costuming, and style of the film reflect the 1950s. Central to the plot, however, are elements of very contemporary urban music and culture (particularly gang activity) and legalized riverboat gambling. This juxtaposition of time frames constructs a general sense of being outside time as well as a deepened sense of rural, small-town isolation. The Coens construct this atmosphere (much as they do in *Fargo*) by having moments of urban and modern life intruding into a very "retro" world. The land of the "big city" exists, but elsewhere.

A general motif of Coen brothers' work is that the opening scenes, as we saw earlier in Barton Fink, are overture and prologue that establish each movie's thesis and theme. The first shot in *Ladykillers* is a wide view of a beautiful sky (suggesting heaven?). After our first look at heaven, the camera pans downward over a gothic bridge spanning a dark river with flat, swampy banks. The bridge is decorated with gargoyles and is a habitat for crows. The camera continues to pan down to the river below. A barge passes (shot now from a stationary position from above – again invoking the divine view) ferrying a load of garbage. The camera pans up to level view, revealing a huge island landfill surrounded by scavenger birds. A godforsaken wasteland, home only to scavengers, lies at the borders of the narrative world we are entering. Our movie will take place on the edge of desolation, in a space briefly invaded by the detritus of the broader world in route to the underworld. Throughout the scene, the soundtrack is an African American spiritual "Let's go back to God."

The setting and themes established, the Coens retreat from the spectacle of the garbage island into the (borderland) region of their small Mississippi town to introduce our main character. Mrs. Munson walks with determination to the (isolated) office of the sheriff. She storms in, disrupting the sleeping sheriff, with her tale of outrage: a local (African American) teen, Wee-Mac, has returned from the Costco at Pascagoula with a portable stereo on which he plays rap music. Not only is Wee-Mac disturbing the peace, the lyrics of his music are laced with racial epithets. Mrs. Munson wants the (African American) sheriff to "reach out" to Wee-Mac. In her outrage she quotes Daniel: *Mene Mene Tekel Uparsin*, quoting from the famous feast of Belshazzar with its central scene of a disembodied finger writing on the wall in Daniel 5:5, 25–28. For Mrs. Munson, the intrusion of the outside world is a sure threat to peace and Godliness. As she leaves, she quotes "Apostle John:" "Behold, there is a stranger in our midst come to destroy us," a quotation that does not appear in any biblical text; in the next scene, we meet Dr. Dorr.

Dr. Dorr is fundamentally a threat because he is an intrusion. Dorr is decidedly opposed to Christianity and piety, indeed to any organized religion. Mrs. Munson is as unfamiliar with the norms and ideals of Dorr's world as he is of hers. When she learns that he studied at the Sorbonne (she sniffs at the quality of an institution called "sore bone") she asks if he is familiar with Bob Jones University. He is not. Later, thinking Dorr, whom she believes is a musician, would be interested, she shows Dorr Othar's handmade fife, which she calls, in Hebrew, a *kalith*. When Dorr asks if Othar ever blew the *shofar*, she is indignant. In another scene, Dorr and Mrs. Munson are enjoying a quiet evening tea while she knits and he reads. Munson observes that Dorr is a "reading fool." He concedes, finding more "currency" in these "dead tongues" than in the newspaper. He finds in them the best of *human* wisdom. Munson, unimpressed, snorts, "Wisdom of man, huh. But what about the Wisdom of God?" Dorr responds that, although he is familiar with the "Good Book," he finds, in the literature of antiquity, many other "good books." Munson's disdainful expression indicates her view.

Munson attends a holiness church on the outskirts of town. After a spirited hymn, her pastor begins his sermon on Exodus 32 and the incident of the

Israelites worshipping a golden calf. This passage is then linked with Daniel 5 via the writing "finger of God." Exodus 31:18 declares that God had given Moses "stone tablets inscribed with the finger of God." The Pastor's thesis is the danger of idolatry. He draws his major metaphor from the nearby garbage island (and riverboat gamblers). His summons is for the people of God to rise up and "smite" the forces of idolatry. Again, in Daniel (as in Exodus 32) the central issue is the lure of idolatry. This preacher is something of a prophet; the bodies of all of Dorr's gang end up on the garbage island, a feast for scavenger birds.

## Jews, and Jewish Bibles, in Hollywood

The influence and impact of Jews in Golden Era Hollywood (or, for that matter, contemporary) has been so widely noted as to be cliché (a cliché that, in many ways, crosses over into defamation given its predominance in anti-Semitic conspiracy theory). Jews were deeply active in many forms of twentieth-century entertainment industries, but also often as deeply reviled (Dixon 2012; Kozloff 2012). In many cases, newly immigrant, restricted socially and economically, and lacking devotion to performative norms of protestant public practice, Jews found a space for economic and cultural influence, even as they were often crassly reviled (Dixon 2012, p. 122) or reduced to caricature (Shandler and Hoberman 2003; Shandler 1999). Jews in film are often reducible to particular types (Hammerman 2018) or used (as per DeMille's *The Ten Commandments*) as ciphers for proto-Christianity (and freedom-loving capitalists).

In 2004, filmmaker Darren Aronofsky turned his attention to the biblical character Noah. Aronofsky pursued biblical and Judaic themes in his inaugural movie *Pi*, a film adaptation of the graphic novel *Pi: The Book of Ants*, by Aronofsky and Edward Ross Flynn, exploring themes of creation, Godhood, chaos, and Kabbalah through the tortured life of its obsessed (and disturbed) central character Maximillian Cohen (played by Sean Gullett. The character's name combines the Latin for highest, with the Hebrew word for priest, "cohen," making Max a quasi "high priest"). Max is a mathematician and number theorist chasing a cosmic algorithm for the meaning of life.

In *Noah*, Aronofsky used the story of Genesis 6–11 to explore the environmental disaster of the Anthropocene. In Aronofsky's *Noah*, God (always distant, often frightening) is planning to destroy humanity because of its evil impact on the environment. Humans are to be exterminated entirely. As he builds his ark, Noah and his family are protected by stone giants. These "Watchers" are figures never present in biblical text, but the centerpiece of cosmic speculation found in the ancient, second century CE Jewish apocalyptic text of 1 Enoch. Noah builds his ark with provision for his family only to save the animals in his charge. Discovering, after the flood (depicted in its full, frankly genocidal, horror) has begun that his daughter-in-law is pregnant, Noah is led to the brink of infanticide and murder. Notably, he sees his own refusal to follow through as a form of failure. God in *Noah* is a haunting, angry, and capricious being. The story, as Aronofsky weaves it, is not the stuff of nursery room decoration.

Indeed, the film was so jarring in its violence, its depiction of God, its inclusion of Jewish fantasy figures, and its overt environmentalism (and, therefore, explicit condemnation of the culture of contemporary consumer capitalism) that it revolted many viewers. In his review for the *Guardian*, Alex von Tunzelmann dismissed *Noah* as "an unholy mess drowning in unbiblical details" (von Tunzelman 2014). Certainly, this was not a radically unique view. Yet, it was also not very reflective. What, exactly *are* the biblical details of the story of Noah, a story that contains various recensions and repetitions betraying a long history of development and that, in its biblical version, is itself an adaptation of ancient near-eastern mythology more broadly. And what would it mean to be "faithful" to the story? To precisely replicate it, word for word (which words?), or to capture its essential truths and history of interpretation?

If the latter, Aronofsky might have done far better than he has been given credit. In his review of the film, Rabbi Paul Tuchman observed how deeply Aronofsky drew from Jewish apocalyptic, mystic, and midrashic traditions from the past. He writes:

> Does "Noah" belong in the Jewish tradition of biblical commentary? Yes, absolutely. If you're not well-acquainted with the literature, you might be surprised at how fanciful – and occasionally downright loopy – midrash can be. There is no sacrilege here, only an earnest attempt to make sense of a very difficult text.
>
> Aronofsky has done us a favor by reminding us that the story of Noah and the flood is not a colorful children's fable. It is a horrifying story of the devastating consequences of evil and violence. It is also a sobering tale of the crushing burden of standing virtually alone against all human-ity while trying to understand and carry out the will of God
>
> (Tuchman 2014, para. 18–19).

In other words, Aronofsky's *Noah* is very much a biblical Noah. Just not a con-ventionally *Christian* one. Turning back, then, to the Coens – their Daniel is, in many ways, a remarkably biblical Daniel (even if, when they turn to actual text and film a page of Bible, the Coens completely invent its words). Their Daniel is resonant with *Daniel's* interests – its rebellion, its challenge to assimilation, its apocalypticism. Their Daniel is a very biblical Daniel, just not necessarily a *Christian* Daniel. Yet: if the biblical book of Daniel is read as a protest against

Jewish assimilation (a protest that recognizes the reality of Jews needing to live and work around sometimes dangerous anti-Judaism), isn't a reconstructed Daniel in a US film who defies traditional Christian reading of Daniel, precisely the same point as the biblical text and, therefore, in many ways the more faithful adaptation?

## (Re)reading the Coen Bible

The book of Daniel, scholarship convincingly argues, was redacted/written late in the reign of Anticohus IV, on the cusp of the Maccabean revolution (Collins 1994; Goldingay 1989; Hartman and Di Lella 1977, etc.). Its two major movements – a series of six narrative midrashim (1–6), and a series of five visions (7–12) – both combine to offer exhortation to a beleaguered community struggling to resist assimilation. As a text narrating events from a past moment of exile written and compiled by a community of indigenous people resisting present-day foreign invasion, Daniel is fundamentally a document of borderlands and Otherspace (Anzaldúa 1987). In the first six stories, Daniel and his companions endeavor to retain their Jewish rituals and faith despite pressures placed upon them from the Babylonians. Often these actions precipitate attempts on their lives. Babylonian kings are presented, again and again, as hubristic and foolish. Daniel's terrifying visions in the second half of the book lay out an arc of history, but Daniel is often unable to understand them without divine interpreters. Daniel must struggle to understand and express his apocalyptic visions, a struggle that takes him to the edge of madness and death.

*Barton Fink* embraces Daniel in its apocalypticism and focus upon visions, dreams, and alienation to construct the film's thesis about the alienation, fragmentation, and risk of art. Barton is a foreigner, as are all the writers he meets in Los Angeles. Fink and Mayhew each allude to Daniel in their writing: Mayhew's book is titled *Nebuchadnezzar* (an allusion to Faulkner's *Absalom, Absalom!*); Fink turns to Daniel 2, the account of Nebuchadnezzar's troubled dream, for inspiration; the rewritten biblical text explicitly links the two. In Daniel, the relocated expatriate Hebrews are trained as seers and visionaries. In *Barton Fink*, all the writers are expatriates to Los Angeles and Fink's typewriter conjures monsters and visions. Lipnick, like Nebuchadnezzar (and Belshazzar) is powerful, mercurial, arbitrary, and a fool. He demands Fink interpret his vision – a Wallace Beery wrestling picture that has "that Barton Fink feeling" – yet, like Nebuchadnezzar in Daniel 2, he gives no detail or explanation. Fink, baffled by his new world, finds his voice through violence and turns back Judaism, particularly Hassidic (kabalistic) expressions. Notably, Daniel does not appear in Reform or Conservative synagogue liturgy; when (if) read in modern Judaism, it is the text of mystics, kabbalists, and hassidim.

The biblical Daniel is also often baffled by his own visions in the latter chapters and needs an interpreter – one in human form, yet who destroys human forms, liberating their "minds" by decapitation and setting free their visions. Yet the moment of liberation, the clarity of the vision, is also a moment that precipitates terrible violence. Fink, dwelling in the Hotel Earle, lives in Otherspace. The terror of Charlie Meadows is separated from Fink's writing desk only by a wall whose paper is sweating down like an unfurling curtain, revealing, unveiling the hidden mystery of life, death, and violence writhing through the body of a "common man," the incarnation of Fink's "life of the mind."

*Ladykillers*, in its turn, captures the interests of the community who redacted and compiled Daniel. Mrs. Munson (though not an orphaned Jewish expatriate) also dwells in the Otherland that is the borders of the wasteland. The underlying purpose of the book of Daniel, indeed the character of Daniel, is to articulate the values of a community of Jews insisting upon fidelity to God in the face of foreign ways and the constant allure of idolatry. In *Ladykillers*, strangers have come that destroy. Both the system of riverboat gambling and the trappings of urbanization are threats. Likewise, Dr. Dorr (his name a homonym for "portal" or "opening" to another space) is steeped in the literature of Paganism. The movie opens with an invocation of Daniel 5. The "finger of God" reappears twice; the preacher's sermon from Exodus and Pickle's disposal of a disembodied finger. As that finger inscribes, all of these evils – intellectual pride, urban culture, wealth, pleasure, glory – have been weighed and found wanting. Its message written and delivered, the finger is no longer needed and is returned to the Outer-world.

The dyptich of these two films invoke the same book, even though they may employ different themes. *Barton Fink* uses the figure of Daniel the seer; *Ladykillers* invokes Daniel the resistant proto-martyr. The biblical Daniel, seen in its context of Jewish history and literature, is a character of both assimilation and protest. Daniel is integral to questions of Jewish identity as "alien" residents within a foreign empire, as immigrants and outsiders trying to find the way to hold onto both their uniqueness and to safety. Both *Barton Fink* and *Ladykillers* focus upon the trickster outsider, the underclass or alien that both struggles with larger culture and seeks a place within it. Both movies argue that humans are under the judgment or protection of larger (divine) forces. Daniel is not merely quoted in these two films. Daniel is fundamental to the logic of their narratives, and their narratives reflect a deeply, intently Jewish history and Bible, reminding us "Bible" is neither singular nor simple, and "faithful" renditions or adaptations of Bible is always already a political conversation.

## Works Cited

Alfaro, M.J.M. (1996). Intertextuality: origins and development of the concept. *Atlantis* 18 (1–2): 268–285.

Anzaldúa, G. (1987). *Borderlands/La Frontera: The New Mestiza*. San Francisco: Aunt Lute Books.

Burnette-Bletsch, R. (ed.) (2016). *The Bible in Motion: A Handbook of the Bible and Its Reception in Film*. 2 Vols, Handbooks of the Bible and Its Reception. Leiden: Walter De Gruyter.

Collins, J.J. (1994). *Daniel*. Hermeneia. Philadelphia: Fortress Press.

Dixon, W.W. (2012). 'A rotten bunch of vile people with no respect for anything beyond the making of money': Joseph Breen, the Hollywood production code, and anti-semitism in Hollywood. In: *Hollywood's Chosen People: The Jewish Experience in American Culture* (ed. D. Bernadi, M. Pomerance, and H. Tirosh-Samuelson), 53–72. Detroit, MI: Wayne State University Press.

Goldingay, J. (1989). *Daniel*, Word Biblical Commentary, vol. 30. Waco, TX: Word.

Hammerman, S. (2018). *Silver Screen Hasidic Jews: The Story of an Image*. Bloomington, IN: Indiana University Press.

Hartman, L. and Di Lella, A.A. (1977). *Daniel*, Anchor Biblical Commentary. New York: Doubleday.

Hicks-Keeton, J. and Concannon, C. (2019). 'Squint against the grandeur!': waiting for Jesus at the Museum of the Bible. *Bible & Critical Theory* 15 (1): 114–127.

Kelso, J. (2007). *O Mother, Where Art Thou? An Irigarayan Reading of the Book of Chronicles*. New York: Routledge.

Kozloff, S. (2012). Notes on Sontag and 'Jewish moral seriousness' in American movies. In: *Hollywood's Chosen People: The Jewish Experience in American Culture* (ed. D. Bernadi, M. Pomerance, and H. Tirosh-Samuelson), 111–124. Detroit, MI: Wayne State University Press.

Kristeva, J. (1980). Word, dialogue and novel. In: *Desire and Language: A Semiotic Approach to Literature and Art* (ed. L.S. Roudiez), 64–91. New York: Columbia University Press.

Lindvall, T. (2016). Ben Hur, Brian, and the Coen brothers walk into a bar: excursions in theology and popular culture. *Journal of the American Academy of Religion* 84 (4)): 1145–1151.

Redmon, A. (2015). *Constructing the Coens: From Blood Simple to Inside Llewyn Davis*. New York: Rowman & Littlefield.

Reinhartz, A. (2022). *Bible and Cinema: An Introduction*, 2e. New York: Routledge.

Scott, A.O. (2009). A serious man. *New York Times* (2 October).

Seesengood, R.P. (ed.) (2022). *Bible and Cultural Studies: Critical Readings*, Critical Readings in Biblical Studies. New York: Bloomsbury/T & T Clark.

Segovia, F.F. (1995). Cultural studies and contemporary biblical criticism: ideological criticism as mode of discourse. In: *Reading from This Place*, Social Location and Biblical Interpretation in the Global Scene, vol. 2 (ed. F.F. Segovia and M.A. Tolbert), 1–17. Minneapolis, MN: Fortress Press.

Shandler, J. (1999). *While America Watches: Televising the Holocaust*. New York: Oxford University Press.

Shandler, J. and Hoberman, J. (ed.) (2003). *Entertaining America: Jews, Movies and Broadcasting*. Princeton, NJ: Princeton University Press.

Sherwood, Y. (2012). *Biblical Blaspheming: Trials of the Sacred for a Secular Age*. Cambridge: Cambridge University Press.

Stefon, M. (2008). That 'Barton Fink Feeling' and the fiery furnace: the book of Daniel and Joel & Ethan Coen's *Barton Fink*. *Journal of Religion and Film* 12 (1): https://digitalcommons.unomaha.edu/jrf/vol12/iss1/1 (accessed 15 October 2023).

Tuchman, P. (2014). Looking at 'Noah' through the lens of Jewish tradition. *Pittsburgh Jewish Chronicle* (11 April). https://jewishchronicle.timesofisrael.com/looking-at-noah-through-lens-of-jewish-tradition/ (accessed 15 October 2023).

von Tunzelman, A. (2014). Noah: an unholy mess drowning in unbiblical detail. *The Guardian* (10 April). https://www.theguardian.com/film/filmblog/2014/apr/10/reel-history-noah-drowning-unbiblical-detail (accessed 15 October 2023).

Walsh, R.G. (2018). *T & T Clark Companion to the Bible and Film*. New York: Bloomsbury Academic.

Walsh, R.G. (2019). Biblical Coens: can we laugh now? *Journal of Religion and Film* 23 (2): 1–29.

## 6

# "Do Not Forsake Me"

Biblical Motifs in Zinnemann's *High Noon*

Any reflection on Bible, film, and US popular culture will eventually turn to the most US-centric of popular film genres, the Western. Film is a modern form of mythmaking (Plate 2017, pp. 21–40), and, as we will see, US popular culture has long expressed its identity and ideology through idealizations of the American West, using the Western as a form of national myth. Westerns have a long history of biblical intertextualities, as we will see, as well. Although the reference to the Bible here is much less explicit than in the last chapter, this chapter will explore the Bible in one Western, a foundational example of the genre, *High Noon.*

## First Verse (Précis)

*Do not forsake me, O my Darlin'/On this, our wedding day.*

For decades the Western was forsaken in film criticism. Westerns are the most generic of genre pics and among the most "pop" of American cultural forms. Yet there is a booming cottage industry of scholarship now reviewing Westerns.[1] As a result, we are better attuned to how the broad appeal of the genre can allow a critical window into American pop culture, itself.

For example, as Jane Tompkins (1992) articulates, Western movies both construct and reinforce American ideology. The American West, it turns out, is spacious enough for etiology. As American popular myth, Westerns exploit America's nostalgia over adolescence to sooth the worried insomnia of American high and postmodern adulthood. As a genre, the Western had its

---

1 For general review, in addition to the sources cited later, note Cawelti 1975; Cunningham 1996; George N. Fenin, *The Western: From Silents to the Seventies* (Fenin 1973); French 1973; Hausladen 2003; Lenihan 1980; Parks 1974; Prats 2002; Tuska 1985; Wright 1975; and Smith 2003. Critique of Westerns has even entered the discipline of biblical studies. Note Koosed and Linafelt 1996; Warrior 1989.

*American Standard: The Bible in US Popular Culture*, First Edition. Robert Paul Seesengood.
© 2024 John Wiley & Sons Ltd. Published 2024 by John Wiley & Sons Ltd.

heyday in movies made between 1946 and 1962, when the United States was dealing with the notion of itself as a superpower (and confronting the rival power of communist Russia). Stanley Corkin's *Cowboys as Cold Warriors* (2004) explores how the flicker of Western films occupied our minds during our collective sleeplessness (Corkin 2004). "Westerns" he observes, "helped mediate [political] shifts by grafting the historical onto the mythic to help audiences adjust to new concepts of national definition" (Corkin 2004, p. 3).

Yet a third example, Peter French's (1997) *Cowboy Metaphysics: Ethics and Death in Westerns,* looks at the motifs of sudden (violent) death in Westerns and suggests *that* threat is really what has been keeping us all awake. In particular, French is looking for what characters in Westerns "give a damn" about (to speak French). French argues Westerns construct a different ethic than Judeo-Christianity; they use but also alter elements of both religious practice and biblical text to ease our worries and our consciences of both threatening and threatening violence (1997, p. 11).

Tomkins has argued Westerns are a form of American myth, exploring identity, gender, and space. Corkin has argued Westerns reflect Cold War struggles and opportunities. French has argued Westerns interpret and subvert Judeo-Christian ethics regarding death and violence. All three scholars identify Zinnemann's *High Noon* as a landmark in the genre and exemplar of how Westerns "work." Are there any biblical motifs in any of the plot, characters, or structure of *High Noon*? If so, how are these used or modulated in the context of larger assertions about American myth and (gendered) identity?

According to Barry Keith Grant:

> genre movies are those commercial feature films that, through repetition and variation, tell familiar stories with familiar characters in familiar situations. They also encourage expectations and experiences similar to those of similar films we have seen. Genre movies have made up the bulk of film practice, the iceberg of film history beneath the visible tip that in the past has commonly been understood as fine art.
>
> (Grant 2012, p. xvii)

Examples of "genre films" would be (among others): film noir, horror, detective movies, family melodrama, screwball comedies, and more. Some genres (such as horror) have numerous and specific subgenres. In essence, the genre is the formula for characterization, plot, theme, and setting. Genre movies "work" by playing to an audience's expectation and by fulfillment of the formula. They function and progress by acquiescence to type. For Westerns, we know immediately how to understand the inner process, motivation, and expectation for characters such as the bad gunman, the noble sheriff, or the saloon prostitute as soon as we see (and recognize) the character type. Genre films delight and sustain interest either in how well they manipulate the formula or in how they deviate from it, changing and challenging our expectations and, perhaps, commentating on our very desire for those expectations. Genre critique explores how the various aspects of a formula function and how a given film complies with or challenges those forms (with occasional commentary on how the compliance or violation shapes an experience for the viewer).

The Western is among the more extensive and important genres explored in genre critique. Tag Gallagher has observed that the Western, "without question ... has been the richest and most enduring genre for genre critics" (Gallagher 2012, p. 298) Grant explains "the first significant essays of film genre criticism, Robert Warshow's articles on the gangster film and the western (originally published in the *Partisan Review* in 1948 and 1954, respectively) and Bazin's two pieces on the western from the early fifties, were all written within a few years of each other" (Grant 2012, p. xvii). Warshow (1979) establishes at the same moment the basic definition of "genre" film and identifies the central characteristics and elements that make up a Western including isolated settings with broad vistas, particular racial characters, rudimentary-but-conventional presentation of gender, male-to-male conflict in a semi-lawless state, stock characters, violence as response to and corrective of violence, tensions between the encroaching civilization and the rugged outdoors, racial simplicity (for example, the absence of round characters who are minority and the reduction – often animalization – of native Americans). Current film theory places the position of gaze and viewer as central themes, critical to the perception of a film's "meaning" or effect. Though genre criticism fell out of critical favor as psychological, semiotic, and structuralist approaches rose in popularity, it should be recognized that genre criticism, like these other approaches, initially was viewer oriented (genre criticism has fairly recently been enjoying something of a comeback as formalist and affect approaches to film theory have emerged). Warshow (and, to perhaps a greater degree, Bazin) also foregrounds the viewer's experience (beyond expectation) and location in his critique.

The principal debate for genre critique of Westerns surrounds how the genre progresses. The conventional, and majority, view is that the Western first develops its types and formulas (silent and early sound eras), then celebrates to the point of exaggeration those types and formulas (particularly war and early Cold War years). As the genre is further refined and explored, these types are then manipulated to articulate an array of themes, including ideological norms and values, often being drawn to the point of cartoonish collapse (the Cold War, "Golden Age" of Westerns in the 1950s and 1960s). This exaggeration and alteration (again, often ideologically driven) result in the dissolution of the genre (the mid-1960s and 1970s); as frustration over genre collapse builds, the films themselves become more violent and gritty. The genre finally collapses into decadence, a ruin fostered by its own deconstruction (in a Derridian sense) and is, effectively, abandoned during the 1980s and 1990s, yet it has begun to enjoy a modest resurgence as new models of affect, gender norms, and psychological influences – and a wave of general cultural nostalgia – work to breathe new life into its conventions.

This narrative of genre development, however, has been seriously critiqued by Tag Gallagher. He argues, instead, that much of this narrative of evolutionary development is critically imposed. Genre critics tend to ignore contradictory evidence, downplay subtlety and nuance in older films, and focus more on the critical narrative and discourse than upon the films themselves.

Though Westerns are a film genre, they need not be approached critically exclusively via genre-critical means. Bazin's 1950s surveys of Westerns were already beginning to explore auteurism. Movies are industrial and cooperative compositions. What results in the final viewing experience is the product of the artistic and creative input of a variety of individuals. Composers, musicians, set and prop specialists, costumers, special effects artists, sound editors, film editors, lighting directors, and more combine their talents with actors, scriptwriters, cinematographers to "compose" the film we see. These various artistic contributions are overseen and managed by directors and made possible by producers.

Auteur criticism explores a film's "meaning" via an appeal to the vision of its "authorship." As James Naremore has observed, "motion pictures and television are often described as collaborative media, but their modes of production are hierarchical, involving a mixture of industrialized, theatrical and artisanal practices." (Naremore 2004, p. 9). Although, as Naremore also notes, several arguments by various critics have been offered to locate the "apex" of that hierarchical production (suggesting authors, actors, cinematographers, and even studio producers), the general consensus has been "for the most part ... associated with directors, who are said to play the most important role in the production process" (Naremore 2004, p. 9). He continues:

> The study of authorship is not itself a theory, only a topic or theme. It can involve a great variety of political positions and theoretical assumptions; and, like all types of criticism, it can be performed well or badly. And yet the discourse on the director-as-author has always been problematic – not only because of the industrial bias of the film medium, but also because the film director emerged as a creative type at the very moment when authorship in general was becoming an embattled concept. At no point

was the irony of the situation more evident than during the 1950s and 1960s, when certain directors in classic Hollywood and the international art cinema became known throughout the world as "auteurs," and when film criticism as whole underwent a kind of revolution. This was the period of the French *politique des auteurs,* or "policy" of canonizing directors in the name of art, and it remains crucial to an understanding of contemporary film studies. ... As its suffix implies, auteurism is less a scientific approach to the problem of the author than a kind of aesthetic ideology or movement.

(Naremore 2004, pp. 9–10)

Auteur criticism arguably emerged from early critique of Westerns, largely as an attempt to move beyond wooden (and somewhat artificial) structures in/of genre analysis. Significant criticism has been devoted to major Western "auteurs," such as Sam Peckinpah, Sergio Leone, John Huston, and Fred Zinnemann.

Peter Stowell's work on John Ford serves as a ready example. Stowell has argued that Ford's body of work, particularly his Westerns, were an exploration by Ford of significant American leitmotifs or archetypes, what Stowell calls American "myths." Following Henry Nash Smith (discussed later), Stowell sees Ford as constructing while also articulating American subjectivity via the construction of certain mythic archetypes, all rooted in the American imagination and American West. Stowell sees six major themes in Ford's work: the myth of the American Adam, the myth of the American Frontier, the myth of American agrarianism, the myth of American individualism, and the myth of American civilization. Ford also constructs a unique American narrative structure, articulating an "American Dream" rooted in Jeffersonian values.

Ford's films express a deep ambivalence with respect to change and stability, past and future, freedom and restriction, individualism and community, wilderness and civilization. These tensions could not be resolved. Only mediation was acceptable, a mediation that was an uneasy alliance held together by the mythic hero. This ambivalence extended to Ford's liberal and conservative ideology. However, on some issues, he had no such qualms. He always favored agrarianism over industrialism, equality over class, the West over the East, empiricism over legalism, and experience over knowledge. To this extent we may describe Ford's ideology as falling within the broad parameters of liberal Jeffersonian democracy.

(Stowell 1986, p. 150)

This (re)construction, built as it is via the images, legends, and romance of America's past, is made a sort of "retroactive" vision. In the mind of the American audience, it is superimposed upon the past. Like a false memory, it is embedded in our national sense of the origin of our values and our ideals. Ford's vision used biblical motifs and characters to construct his American ideal. His West is populated with largely Christians or, at any rate, those of white European descent, aware of Christianity, either embracing it as a good basis for values – the women – or grudgingly acknowledging its merits while also aware of its limitations, particularly in terms of peace and love – the men.

Americans have long articulated their national identity not only by symbolism, but expressly via images, and romanticized stories, of "the West." In *Virgin Land: The American West as Symbol and Myth*, Henry Nash Smith (1950) catalogs and chronicles the use of narrative, fiction and images are knit together to form a "mythic" sense of American subjectivity. He uses the term "myth" fully within its broad, religious studies sense and context – as a collectively authored form of popular "meaning-making" story, rich in symbols that speak to the establishment etiology, cosmogony, anthropology, soteriology, and even the progress of historical "meaning" and eschatology. John G. Cawelti's *Six-Gun Mystique* (1975) supplemented Nash Smith with a turn toward popular culture. Cawelti's findings reinforce Smith's notion of the West as American mythic space but argue that the West appears more, and more forcefully, in pop media of pulp fiction, television, and movies. Cawelti engages the Western as both myth but also as genre. Cawelti also poses the question regarding the genre of Western and American values: does the Western create or reflect American values, norms, and expectations?

An array of scholarship has argued that Westerns both simultaneously reflect and articulate national norms. The most significant of this critique has explored construction of masculinity and femininity. Patricia Nelson Limerick (1987), in *The Legacy of Conquest: The Unbroken Past of the American West*, sees clear affinity between the construction of racial "Other" and the characterization of stereotypical masculinity and femininity in Westerns. Linking feminist concerns for the suppression of women to broader cultural concerns for systemic, national language of conquest, Limerick problematizes the way Westerns depict not only women but racial minorities (particularly Latinos, Native Americans, Blacks, and Asians) and the conquest of the very landscape. Westerns as a genre overwrite or erase complex notions of race and identity.

In terms of political and cultural critique, Westerns have been seen as a particular American mythology, worked out in the context of the American identity crisis following World War II and during the Cold War. Discovering itself a nuclear "superpower" and engaged in international politics to spread American ideals into "third world" areas, Americans at home were left wrestling with tensions arising from their own national prominence, power, and opportunity. According to Stanley Corkin (2004), Westerns reinforced American expectations and self-perceptions, linking those values in a mythological past and space. The production of Westerns exploded during the Cold War years while the genre also expanded significantly in complexity. Both John H. Lenihan (1980, *Showdown: Modern American in the Western Film*) and Richard Slotkin (1992, *Gunfighter Nation: The Myth of the Frontier in Twentieth-Century America*) have argued that Westerns explore American infatuation with violence, generically. This violence, Slotkin argues, is the direct manifestation of the disorientation and disenfranchisement from American broad political and economic frustration in the 1950s and 1960s.

These studies have each articulated how popular film, in general, and Westerns, in particular, both reflects (because of box office needs) the values, ideals, and structures of culture and perpetuates and modifies (by the need to innovate as well as the simple rearticulation in film) those assumptions. In other words, film simultaneously reflects and constructs popular ideology. Westerns, in particular, have a pivotal role. Set as they are in the era of American expansion and settlement, they construct a national "myth of origins."

## Second Verse

*The noonday train will bring Frank Miller./If I'm a man I must be brave.*

*High Noon* (1952) was directed by Fred Zinnemann, an Austrian-born Jew from a script by another European Jew, Carl Foreman. Zinnemann and Foreman were both initially eager to produce a Western but were not encouraged by many. John Wayne, who famously despised *High Noon* as "unAmerican," remarked pointedly that one could not expect a "real" Western from the likes of two "foreign Jews."

The film garnered mixed reactions from the film community. On the one hand, *High Noon* (eventually) benefited from general critical acclaim. Yet the film ignored, flaunted, or inverted standard themes and motifs of the Western. Costumes, shots, and dialog are all very unconventional for Westerns of its time. There are no Indians, few horses, and no vast prairies. There is a comparative lack of action; nothing happens for most of the movie. Indeed, that is a critical element of the plot: the population of the town of Hadleyville refuse to act to face down an impending threat.

The central hero, marshal Will Kane (Gary Cooper), doesn't fit the standard type. He is pensive and worried as he prepares for the gunfight to come. He writes his last will and testament. He is unable to control his wife. He is unsure as a gunfighter. He is tempted to flee. The townspeople are not much better. They are cynical and uninterested in doing "the right thing." In this Western, the "action" is largely internal; the showdown is delayed and almost anticlimactic. Dimitri Tiomkin (another "non-American") produced a musical score that was, compared to other Westerns, restrained and built around leitmotifs. The main theme, "Do Not Forsake Me, Oh My Darling: The Ballad of High Noon"[2] not only expresses the entire plot of the film but is nearly a constant presence in the film's score; the song is reprised more than 25 times in the 86-minute movie.

The basic plot of *High Noon* is relatively simple: Frank Miller, a convicted murderer, has been pardoned from hanging and released from prison. He is returning to Hadleyville on the train; three of his former gang will meet him. Together, the four plan to ride into town and kill Kane (who arrested Frank). The train is to arrive at noon on Sunday.

That very Sunday morning, Will Kane has married Amy Fowler (Grace Kelly), a beautiful young blond-haired, blue-eyed woman, in the office of the town's justice of the peace. As a Quaker, Amy has insisted Kane also take an oath of non-violence; he is resigning his post as marshal and planning to move away and start a general store with his pension. Kane learns of Miller's pardon (and return) via a telegram delivered just after his wedding. The new marshal is not due to arrive until Monday. Kane is urged to flee. He feels, however, that flight would be cowardly. To flee is to face "lying a coward in my grave." Amy insists that if Will stays, she will leave him (and buys a train ticket to St. Louis to make her point). Meanwhile, Kane begins trying to round up a posse of deputies; he has just over an hour.

No one in town will help Kane. His current deputy, Harvey (Lloyd Bridges), resigns because Kane will not allow him to parlay the current crisis into a promotion for Harvey. The town justice of the peace flees. Many other citizens refuse because of fear. The bulk of the film unfolds, in real time, over the last hour before the noon train arrives. As the minutes tick by, Kane goes from location to location seeking help – saloons, hotels, private homes, city hall, the church, and city streets. As the film progresses, Kane becomes increasingly conflicted, distraught, and alone. The tension is highlighted by sweating people (it is a very hot day) and frequent shots of clocks (one in nearly every scene).

Frank does, indeed, arrive on time and comes looking for Kane. Kane is forced to hide and use his wits to pick off the gang. At a critical moment, he is aided by Amy who, as the first shots ring out, decides her love for Kane is stronger than her ethic of nonviolence and returns. She, herself, kills one of the gang members by a shot to the back. She also physically attacks Frank Miller in the climactic scene, distracting him and allowing Kane to shoot Miller. The conflict now resolved, the citizens return to offer thanks and praise. Kane throws his badge onto the ground and rides off in a wagon with his new bride toward a new life.

---

2 Lyrics by Ned Washington and performed by Tex Ritter – the movie's only appeal to "conventional Westerns." On the song and its impact on film, see Deborah Allison, "Do Not Forsake Me: The Ballad of High Noon' and the Rise of the Movie Song." https://www.sensesofcinema.com/2003/cinema-and-music/ballad_of_high_noon/ (accessed 15 October 2023).

*High Noon's* plot is "fraught with background" that is fleshed out in the intricate and subtle relationships between characters. Miller's motives are more than "getting even" for arrest, and Kane's are more than just "duty." The center of this matrix of relationships is Helen Ramirez (Katy Jurado). Ramirez is a Mexican woman and widow. She owns the town's saloon and is silent partner in the general store. She lives on the second floor of the town hotel. Ramirez, as the film begins, is deputy Harvey's lover. Five years prior, she had been the lover of Frank Miller. After Frank, she was Will Kane's lover for about four years. Indeed, much of Harvey's refusal to help Kane arises from jealousy. There are hints that Kane, in the past, was a heavy drinker and regular at the saloon. His motives to capture Miller arose in part from his desire for Helen. Will and Amy's marriage is also understood more clearly against this back story; in many ways, the marriage marks his desire to put away an old life of violence. That new hope, however, is threatened in every possible way by the sudden return of his past and concerns that flight aborts his own rebirth.

Nearly every major character in the film pays a visit, at some point, to Helen's hotel room. She first appears in a scene in her room where she, in nightgown and robe, is with Deputy Harvey. Later, Kane visits to warn her of Miller's return (and Miller's likely revenge against Helen, after finishing with Kane). Even Amy, intrigued by this mysterious presence who seems to be so involved in everything disrupting her new life (and who was, she learns, a former lover of her current husband) pays a visit. Helen's dialog with all three explicates Kane's behavior and turmoil; Kane, himself, rarely speaks. Helen also is the most direct and unapologetic about her plans to leave town (as well as about her own sexual past). She knows she is a strange and foreign woman in Hadleyville.

The film also explores themes of duty, honor, and integrity among the general citizenry. What is the "right path:" love or duty? Will "Will" stand firm despite standing alone? Who controls "law," the citizenry or "the professionals?" What is, in other words, the virtuous and wise path, particularly for citizens in a newly pacified world? Carl Foreman was very vocal about his script's political implications. Caught in the web of the House Committee on Un-American Activities hearings, Foreman would, by the film's release, be officially "blacklisted." It is unclear to what extent Zinnemann intended the film to be political. Foreman, however, was clear that the film was about a cowardly, inactive, and dishonorable film industry and political witch hunt. Foreman saw Kane's honor as an indictment of American passivity and cowardice. For others (notably Corkin), the film is clearly a commentary on the harsh burdens of military power and liberty.

The contrast between Helen and Amy is drawn in broad strokes. Both women are loved by Kane. Kane was Helen's former lover (though he did not marry her). He is Amy's present husband (though, as yet, they do not appear to be lovers). Helen knows Kane will stay and fight. Amy insists Will flee with her. What Helen finds attractive about Kane – the essence of his manhood – Amy detests and fails to understand. Helen is infinitely practical; she advocates doing what one must to survive. Amy is naïve in her ideals and virtue. Helen is openly sexual. Amy is a virgin. Amy is, throughout, dressed in her wedding garments. Helen is first dressed in a silk sleeping gown and robe, then in exotic clothing. Amy is blond with blue eyes and from "back east." Helen is dark haired with dark eyes and skin; she is from Mexico. Amy speaks with proper elocution. Helen has a strong Spanish accent. Amy is thin and graceful. Helen is Rubenesque. Amy appears, most often, to the strains of "Do not forsake me." The music for Helen is a mariachi-inspired samba. In short, everything about the presentation of Helen (even her name) speaks to sexuality and exoticism, to foreignness, strangeness, and temptation. Everything about Amy, including her name, invokes love, chastity, devotion, values, and "whiteness." Kane is positioned exactly between these two, one marking his former self, the other embodying his hopes for the future.

## Bridge

*O to be torn "twixt love and duty!/S'posin" I lose my fair-haired beauty!*

There are two explicit references to biblical text in *High Noon*, and both occur within the Hadleyville Church. The 11:00 worship hour corresponds to the tense wait for the noon train. In the first scene, the congregants are singing the first verse of the "Battle Hymn of the Republic." This (period relevant) hymn alludes throughout to the Apocalypse of John (particularly 14:17–20). We next see the church interior when Kane interrupts the sermon seeking volunteers for his posse. The pastor announces his text for the day and begins the reading from Malachi 4:1–4, a passage about the Day of the Lord:

> For, behold, the day comes, burning like an oven, when all the arrogant and all evildoers will be stubble; the day that comes shall burn them up, says the Lord of hosts, so that it will leave them neither root nor branch. But for you who fear my name, the sun of righteousness shall rise, with healing in its wings. You shall go forth leaping like calves from the stall, and you shall tread down the wicked, for they will be as ashes under the soles of your feet, on the day when I act, says the Lord of hosts.[3]

This reading predicts the denouement of the film. Kane and Miller are to meet at noon, the sun's highest point on an already hot day. Kane, during the ensuing gun battle, hides in the town stable, which Miller sets aflame; Kane escapes by

---

3 English translations here, and throughout, are from the Revised Standard Version, modified by me (using the standard, *Biblia Hebraica Stuttgartensia* [Stuttgart: Deutsche Biblegesellschaft, 1990]).

releasing the stock inside and rushing out in the confused stampede. By the end of the battle, all four of the Miller gang lie dead in the streets. Will and Amy are reunited, their love reaffirmed and their relationship healed. Will has acted as God's agent, destroying the wicked on the Day of the Lord.[4] Kane's violence is God's judgment. Kane is God's Will.

*High Noon's* original song with its insistent plea, "do not forsake me," reverberates with yet another biblical echo. The motif of "forsakenness" (Heb. *'āzab*) occurs more than 50 times in the *Ketuvim*. It frequently marks the pleas of the tormented to God (viz. Ps 27:9; 38:21; 71:18. Perhaps, most famously, Ps 22:1). Left alone and "be-set by evil men," who seek the life of the innocent and revel in violence, the voice of the Psalmist cries, again and again, to God, begging against being "forsaken." The trauma of abandonment (by his wife, by his friends, by the townspeople) surrounds Kane throughout the film.

A second locus for *'āzab*/forsakenness is God's pleas for fidelity in worship. Deuteronomic writings (viz. Deut 4) express the covenant between God and God's people via metaphors of marital fidelity; idolatry is likened to adultery. The motif is central in the prophets, perhaps most aggressively in Ezekiel 16–18 or Hosea 1–3. A breach in marital loyalty is a major element of forsakenness in *High Noon*. The tension of this rift is even more acute with the presence of Kane's former lover, Helen. Will is, at least ideologically, betraying his new bride; Helen knows he will stay to face Miller at any cost, revealing that Helen knows and understands him with a greater intimacy than Amy's (a major portion of "the cost" Kane is risking).

But there is, still yet, a more relevant use of *'āzab*/forsakenness in Hebrew text. The book of Proverbs opens with a nine-chapter celebration of the virtues of Wisdom (my readings of Proverbs are very much informed by McKane 1970; Scott 1965; and Van Leeuwen 1997). Wisdom (*hokma*, in later Greek, *sophia*) is a gift from God and very often articulated in terms of knowing submission to God's will and divine instruction (*torah*) and reproof (1:7; 3:11; etc.). The prologue to Proverbs is framed as a father's remarks to his son (1:8; 2:1; 3:1; etc.). There is substantial debate regarding the origins of Hebrew wisdom traditions, whether they be public or private, court or main street, school or home (see Fox 1996, pp. 227–239; Westermann 1995; or, for summary Crenshaw 1998, pp. 35–54). Whatever the exact origin, this discourse, couched as fatherly advice, is reflecting a discourse of men, about "manly" experience and interests.

---

4 As for the congregants, they initially arise to help. They decide it is best if Kane simply go away. As Miller and his gang arrive in town, the congregants are seen inside the church, fervently in silent prayer. Miller, evil, still arrives at their town and is driven away only by Will's "righteous" response of noble violence. One is left wondering if their prayers have been answered.

Fidelity/marital metaphors surround the advocacy of wisdom. Wisdom, personified as an actual woman, is celebrated as "good wife/partner" (Murphy 2002, pp. 133–149). She first appears in 1:20–33 where she "cries aloud in the street" as she searches the city, promising rewards to those who embrace and keep her. Again, in 8:1–31, we see her searching the streets, the markets, the houses of government, and the holy places calling for those who are wise to embrace her. She is a good partner, always providing insight and ability. In 4:1–9, the father's pleas become earnest:

> Hear, O sons, a father's instruction … When I was a son with my own father, a tender youth, the only child of my mother, he taught me and said to me, "Let your heart hold fast to my words… Get wisdom… *Do not forsake her, and she will defend/protect you; love her, and she will love you.*" (4:1–4; ital. added)

The metaphor is clear: as a father counsels his son to "find a good woman" and set up a peaceful home, he just as urgently pleads with his son to embrace wisdom.

A second woman appears in Proverbs. Occasionally called "Dame Folly," she is the antithesis of Wisdom (Camp 1985).[5] Like *Hokma*, she can be seen in the streets, enticing men inside (5:1–6), but she promises only fleeting and dangerous pleasures. She is sexually experienced and alluring, but she is an adulteress and will not remain faithful. In the end, she will forsake her paramours to face violent death (5:8–14).

Dame Folly is described as a "strange" or "foreign" woman (Prov 2:16; 5:3, 20; 6:24; 7:5 and, beyond the prologue, 20:16; 23:27; 27:13).[6] In part, the "strange woman" (*'ishah zara*) may linguistically imply "a woman who is an inappropriate sexual partner for you" or "someone else's wife." Clearly, however, issues of "foreign-born" women as inappropriate wives can be found in biblical text (viz. Ezra 9–10). Further, the primary issue in Proverbs is the embrace of a *Jewish* ethic as "wisdom." "Other," "foreign," and "strangeness," in this light, take on more ethnically charged connotations.

Within *High Noon* this contrast is reflected in the contrast between Helen and Amy. Helen's advice and insight, at first seemingly vital and accurate,

---

5 The trope of Wisdom vs. Folly is often referred to as the "Two Woman Motif" of Proverbs. It is, by no means, exclusive to that book, nor even to the Hebrew Bible. Notably, see Rossing 1999 where she follows the theme into the New Testament's Revelation to John.

6 See, for an excellent survey on the topic, Streete 1997. Streete, interestingly, argues that the original context of the material for 1–9 was concerns regarding tribal/ethnic identity and marital stability. This structure was then articulated in and later made allegory for Hebrew Wisdom.

will, in the end, leave Kane alone to face mortal danger (and result, inevitably, in the death of at least one of her former lovers). Helen, though not specifically associated with adultery, is certainly sexually experienced. She abandons Kane and has honeyed speech. She is very literally "strange" and foreign to the world of Hadleyville.

Amy, however, pleads for mercy and, initially, offers a suggestion that isn't completely imprudent – with a deranged gunman bent on revenge due to arrive on the next train, flight is certainly reasonable. She speaks the truth (as she knows it). She is a virgin; she spends the entire film dressed in a wedding garment. She is, also, very much *not* foreign or "strange" – in either sense of the word. Finally, she plays a critical role in Kane's final victory.

## Refrain

*Do not forsake me, O my Darlin,'/You made that promise when we wed.*

In some ways, the characters of Helen and Amy exemplify the classic "two woman" trope of Proverbs. Helen, very literally a "strange" and "foreign" *'ishah zarah*, represents Kane's violent and sexual past. Amy represents Kane's turn to wisdom; she is the classic 1950s view of the "Virtuous Wife" (*'ishah hayil*).[7] In many ways, Kane performs the dichotomy the two women embody. He speaks wisdom. Flight would damage Kane's honor and prevent him from putting away his violent past. Like both *hokma* and the *'ishah zarah*, Kane searches the streets, neighborhoods, markets, public houses, courtrooms, and temples seeking followers. His is the voice of the title song.

Yet, Kane cannot really embody the two-woman trope alone. To begin, gender is essential for his character. "Manhood" is the core thesis of the film and essence of all inner conflict and turmoil. Kane is able, however, to connect with the motif through both women. As past and future lover of the two women, Kane divides and conflates them both. Having absorbed both women into himself, the new triad unites to demonstrate "wisdom." Both women nuance Kane's struggle to be authentically male.

Such, unfortunately, is also reminiscent of the biblical trope. In Wisdom literature, the function and gender of women are controlled and scripted by their relationships and their value to men (Camp 1985. See also Brenner-Idan 1995). In key ways, both texts – the film and the wisdom writings – perform a dynamic

---

7 The *'ishah hayil* of Lemuel's poem in Prov 31 is, within Proverbs, distinct in both origin and theme from *Hokma* of 1–9. The two are often, however, conflated by later interpretive communities and perhaps even by Proverb's redactors. See Camp 1985, pp. 124–139.

articulated by Tomkins. Tomkins observes that women, in Westerns, queerly construct male identity. Women are the "language of men." Tomkins observes that women in Westerns are "masking the fact that what the men are really interested in is each other" (Tompkins 1992, p. 40).

In *High Noon*, Amy-as-Lady-Wisdom is, herself, instructed and changed. Amy's choice not to forsake Kane, in the end, brings her to forsake her own value of nonviolence. To defend Kane, Amy must "cross over" into his argument, into *his* message of wisdom. In essence, Kane has taught wisdom to Wisdom. This conjoined queer matrix of Kane-Amy-Wisdom has an ominous moral: to eschew violence is ultimately to forsake because it is to be dishonorable, to be unwise. As Tompkins also observes, "the genre [of Westerns] exists in order to provide a justification for violence" (Tompkins 1992, p. 272). That justification, indeed, sums up *High Noon* very neatly and certainly permeates American Cold-War era politics, government, and gender roles.

*High Noon* uses biblical motifs of the Day of the Lord, "forsakenness," and the personifications of Wisdom and Folly as women to articulate that violence is necessary for true peace, civility, liberty, and honor. Such violence is likened to divine judgment. Understanding this is divine wisdom.

The film ended, the voice of Tex Ritter soft in our mind's ear, our American (post)modern angst is, once again, assuaged enough, at least, for us to switch off the TV and turn to sleep.

## Works Cited

Brenner-Idan, A. (ed.) (1995). *Feminist Companion to Wisdom Literature*. Sheffield: Sheffield Academic.

Camp, C. (1985). *Wisdom and the Feminine in the Book of Proverbs*. Sheffield: Almond Press.

Cawelti, J.G. (1975). *The Six-Gun Mystique*. Bowling Green, KY: University of Kentucky Press.

Corkin, S. (2004). *Cowboys as Cold Warriors: The Western in US History*. Philadelphia: Temple University Press.

Crenshaw, J.L. (1998). *Old Testament Wisdom*. Rev. ed. Louisville, KY: Westminster John Knox.

Cunningham, E. (1996). *Triggernomitry*, 2e. New York: Causton Printers.

Fenin, G.N. (1973). *The Western: From Silents to the Seventies*. New York: Grossman.

Fox, M.V. (1996). The social location of the book of proverbs. In: *Texts Temples and Traditions* (ed. M.V. Fox, V.A. Hurowitz, A.M. Hurvitz, et al.), 227–239. Winona Lake, IN: Eisenbrauns.

French, D. (1973). *Westerns: Aspects of a Movie Genre*. New York: Viking.

French, P.A. (1997). *Cowboy Metaphysics: Ethics and Death in Westerns*. New York: Oxford University Press.

Gallagher, T. (2012). Shoot out at the genre corral: problems in the 'evolution' of the Western. In: *Film Genre Reader IV* (ed. B.K. Grant), 298–312. Austin, TX: University of Texas Press.

Grant, B.K. (ed.) (2012). *Film Genre Reader IV*. Austin, TX: University of Texas Press.

Hausladen, G.J. (2003). *Western Places, American Myth: How We Think about the West*. Reno, NV: University of Nevada Press.

Koosed, J.L. and Linafelt, T. (1996). How the west was not one: Delilah deconstructs the Western. *Semeia* 74: 167–181.

Lenihan, J.H. (1980). *Showdown: Confronting Modern America in the Western Film*. Champaign, IL: University of Illinois Press.

Limerick, P.N. (1987). *The Legacy of Conquest: The Unbroken Past of the American West*. 2 Vol. New York: Norton.

McKane, W. (1970). *Proverbs*, Old Testament Library. Philadelphia: Westminster.

Murphy, R.E. (2002). *The Tree of Life: An Exploration of Biblical Wisdom Literature*, 3e. Grand Rapids, MI: Eerdmans.

Naremore, J. (2004). Authorship. In: *A Companion to Film Theory* (ed. T. Miller and R. Stam), 9–24. London: Blackwell.

Parks, R. (1974). The western hero in film and television: mass media mythology. Ann Arbor, MI: UMI Research. PhD thesis. Northwestern University.

Plate, S.B.R. (2017). *Religion and Film: Cinema as the Re-Creation of the World*, 2e. New York: Columbia University Press.

Prats, A.J. (2002). *Invisible Natives: Myth and Identity in the American Western*. Ithaca, NY: Cornell University Press.

Rossing, B. (1999). *The Choice Between Two Cities*. Harrisburg, PA: Trinity/T & T Clark.

Scott, R.B.Y. (1965). *Proverbs, Ecclesiastes*, Anchor Biblical Commentary. New York: Doubleday.

Slotkin, R. (1992). *Gunfighter Nation: The Myth of the Frontier in Twentieth-Century America*. New York: Atheneum.

Smith, H.N. (1950). *Virgin Land: The American West as Symbol and Myth*. Cambridge, MA: Harvard University Press.

Smith, A.B. (2003). *Shooting Cowboys and Indians: Silent Western Films, American Culture and the Birth of Hollywood*. Boulder: University Press of Colorado.

Stowell, P. (1986). *John Ford*. Boston: Twayne Publishers.

Streete, G. (1997). *The Strange Woman*. Louisville, KY: Westminster John Knox.

Tompkins, J. (1992). *West of Everything: The Inner Life of Westerns*. New York: Oxford.

Tuska, J. (1985). *The American West in Film: Critical Approaches to the Western.* Westport, CT: Greenwood Press.

Van Leeuwen, R.C. (1997). The book of Proverbs. In: *The New Interpreter's Bible*, vol. 5, 195–262. Nashville, TN: Abingdon.

Warrior, R.A. (1989). Canaanites, cowboys and Indians: deliverance, conquest and liberation theology today. *Christianity and Crisis* 49 (12): 21–26.

Warshow, R. (1979). Movie chronicle: the westerner. In: *The Immediate Experience*, 135–254. New York: Atheneum.

Westermann, C. (1995). *Roots of Wisdom.* Louisville, KY: Westminster John Knox.

Wright, W. (1975). *Sixguns and Society: A Structural Study of the Western.* Berkeley, CA: University of California Press.

# 7

## God's Dice

### The Bible in/and Sci-Fi and Fantasy Gaming

Characters, plots, motifs, and memes from mythology, in general, frequently appear in fantasy role-playing games, with biblical characters, allusions, and themes easily holding pace with those of Greek and Roman mythology. A particularly popular set of cameos include Satan and his demonic allies and the plot device of a cosmic "war in heaven" that results in powerful spiritual warfare hidden behind the events of our realm. What humans perceive as "real," it posits, reflects – but does not exhaustively entail – what is in the hidden-but-really-real cosmic/spiritual realm; essentially, what we experience as reality is actually a proxy war between supernatural forces of Good and Evil. At stake is the outcome of both realms.

By use of these allusions to symbol, character, and theme, fantasy role-playing games create plots that also treat a narrative theme of conflict between "order" or "law" and disaster, or "chaos," sometimes even framed within a moral/ethical continuum as good vs. evil. Doing so adds richness and complexity to the experience of play and fosters an affective engagement with the characters and outcomes. Yet the games also explore the ambivalence within that struggle. What, really, constitutes "good" or "evil?" Is it possible that defense of Order can become a means of oppression? Who determines the permissible range of variation and freedom? The forces for order often use similar tactics, stratagems, and weapons as those of chaos; when is this problematic?

These sorts of worries appear in biblical text, as well. More accurately, they arise and have arisen from historic interpretation or other cultural use of biblical text. Scholars note, for example, the ways in which the characters of God and the Lamb in the New Testament's Book of Revelation pour out wrath in demonstrably terrible ways in Revelation (more on this later).

It is not, coincidental, I will argue, that gaming's allusions to biblical text cluster around characters and themes from books or narratives that reflect these tensions and ambivalence. In what follows, I want to offer first a review and analysis of

*American Standard: The Bible in US Popular Culture*, First Edition. Robert Paul Seesengood.
© 2024 John Wiley & Sons Ltd. Published 2024 by John Wiley & Sons Ltd.

some examples of the Bible in sci-fi and fantasy role-playing games, with a focus on the games of *Dungeons & Dragons* and *Warhammer 40k*. Next, this chapter will explore the ways both games have, at times, become touchy spots within culture, in some circles regarded as "Satanic" and dangerous and not appropriate for Christians to play or participate in; the most notable example, which I will survey, is the role of *Dungeons & Dragons (D&D)* in the "Satanic Panic" of the 1980s. Next, the essay will turn back to the Bible and its reception, noting in particular the development of the character of Satan and the turn in recent scholarship to articulate the ways that Bible, itself, is similar to the genre of fantasy literature (e.g. the work of Aichele) and offers views of God and the forces of "Good" that are unnervingly similar to Chaos. In the end, I will argue that the themes, memes, and motifs of Satan, the demonic, and John's Revelation appear in these games certainly to add narrative "thickness" and depth but also as a means of the game exploring the tensions within its (and the Bible's) own narrative logic.

I have selected the two examples of *D&D* and *Warhammer*, in part, because of their broad familiarity, but more because of their "foundational" status within the genre. Both, as well, have generated a massive body of creative content including role-playing games, tabletop games, and video games, as well as a range of supporting entertainment content (fiction, film, merchandise) and supplementary, "second-order" commentary and games ("how-to" manuals, play tutorials, and online social media communities). Readers are invited to explore these, though this particular essay will treat them only in broad strokes, both for reasons of space but also due to my larger interest in structure over detail. Finally, I have chosen these examples because they are center-genre for the themes of my focus: games that revolve around narratives of Order/Good vs. Chaos/Evil. Both as well struggle implicitly with worries of whether or not these options, presented as binary, are as separate as one might hope, or whether there are troubling points of overlap. I am arguing that the use of biblical characters and themes in fantasy role-playing games is actually a form of biblical interpretation. Attention to the moments of intersection also provides an opportunity to explore a fundamental aspect of culture and cultural studies: game creation and play. I will argue that the character of Satan and the divine war motif that is featured most prominently in Revelation is appearing in fantasy role-playing games that struggle with the ambivalence of a War against Chaos narrative. As such, tensions within Revelation itself are being intuitively noted by these games. When we create and play games, we are engaging in an activity that is drawing from the "genetic code" of the creation of societies and cultures and their products, including religion and, indeed, the Bible. When we create and play games that allude to Bible, we are also interpreting Bible, and what emerges is both a commentary on biblical text (a space to perceive or learn a level of its meaning otherwise implicit in academic or confessional interpretation) and an opportunity to reflect on how religion, Bible, and imagination, themselves, function.

## *Dungeons & Dragons* and the Birth of a Genre

In Wisconsin, in the early 1970s, two friends, Gary Gygax and Dave Arneson, had been looking for ways to engage their favorite fantasy novels more deeply, J. R. R. Tolkien's *The Hobbit* and *The Lord of the Rings*. They adapted rules from a tabletop wargame called *Chainmail* into a role-playing game set in a high-concept fantasy world very similar to Tolkien's Middle Earth and called *Dungeons & Dragons*, which they published in 1974 via their own colophon of Tactical Studies Rules (TSR). Their game would evolve into multiple editions, eventually being bought by Wizards of the Coast (a subsidiary of Hasbro toys since the 1990s). The game has entered mainstream awareness and spun off hundreds of books, merchandise, television, and film. In 2023 Paramount Pictures released *Dungeons & Dragons: Honor Among Thieves* (directed by John Francis Daley and Jonathan Goldstein) with a production budget of $150 million. Its gross of slightly over $200 million was somewhat lackluster, but its contribution to renewed interest in the game spilled over to a 40% growth in annual sales of *D&D* products and games by Hasbro (an annual revenue stream in the hundreds of millions). Notably, *D&D* has grown from its simple midwestern origins into a global phenomenon that is no doubt quickly recognized and culturally mainstream.

Gygax and Arneson's innovation was a game that could be played on a tabletop but need not. Certainly, many players build or paint customized miniature figures representing their character; many others design elaborate scenery sets or create models of enemy or neutral players in order to better visualize game scenes or combat. However, unlike previous tabletop wargames, what sets *D&D* apart is a continuity of campaign play enabled by its more narrative style. Players can very literally do anything, limited only by their imaginations and agreed upon convention.

*Dungeons & Dragons* takes place in a world inhabited by humans but also various races of demi-humans such as elves, dwarves, gnomes, halflings (hobbits), orcs, and, of course, dragons and other monsters and creatures. Magic is common. Technology is limited to essentially that of medieval Europe. A game leader called a "Dungeon Master" sets up the particulars of an individual game's narrative, objectives, and themes and envisions (and "populates") the immediate world in which events will take place – all by creation of story following general conventions and guides published as "rules." (TSR also publishes prewritten worlds/scenarios for making the creative life of Dungeon Masters a bit less exhausting). Other players create "characters" – an identity they will assume within the game. Characters are chosen among an array of racial options, with an equally complex array of skillsets or classes (wizard, warrior, knight, rogue, cleric), each with its own abilities and limitations and an infinite array of secondary skills, backgrounds, or attributes. The game is collaborative, without winners or losers. Characters normally begin as relative novices but can gain powers, abilities, and useful items as play progresses.

As play progresses, the Dungeon Master narrates a series of circumstances ("You follow a path into the dark woods that terminates in a small clearing containing a simple, small house. You can smell something burning, perhaps cooking, inside. What do you do next?"). Players respond by stating their character's actions ("I try to creep up to a window or door of the house unseen and listen or peer inside undetected."). The success or failure of a choice is determined by rolling special dice, most commonly a 20-sided die or d20. Players modify their die roll up or down based on a variety of factors (for example, a large, muscular hero in armor will have trouble with stealth). The Dungeon Master then tells the players what happens next ("As you approach, a harsh voice from inside cries out in alarm, and a terrible looking Ogre bursts open the door and roars at you."). Characters can engage in combat via a series of elaborate tables and rules scaling effects and skills, with success or failure again mitigated by rolling specialized dice ("We attack the ogre!" "Ok, let's roll for who gets combat initiative...").

The narrative world of *D&D* varies greatly. One of the strengths of the game has been its somewhat "open source" nature. "Rules" tend to be guidelines and case studies for resolving potential scenarios. Books containing predetermined monsters, characters, weapons, magical spells, and more – all with their various needs, limitations, and effects – can be purchased, but even there function more as a "tool chest" or set of guidelines for player or Dragon Master adaptation. *D&D* has fostered a very ingrained culture of local adaptation that helps the game thrive, even as it produces an array of player support products (books, dice, miniatures) that can enhance play.

Among the array of monsters and creatures encountered, one finds multiple allusions to classical myth and Jewish and Christian literature and tradition. Demons and the demonic appear with regularity (indeed, many of the demons are named, and in some scenarios players can travel through other realms of existence, including Hell). The moral system of the game essentially pits forces of law against forces of chaos. Player-characters, like the beings they encounter, have a personal "alignment" – a place on the spectrums of Good or Evil, Law or Chaos. Dungeon Masters are encouraged to make sure that player-characters actually behave consistently with their alignments ("lawful good" characters, for example, would not torture; "chaotic evil" characters will not act out of pure altruism).

Through the game, players can inhabit identities and roles that use sorcery or magic (including harmful or even overtly demonic varieties). They may find themselves in a battle against the undead or demonic. They may, themselves, engage in troubling fantasy behavior such as theft, murder, or rape. These aspects of the game, its potential to be a space for the – public – indulgence in dark fantasy and the ever-present worry that what is fantasized about in the game might be experimented with one day in "reality," as we will see, have generated occasional discomfort among many nonplayers.

## The Lore of the God-Emperor: *Warhammer 40k*'s Narrative Frame

In 1975, three friends, John Peake, Ian Livingstone, and Steve Jackson, pooled their mutual funds to turn their mutual hobby into a business and founded Games Workshop, a UK-based mail-order catalog for all things related to fantasy literature and games. The trio, like Gygax and Arneson, were particularly enamored with the rich, high-fantasy world of J. R. R. Tolkien's Middle Earth. In two years they grew into publishing *White Dwarf Magazine*, initially a hobby magazine for sci-fi/fantasy games in general, and opened their first physical game store in Hammersmith, London one year later. (On the array of products, see their product site, www.games-workshop.com.) In 1979, Games Workshop entered into partnership with Citadel Miniatures, a company making 35 mm scale models (initially molded out of lead) of monsters, heroes, and other characters common in sci-fi and fantasy games. Consumers would purchase the miniatures, often painting them by hand to suit their tastes, and collect them or use them in various role-playing games.

By 1983, Games Workshop had devised its own, distinctive model series and a set of rules adapted from generic tabletop, model wargaming and such is the origin of *Warhammer 40k*. Currently, Games Workshop has over 500 stores worldwide (largely in the United States, United Kingdom, and other parts of Europe) and extends license to sell its products in thousands more small, local game shops. In addition to their game system and models, gaming magazines, and modeling supplies (specialty glues, paints and brushes for building and hand-painting models), they have launched a series of pulp fiction novels (the Black Library) and, since 2004, a best-selling series of video games based on their tabletop role-playing characters. The tabletop gaming industry in the United States is modest (compared to other hobby, entertainment, and leisure markets), earning about $25 billion annually and with projected growth of 11–12% annually. Although sales figures are closely guarded within the industry, and complicated by multiple forms of content and merchandise sold by the game manufacturer, without doubt *Warhammer* commands a significant portion of that market.

To play *Warhammer 40k* players assemble two "armies" of collectable 35 mm scale models, which "fight" against one another on a table surface, waging battles set in the fortieth century and within a gaming world that spans galaxies. Armies include humans, demi-human alien races (many based upon traditional fantasy races such as elves and orcs), stranger alien monsters (the savage bug-like Tyrannids), and cyborg races, with a host of mechanized weapons for each. (the current iteration of rules, the 10th edition, was released by Games Workshop in summer 2023, sold as part of a boxed set of miniatures, cards, and books under the title of *Leviathan*).

At its simplest, players take turns attacking. They announce which model is attacking which (shooting at it, or perhaps rushing forward into melee) and roll a six-sided dice to determine success (with additional dice rolls to assess damage). Models are highly variable (indeed, most gamers build their own armies out of kits, which are sometimes customized), different weapons or armors result in different plus or minus numbers to the die roll outcome, making some weapons much more powerful and some defenses much more vulnerable. The Games Workshop system are a series of rules indicating weapon and armor strength, various secondary metrics (e.g. how far – measured in tabletop inches – a given model can shoot or move, how many wounds a model may sustain before it is inoperative, etc.), and special rules for each army or to resolve common scenarios (e.g. can characters ride inside of other model vehicles and, if so, can they be wounded?). These rules are published in large bound books, updated periodically (the game is currently in the 10th edition) along with several other books (sold as "codices") containing rules for specific armies. In each edition and codex, Games Workshop publishes pages and pages of tables and rules (called by players "the Crunch") and hundreds more pages with the backstory for armies and events (called the "Lore" or, more cynically, "the Fluff").

In their original gaming system, *Warhammer* was a traditional high-fantasy aesthetic where players chose armies of humans, elves, dwarves, orcs, ogres, or other monsters. Play was roughly based upon Tolkien's Middle Earth. With the development of its iconic "space marine" character line, *Warhammer* developed its own unique narrative context, officially designated "*40k*" to distinguish it from the traditional fantasy world, set in the "grim dark" future where "there is only war." "Unique" is something of a qualified term with *Warhammer*. In terms of models, *Warhammer 40k* still borrows heavily from other sci-fi franchises. They offer, for example, an army of Aeldar (which are simply space elves), Ogryn (which are large demi-human brawlers, essentially ogres), "squats" (which are a stocky, diminutive demi-human race that excel at mining – in other words: dwarves), and orks (spelled with a terminal k, rather than the conventional "orc," yet essentially a space-going, gun-toting version of the same fantasy game character type). Games Workshop, ever attuned to business needs, well knows that "Ork" can be copywritten (as opposed to the public domain "orc." Games Workshop, unlike other game-systems, is fierce about protecting intellectual property and creative content, going to great lengths to inhibit copycat products or player-created content). Games Workshop reintroduced their Lord of the Rings model series (under exclusive license) in the early 2000s, shortly after the series of film versions of the novel directed by Peter Jackson. In recent years they have initiated another product line subtitled "Age of Sigmar," which returns to a high-concept fantasy world. These series, Lord of the Rings and Sigmar, run concurrent to *40k*, though there is little overlap between them.

In addition to borrowing character trope and vocabulary from genre, in the construction of its narrative world, *40k* draws heavily from other popular science fiction/fantasy novels and fantasy worlds. *Warhammer 40k* draws its iconic character, the space marine, from Robert Heinlein's *Starship Troopers* and its narrative world draws key components from Frank Herbert's *Dune* saga. Visually, the models and art for *40k* draw from a mixture of medieval European Catholicism, Roman imperial insignia and heraldry, British Empire era navy, and World War I and II European theater armaments and uniforms. What makes *40k* unique, then, is the way in which it synthesizes and organizes an array of other sci-fi/fantasy traditions and memes. It is, to its core, an allusive, bricolage (or "patchwork") world.

## The Devil in the Details: Satan and the Cosmic War Motif in *W40k* and *D&D*

The narrative world of *Warhammer 40k* that emerges from this allusiveness draws both from low-concept fantasy (where the world the characters inhabit is our own reality, but some form of travel or discovery takes them into the fantasy space. *The Wizard of Oz*, for example) and magical realism – where there are strange and mysterious, magical elements which interrupt our world (e.g. the novels of Gabriel Garcia Marquez).[1]

The central character in its lore is the "God Emperor." Born in eighth century BCE Antatolia, the emperor was both psychic and immortal. Human history progressed as our own has, through the present and into a future where space colonization was active and prosperous. Humans colonized other worlds, normally living in densely packed "hive cities" populated by billions of our species. A few alien races – notably the aeldar/elves and orks – were encountered and conquered. The tremendous expense and wealth, along with the tremendous grown in populations, resulted in vast economic disparity and

---

1 Fantasy's other option is the "high-concept" world, such as Lord of the Rings, where there is much less correlation between the fantasy reality and our lived world. Magic or some other power is common, races of demi-humans exist alongside humanity, and wild or treacherous monsters and beasts abound.

a return to feudal governance. The great families, as they do, began to fight amongst themselves. Using terrible weaponry, the result of their great engineering (centered around the factories and tech schools of earth/Terra's first colony: Mars), they waged terrible wars, killing billions and threatening the very survival of our species.

Enter the Emperor. Rising in power, first by conquering Terra, then by pushing through the other colonies, the Emperor established a peaceful kingdom, settling the various internecine disputes among the various lords. The Emperor was a powerful psychic. He discovered ways to manipulate and move through the Warp. The Warp is a dimension above-and-alongside our own. Through it, via wormhole portals, one can travel unimaginable distances as well as send psychic messages. A few individuals can also manifest warp energies in our own reality in ways that seem magical. Yet the Warp is also extremely dangerous. It is a dimension of pure chaos. Travel through it always involves the risk of appearing in the wrong space-time; travel through can be negotiated only by the assistance of a psychic navigator (who follows psychic "beacons" generated by the Emperor). Further, the Warp is populated by an array of powerful beings who revel in Chaos and would greatly desire to enter our reality and unleash terror. Indeed, the realm of the warp is very, very like the realms of Hell and the underworld. The walls of the Warp are also quite thin in places. Moving in and through it can disrupt the barrier rigidity and allow "rifts" in space–time reality. Through these gaps, an array of dark armies and other forces can emerge, as well as a general chaos "infection" that drives some humans mad and bends them to the end of seeking the ruin of our own reality.

The Emperor seized power over earth and spread outward, bringing as well his redemptive ideology. He brought lessons about the Warp but also forbade religion and the use of many technologies. Necessary (read: martial) technology was reduced to ritual. Hundreds of servitors (*40k* draws heavily from medieval ecclesiastical Latin for its language. The Emperor's symbol is an eagle, his aquila. The armies of the Empire are the Astra Militarium, etc.) were trained in religious rituals and devotions to the "machine spirit" (or "Omnissiah," the "Machine God") of their vessels, tools, and weapons. They, through ritual, maintained technology they could no longer understand (or modify, which was the goal), becoming a large, quasi-ecclesial body called the Adeptus Mechanicus (a group distinct from the "Ecclesiarchy," which is the governing bureaucracy or the Inquisition that enforces the necessary rule and secrecy total control the Imperium requires).

The God-Emperor was also preternaturally intelligent. He took a portion of his own DNA and genetically engineered a class of warrior, the Space Marine (Adeptus Astartes). The Emperor initially designed 20 heroes, each with his own character and aspect of the Emperor. Significantly larger, stronger, faster, and tougher than normal humans, the archetypical heroes were, in turn, genetically engineered to produce vast armies for the Imperium of Man. Clad in ultra-powerful armor and using extremely effective weapons, they were sent out by the Emperor in Crusades to effect the dominance of humanity over the "xenos" (the alien races found in the galaxy). There seemed no end to humanity's potential.

Yet, the power of the Warp remained. Its energies and madness infected one of the Emperor's most beloved space marine heroes (his "Children"), Horus. Horus turned upon his father and the Imperium and led a revolt against Terra with some other chaos-infected heroes (with their chapters and army factions), causing a great civil war within the Imperium called the "Horus Heresy." The God-Emperor was himself eventually able to stop Horus, but was gravely injured as a result. He was placed upon the great Golden Throne, a life-sustaining machine, where he lay in state, existing only as sentient warp energies, tied to a desiccated and fragile body sustained by machines, an apparent corpse. The empire he left behind has struggled on, a shadow of its former glories. The empire's governance, like its technology, are perpetuated by rituals that perpetuate the emperor's teachings. The space marines remain, but they have been fragmented into hundreds of chapters, unable to unite again as a common force. With his passing, various rifts in the Warp have opened and unspeakable monsters have emerged. Other alien races have resurged, as well. And humans now battle among themselves, with the Imperium at war against the Heretics. In this gloomy space, humanity is no longer waging crusades of conquest but battling daily to simply exist, beset by the challenges of the "chaos, the Xenos, and the Heretic." With little hope for victory and peace, there is "only war."

The *40k* lore refers, again and again, to the present world as "grim dark" (sometimes "grimdark" in fan literature). It is a world wrestling with the traumas of ecological collapse and climate disaster, ghastly weapons of mass destruction, genocide, overindustrialization, vast disparity of wealth, urban sprawl, governmental incompetence and corruption, oppressive and inquisitorial disciplines, and more. The world of *Warhammer 40k* struggles with themes of racism and xenophobia, violent oppression and fascism. These energies, like the Warp energies, spill out of the game, as well. Among the culture of its fandom, there are more than occasional glimpses of racism. The models, like the lore, almost exclusively feature (white) males. Fans on Reddit expressed outrage in 2020 over the inclusion of people of color within newer models for space marines and the release of new models for a women's army, the Adeptus Sororitas (even though these models, like most depictions of women in sci-fi/fantasy, are buxom and beautiful and often revealingly clad). More disturbing, perhaps, are the models of the Sororitas themselves, which are often modeled as "penitents" (people "repenting" of some "heresy" against the Imperium), sometimes actively undergoing (self) torture.

As the game draws from larger sci-fi/fantasy franchises for its symbolism and lore in order to craft its narrative of Order vs. Chaos, it draws very heavily, as well, from biblical text, particularly the apocalypse. The creatures from the Warp are known as daemons and they, and their leaders, draw heavily from art and tradition describing the demonic. The Emperor is not only messianic as a figure, he is openly Christ-like (and, indeed, referred to more than metaphorically as a God-Emperor). The battles against chaos happen on worlds with names like Abaddon and Armageddon. Alien armies, such as the waves of marauding orks, are led by a monstrous, ethereal master known as "the Beast."

The lore of the game amalgamates various sci-fi traditions to create a world facing the social and moral ills of the twentieth century, drawn out to caricature scale. In doing so, it also heavily interjects Christian images, ecclesiastical symbol and history, liturgy and allusion. Notably, these images and memes are interwoven around the main narrative of the lore and are, themselves, intersecting with the theme(s) of God's divine warfare against Satan.

## The "Satanic Panic" and the Dissonance Between *D&D* and Some US Religious Circles

*Dungeons & Dragons*, as a game, was populated with fantasy creatures and scenarios drawn, as we've seen, from other fantasy franchises (such as Tolkien), ancient mythology, but also Christian tradition and the Bible. *D&D* players face orcs and dragons but also monsters such as demons, witches, vampires, and an array of other beings. Shortly after its origins, *D&D* became the target of concern among many Christian leaders (and not a few parents. Or sometimes both. My own mother had me speak with a local youth minister about my interest in the game when I was 14).

For many, the game was thought to be a gateway into the occult. For some, the invocation of Satan's name, as well as other evil entities and demons, was potential invitation for those beings to attend to a hapless teen, perhaps even via possession. Teens and other impressionables could also engage in an array of troubling fantasies within the game. There was general concern that lowering the threshold of moral/intellectual opposition to certain behaviors via imagining them (particularly, doing so in groups of other teens and perhaps receiving acclaim or approval) could lead to actualizing those behaviors. Many feared that role-players would move to "next level" game engagement via "live action role play" (or "LARP") where any number of dangerous activities could ensue. Such fears, for example, were aggressively pushed by the evangelical Christian tract (and comic book) author and publisher Jack Chick.[2]

There were, as well, widely publicized, accounts of disturbed or violent behavior exhibited by *D&D* players (most notoriously, by the teenaged assassins at Columbine High School) and accounts of suicide resulting from trauma arising from game-play. Notably, however, many of these accounts turn out, upon review, to be more urban legend than actual fact, and the correlation of dysfunctional behavior by/among role-players was never advanced to causational.

Writing of the controversy, Laycock notes:

> [C]urious is the fact that Christian critics of fantasy role-playing games appeared alienated form the game's obvious provenance in Christian cosmology. The creators of D&D were themselves Christian, and many of the supernatural elements of the game are inspired by the Bible and Christian tradition. More than any other fantasy role playing games, D&D frames the world in stark terms of good and evil.... However, Critics saw these elements not as evidence of the games provenance in Christianity, but rather as its link to satanism.
>
> (Laycock 2015, p. 23)

Indeed, he notes "a paradox: the admittedly Christian elements of D&D prove [to its critics] that it is an anti-Christian, 'occult' game" (p. 23).

Far from the days when religious leaders and experts generally expressed (at least mild) concern about the influence of role-playing games on morality and ethics, fantasy gaming in current professional educational and religious scholarly discourse is generally considered harmless fun, and indeed often advocated for as a tool for general education (Fehleison and Eurich 2019; Leeson and Gibbs 2019; Porter 2008), therapy (Howard 2018), and even interfaith encounter (Inoles et al. 2016, 2018; Feltmate 2010) and liturgy (Durheim 2021).

What has changed in the interim is, perhaps, a longer-standing experience with the games (and the fact that the overwhelming majority of teen players in the 1980s are now quite well-adjusted adults with children of their own), but also a changing of the larger political conversation (or at least its focus within culture). Most new technologies or entertainment venues in the United States

---

2 One of Chick's more famous comic-book tracts was the 1984 *Dark Dungeons*. In it, Chick depicts two young women who are drawn into role-playing from a need to fit in socially. They become adept at the game, quite literally, falling under the mentorship of an actual witch who is using the game as a means of recruiting young people into occult practices and rituals. Eventually, one of the young women is intentionally goaded into suicide as a sacrifice to Satan. The tract was adapted into a satirical film of the same title. See RGP Advocate @ *The Escapist.com* – http://www.theescapist.com/darkdungeons.htm (accessed 23 October 2023).

have been considered evil or "gateway" to evil; for example, radio, film, television, and internet have each, upon arrival, been denounced as harbingers of moral and cultural decline. Laycock also sees responsibility in the rise of the "New Christian Right" in the 1980s. He notes:

> The conservative evangelical movement that formed in the 1970s emphasized biblical literalism and promoted leaders who derived their charisma from their personas as postbiblical characters. Biblical literalism adopted the modernist assumption that stories have value only if they are true in a historic and scientific sense. The project of biblical interpretation is paradoxically a "generative" one, as literalists are constantly required to "discover" new truths in a text that is allegedly simple and unchanging.... These distortions were not regarded as dishonesty; instead they were a sort of creative confusion between literal and creative frames of communication. In other words, conservative evangelical culture during the decade of the panic was attempting to be creative and literal simultaneously.... Satanic conspiracy theories can be read as an extreme example of this tendency to creatively confuse frames and to treat metaphorical claims as literal truths.
>
> (2015, p. 21)

Several of Laycock's themes have been treated in previous chapters, but one aspect stands out: there was, among Christian opposition to fantasy role-playing, a clear perception that the very nature of fantasy itself was an intrusion and a threat to Christian practice. Laycock notes, in his significant analysis of the opposition, that "several Christian critics .... concluded that the imagination itself is heretical because imaging another world amounts to a rejection of God's" (p. 23. Cf. pp. 24–25). He continues, noting that the "realization that a game of imagination can resemble a religion naturally leads to a suspicion that one's religion could likewise be a game of imagination" (pp. 24–25). The persistence of fantasy, and the observation implicitly made about its uncanny resemblance to systems of faith and religion, provoked a crisis among many Christian literalists.

## The "Origins of Satan" and the Bible as Fantasy Literature

For many readers of the Bible, the character of Satan is both instantly familiar but also mysterious and arcane. As with any good villain, Satan's motives and "origin story" are, in biblical text, quite vague. This vagueness has enabled a long history of speculation and tradition to develop. Neither Moses nor the Jews encounter Satan during their wilderness wanderings and the Garden serpent is not, in Genesis, identified as Satan. Indeed, the word "Satan" is completely absent from Genesis and occurs only once in the entire wilderness wandering epic, and there Satan is clearly working for God. In Numbers 22:22, God, angry at the mercenary prophet Balaam, sends an angel to be "his" (Balaam's?) "Satan" (stopping him on a wilderness road). Famously, this Satan is seen by Balaam's donkey who refuses to go further. In other words, the only appearance of Satan in the biblical wilderness narrative is a *positive* encounter that effects God's will at God's behest.

Most scholars are, of course, not surprised at this semi-positive role for Satan (see, for a survey, Pagels 1995; Russell 1987a). The character of *ha-satan* develops over the course of the biblical canon and through the intertestamental period (Russell 1987b). *Satan* simply means "to oppose" in Hebrew. Etymologically, the Greek equivalent, *diabollos*, means to "cast against" or "oppose." As Hebrew Bible develops, we find passages that describe a figure in the heavenly court who works as "opposing counsel" for God's deliberations, occasionally testing humans such as Job (see 1 Kings 22:19–28; Job 1–2). In time, this occupation is ascribed to a particular individual "the accuser" or *ha-satan* (Job 1–2; Zech 3:12). In the (very late) book of 1 Chronicles, the generation of Satan from a divine role to a specific character seems complete (1 Chr 21:1). Ancient Judaism has no stable category for "Satan" or "the devil" as a fixed, specific character; engagement with the binary structures of the religions of Babylon crystallizes this opposition to (in?) God's will into a specific character (note Pagels 1995; Wray and Mobley 2005; and Russell 1987a, b). During the second temple period, the figure develops more clearly. Daniel 7 describes a conflict between God's angels and angels of the Greeks and "the Prince of Persia." In this later literature, Satan emerges as a malevolent being of significant power opposed to the will of God. In other words, the formation of "Satan" into a unique character is part of the oral traditions that arise during the late second temple era – traditions that also include the resurrection of the dead and messianic expectations. By earliest Christianity, Satan was a figure clearly at odds with the work of God, in no way a part of God's courts. By late antiquity, the roots of the legend of the fallen angel were well established (Russell 1986, 1990). Satan as a character emerges from tradition, a collective process of interpretation by storytelling that uses an array of prior and contemporary cultural themes and means as its building blocks.

The Satan that Jesus encounters in the Gospels (e.g. Matthew 4:1–11; Mark 1:12–13; Luke 4:1–13) is also a hybrid figure who has ancient Jewish and pagan trickster deities in his own lineage. He is also clearly an aspect of the "oral Torah" culture of the late second temple and one of several markers that indicate the earliest followers of Jesus (the Q community) had much more in common with the Pharisees than the Sadducees. There are other hybrid moments in the encounter. As we have noted, consensus seems to be that the genre of Jesus and Satan's debate is midrashic haggadah, a favored exegetical technique of the early rabbis (see, for example, Davies and Allison 1988, pp. 352–354). The pericope may have its roots in Pharisee, pre-rabbinic Oral Torah communities of Jews who became convinced of Jesus' prophetic significance (if not his outright messiahship). Jesus' character is being defined by this scene that draws from earlier traditions of the Devil in ways that establish both compliance with a dominant narrative and deviant subaltern alteration.

The serpent in the Genesis 2–3 narrative has been identified as Satan through the reception of the narrative, yet notably is not identified as such within the Hebrew Bible. At the other end of the Christian canon, its final book, John's Apocalypse (or Revelation to John), Satan does appear in somewhat serpentine form. In Revelation 12, John of Patmos has a vision of a pregnant woman in the sky; a "great red dragon" (Greek) appears as well.

> And there was war in heaven: Michael and his angels fought against the dragon; and the dragon fought and his angels, and prevailed not; neither was their place found any more in heaven. And the great dragon was cast out, that old serpent, called the Devil, and Satan, which deceives the whole world: he was cast out into the earth, and his angels were cast out with him.
>
> (Rev 12:7–9; NKJV)

As the woman goes into labor the dragon attempts to devour her newborn child. The child is saved by cosmic forces that summon a protective stream of water, and the enraged dragon summons a monster from the seas, the infamous "beast" of Revelation 13 who rules the earth, forcing humanity to take its seal upon themselves in the form of a mysterious number "sealed" (Written? Branded? Tatooed? Microchipped?) on their foreheads (Rev 13:13). The savage beast imitates the "slaughtered lamb" (an avatar of Jesus throughout the Apocalypse) and leads many astray (Rev 13:14–17), kindling God's wrath and prompting an array of catastrophes and judgment.

Events come to a head in Revelation 20:1–7:

> Then I saw an angel coming down from heaven, holding in his hand the key to the bottomless pit and a great chain. He seized the dragon, that ancient serpent, who is the devil and Satan, and bound him for a thousand years and threw him into the pit and locked and sealed it over him, so that he would deceive the nations no more, until the thousand years were ended. After that he must be let out for a little while. Then I saw thrones, and those seated on them were given authority to judge. I also saw the souls of those who had been beheaded for their testimony to

Jesus and for the word of God. They had not worshiped the beast or its image and had not received its brand on their foreheads or their hands. They came to life and reigned with Christ a thousand years. (The rest of the dead did not come to life until the thousand years were ended.) This is the first resurrection. Blessed and holy are those who share in the first resurrection. Over these the second death has no power, but they will be priests of God and of Christ, and they will reign with him a thousand years. When the thousand years are ended, Satan will be released from his prison and will come out to deceive the nations at the four corners of the earth, Gog and Magog, in order to gather them for battle; they are as numerous as the sands of the sea. They marched up over the breadth of the earth and surrounded the camp of the saints and the beloved city. And fire came down from heaven and consumed them. And the devil who had deceived them was thrown into the lake of fire and sulfur, where the beast and the false prophet were, and they will be tormented day and night forever and ever.

(NRSV)

The "War in Heaven" in John's apocalypse happens in two campaigns. First, Michael the archangel leads Heaven's forces against the Dragon (identified as Satan) and his legions (never further identified); this first wave is successful enough to cast the Devil to Earth. Unlucky us, Satan shifts the direction of his rebellion to seducing humans away from loyalty to God. After horrible wrath being rained upon the disloyal humans (to woo them back? More likely to cowl them into submission again) without success, God decides to attack Satan. Satan is seized and cast into a deep pit allowing a respite, but he escapes to again cause trouble. The third and final wave of the campaign is a Satanic siege against God's "beloved city." God intervenes directly this time, and the conflict ends with surprising abruptness given its buildup. With Satan finally dispatched, the New Jerusalem, a gigantic city with massive walls and golden streets, descends to the earth and God lives with the faithful (and victorious) humans forever in bliss.

The Revelation to John, as we will discuss much further in Chapter 9, belongs to the genre of "apocalyptic." The genre names arises from the book's title, a Greek word that means "to uncover" or "to reveal." Though strange and mysterious to us, the genre was fairly common among late second temple period Jews and was, by design, ironically intended to make the cosmos more clear (not more confusing). As a genre, its function (again as we will explore in more depth later) was less to reveal mysteries of the future, and much, much more to unveil the (spiritual) realities of the present. As such, Revelation's key theme is that things in this world are not what they seem; instead, we are seeing the physical manifestation of a great "War in Heaven" campaign. God, as leader of Good and Order, is at war with the devil, Satan, master of the forces of Chaos and Evil.

Cosmic war motifs are common in ancient mythology, and commonly invoked in apocalyptic literature. Adela Collins has documented the cosmic war elements of Revelation alongside their antecedents in other ancient near eastern myth (Collins 2001). Dragons and serpents are frequently monsters of Chaos (note Ogden 2013a, b, 2021). The developing character of Satan is born from a series of borrowed traditions itself (Russell 1987a), most coming from an array of stories and traditions about cosmic, para-natural warfare among supernatural beings. These motifs were developed within the ancient, nascent Christian community, even as they expanded even further in later European literature and culture.

Most professional, scholarly commentators on Revelation see the book wrestling with the tensions between the emerging Jesus movement and the Roman State. A particular challenge was the Roman Imperial Cult – a system of religious rituals and practices that celebrated the power of the state as supreme and the emperor as implicit deity (certainly many may have – excusably given the rhetoric – understood that the claims were of the *actual* divinity of the emperor). The great "Beast from the Sea" is the Roman Empire. Revelation argues that empire is (i) actually a puppet regime led by Satan; (ii) doomed to lose and be destroyed (see, for example, Aune 1997–1998; Rossing 1999).

Of course, these are hardly the only contemporary interpretations of Revelation's strange war, nor are they the most popular (see Wainwright 2001). As the reception and interpretive history have developed, the War in Heaven has moved to an earlier point in cosmic history, indeed even prior to the creation of an inhabited earth, a reading made beautiful narrative by John Milton in his *Paradise Lost*. Satan/Lucifer, the most beautiful of archangels, falls victim to his own pride and rebels against God, only to be cast down into Hell. Enraged at his defeat, he turns his anger toward spoiling God's creation, beginning with God's favorites, humanity. Eventually, God steps in and brings a decisive end to Satan and those whom Satan has seduced into loyalty. In addition to this narrative, Revelation 20 has also become a focus for readings about Jesus's second coming and God's judgment of the earth, and the potential (and place) of a millennial, 1000-year reign by God (Wainwright 2001, pp. 21–106 for an overview; Rossing 2004 for a historical critic's rebuttal of "rapture" readings).

When Revelation uses a tale of a cosmic battle between a hero and a (serpentine) monster to represent a cosmic battle between the Divine and Chaos, it is patching into a long-standing, very ancient motif, a motif so common that scholars have given it a unique name and study: *chaoscampf* (the German for "Chaos war," Beal 2023, p. 3). Monsters are harbingers of (anti-divine) chaos and would be part and parcel of Apocalyptic. Indeed, Beal notes that the very word "monster" is from the Latin *monstere* for "vision" or "omen;" he continues, describing monsters as "otherness personified... imbued with agency they act, or threaten to act, imposing their otherness on our familiar understanding and experience of sameness and order" (p. 4). Beal notes that monsters and the monstrous, in the writing of Sigmund Freud, represent the *unheimlich* – often translated "the uncanny," but very literally, "unhomeliness." Monsters represent chaos, but a chaos that is already, to use a common horror trope, inside our own homes. They are omens of the chaos within; they are what we fear *we* are. Certainly, when monsters are battled within any fantasy space, whether role-playing game, film, or ancient religious text or mythology, they are symbolizing our war within ourselves, what we worry we might become.

Is this true of Revelation's monsters (or other biblical beasts)? If so, what is the fear? Revelation draws its dragons from out of the waters of other Hebrew Bible texts, pulling to the surface other traditions and beasts suggested in the Bible, much as Revelation builds, through bricolage, its worldview via citation and allusion to other bibles. Beal notes, for example, how the red dragon/Satan is resonant with the Hebrew Bible's Leviathan (Beal 2023, p. 75). Revelation creates a story of the world's impending transition with references to how it has transformed before and via assertions that it is God behind the transformation. Beal writes that Revelation is creating a narrative world where "the cosmogonic beginning becomes *chaogonic* ending" (Beal 2023, p. 76. Emphasis in original). The world's seeming order is a veneer; beneath it is a churning chaos.

Yet, Beal continues, "in this state of disorientation, it is often difficult to distinguish God from monster" (p. 77). Much of the horror, destruction and death in Revelation indeed does *not* originate from the dragon or his Beast. Quite the opposite, they are seeking to establish a whole *new* order (in rival to God's). Beal writes:

> In this state of disorientation, it is often difficult to distinguish God from monster... Each new vision, each new monstrous portent, disturbs whatever certainty might have been achieved up to that point. Is that [monster] one of "ours" or one of "them"? It does not help matters that at least as much cosmic devastation and human suffering are being meted out by God and God's angels as by God's murderous opponents.
>
> (p. 78)

He concludes that Revelation "is neck deep in human blood, much of it spilled by God and God's sickle-swinging, plague-bearing angels" (p. 84).

In Revelation's fantastic vision, there is a real fear of monsters and chaos, and God meets these firmly. But, perhaps, there is such firmness that a reader could be fairly left with the question about whether the medicine might be as severe as the disease. In a war against an enemy as evil and as chaotic as Satan, can one remain free of violence and chaos oneself? When one battles monsters, does one become monstrous as well? If it is *God* battling the monster, what then?

Satan and sinister forces are at war with God. Yet the forces of Heaven and God act in deeply intimidating and violent ways to suppress Satan's forces. In more than a few cases, their assaults are as terrible, if not more terrible, in effect upon the Earth than those of Satan. God as the force for Order and Good certainly provokes a great deal of suffering and Chaos. The result is a very ambivalent situation where God is less condemnatory of Satan's/Rome's rule, qua the imperial rule itself, but mostly concerned that it is not God who is ruling. In other words, the issue is less *what* empires do, or *how* they effect and secure rule, but much more *who* is in charge as emperor. As Beal writes, the issue is less that Satan is a monster, and more that he's the wrong sort of monster. God, in suppressing Satan, becomes even more fierce. God out monsters the monster Satan.

## Playing (with) the Devil

J. R. R. Tolkien, in his lecture, latter essay, "On Fairy Stories" addresses head on the question of whether fantasy writings are reducible to Children's literature (Tolkien 1947). Tolkien argues against such an idea. Certainly, the stories we categorize as "fantasy" are stories often told to children, and they do, indeed, very often have plots revolving around magic and magical intervention. Further, more than a few fantasy stories, like myth, have heavy elements of "coming of age" narrative integral to their plots. Yet, Tolkien continues with metaphor to argue that, if fantasy is indeed the furniture found in the nursery, it is there because of its age and function (Tolkien 1947). Fantasy, Tolkien argues, may be a genre beloved by children and adolescents, but its origin as a genre is far more adult, and quite ancient. Fantasy stories are among our most primal and powerful forms of storytelling.

Perhaps one additional factor is the association many build around fantasy and mythology given their own encounter and experience. These are stories we most often meet in childhood (Pyper and Vander Stichele 2012; cf. Fewell 2003). Because of this, there tends to be an element of "childish things" associated with them which serious minded adults must "put away." Or, at least, that seems to have been the conceit of modernism. Late twentieth century has seen a blossoming of fantasy literature, popular in film and fiction, with hundreds of millions of avid, adult readers. Indeed, a quick visit to a local game and hobby store will clarify that the majority of consumers are, demographically, adult white males.

The parallels between Biblical literature and fantasy, as genres, have been examined for some time now, a line of inquiry focalized in the work of Aichele and Pippin and others (Aichele and Pippin 1992a, b). Fantasy, as a genre, they note, is a form of commentary. Fantasy functions by the creation of alternative narrative worlds, worlds that often resemble our own, but that have key elements of difference – normally elements of magic and wonder. Science fiction, as a genre, has been long understood to be a commentary on present-day social and technological reality via speculation (Vint 2016). In science fiction, writers explore where we are trending; they critique what we assume and show the trend lines of culture. In many ways, science fiction as a genre resonates with the biblical prophecy mode of Apocalyptic (as we will explore elsewhere in this book). In a similar way, Fantasy is a commentary on the world we currently inhabit. In its alternative vision, it is an examination of the limits of our "natural" world, and an articulation of our hopes for what the world might become (or our fears).

Fantasy role-playing games are a particularly powerful mode of engagement with the genre of fantasy. The alteration is subtle, but significant. In fact, several scholars of fantasy gaming have argued that, as a collective form of storytelling and world building, Fantasy role-playing games are actually a new, collaborative art form (as surveyed by Laycock 2015, pp. 11–12). Rather than passive consumer of the narrative, participants enter, themselves, into the world being created, a shift of engagement that dramatically increases the affective encounter with that world, facilitating even more direct levels of participant attachment and emotional investment. Indeed, during the 1980s "panic" over fantasy gaming, this heightened, affective entanglement was frequently cited as one of the chief risks posed by the games; players would immerse themselves so deeply within the game that they would lose the ability to differentiate "reality" from fantasy (or would find fantasy so much more engrossing that they become emotionally and psychologically unable to persist in more mundane experience).

In the early twentieth century, cultural studies critic Johan Huizinga engaged in a rigorous analysis of what, precisely, humans do in the creation of games and in play. In Huizinga's foundational *Homo Ludens*, he introduces "Ludology" (from "ludos," "play") as a heuristic for understanding the whole of human culture (Huizinga 1931). Humans create games, elaborate systems of rule-driven engagement and shared participation, as ways of not only diversion and recreation but also for organization and collaboration. The "games" we play are assembled from rules and practices found from among other games and systems, adapted and refreshed again and again in a bricolage. Our "games" include economic and political systems, religions, and fields of academic inquiry as well as arts, music, social sets, and (sub)communities.

Religion is, on a psychosocial level, the creation of an alternative world, a fantasy space. Fantasy worlds, arising from creative play, art, fantasy genres, or religion are creations of "paracosms" – worlds that lie beside or in alteration with our current cosmos. In paracosms, we explore not only new and creative realities, but learn, by difference, more about our own and imaginatively create idealized spaces as forms of escape, compensation, and experimentation. Laycock summarizes Huizinga: "Huizinga sees clear connections between play and religious rituals, both of which he describes as occurring within a 'magic circle' separated from ordinary life... Durkheim's 'sacred'" (Laycock 2015, p. 16). Laycock, having analyzed and reflected at length upon the religious opposition to fantasy role playing games identifies a core motivation that possibly lies beneath much of the antigaming ardor: "the realization that a game of imagination can resemble a religion naturally leads to the suspicion that one's religion could likewise be a game of imagination" (pp. 24–25). Much more than arguing that biblical narrative has generic similarity to fantasy literature, it seems there are credible lines of argument that the borders between games, particularly fantasy games, and religious expression itself are not so strictly separate.

Like the genre of apocalyptic, the genres of sci-fi and fantasy can be easily misunderstood. Science fiction, at its core, isn't really about exploring the future. Instead, it is the extension of the present – with its various social features, technologies, potentialities, and limitations – extended forward. We see in its vision a glimpse of where we could be heading if we don't change course. Sci-fi is like apocalyptic in that it is a revelation of the present as warning for the future. In a similar way, fantasy is not just escapism. It is, instead, the construction of a hypothetical reality that, in its construction, becomes commentary upon our present one. Fantasy reveals what we'd like the world to be which, implicitly, reveals what we feel the present world is lacking. That is, fantasy does this when it's not doing the opposite: in showing us what the world could become or in revealing the darkness of the world as it is, but that we don't notice due to familiarity.

Taking *Dungeons & Dragons* and *Warhammer 40k* as generic examples, sci-fi and fantasy role-playing games use the characters, themes, and motifs in part to establish a "thickness" to their narrative worlds, a technique that increase gamers' attachment to characters and play. These biblical themes benefit from the ubiquity of the Bible's influence. Players who may very well never have read the actual words of the Bible are still familiar with the characters and some of the story lines. The result is a widely accessible, instantly intelligible system of allusions.

Yet these allusions are also functional religious symbols. As such, they are engaged and engaging in ways that outstrip themes and memes from Greek and

Roman mythology. Players not only know *about* these themes and character but also encounter the *affects* associated with them. In particular, they enter into a richly symbolic world that is itself permeated with a narrative of Good vs. Evil, Order vs. Chaos. This affect spills over into the games, as well.

There are inherent problems with the narrative of Chaos vs. Order. Are sides divided so clearly? Is there spillover between techniques or strategems between sides? Can one easily tell the difference between Good and Evil when looking simply at outcomes? When does the need for order and community good fade over into fascism and suppression of the individual?

"Darkness and Light" as metaphors can all too readily become signifiers for xenophobia and racism, and "cosmic war" can easily drift into toxically gendered tropes. These concerns arguably appear within the biblical narratives but certainly appear in the history of reception. The character of Satan evolves in both scholarship and tradition and within western art and literature. Satan's character is probed for the cause of his "fall" or rebellion. He becomes, in the hands of Milton for example, an almost heroic figure, whose power and beauty are overridden by his arrogance and misdirected will. He is ascribed an array of moral limits, none of which appear within biblical text. Satan provides a foil for the goodness of God. Evil exists in the world; if one believes in God, this poses an initial problem of theodicy: can God not stop the evil? Why does God allow evil to happen? A figure such as Satan absolves God of some of the responsibility: Satan, not God, is the source of the evil. God tolerates Satan, however, raising a different sort of problems: is God too passive and permissive? Is God being more patient with Satan than God is being with humans? Is God really unable to hold Satan for long? And, ultimately: Does Satan really, in the end, accomplish God's will by other means; is Satan just another tool of God, meaning God is *really* the one behind all the suffering.

In part, the role-playing games are implicitly importing these affects and allusions alongside the cultural "thickness." The games, then, influenced by energies that very likely drove the composition and collection of the biblical text, use biblical text to create an affective system that probes these complex narratives. Like biblical text, as well, they provide, as participatory fantasy narratives, a sort of personal and protective release. Fantasies can compensate for "real world" frustration. An individual's darker energies and more harmful desires can be vented off safely. The game also provides a new "lab space" for testing desires, impulses, and urges in ways that allow one to explore potential implication and ramification but that also do not cause as significant, direct physical harm. As with the individual, so also the community. These games, and their biblical allusions, provide a space for larger scale reflection on social order, regulation, and the ever-looming risk, alongside the potential blessing, that comes along.

# Works Cited

Aichele, G. and Pippin, T. (ed.) (1992a). *Fantasy and the Bible*, Semeia Studies, vol. 60. Atlanta, GA: Society of Biblical Literature Press.

Aichele, G. and Pippin, T. (ed.) (1992b). Introduction: why the fantastic. In: *Fantasy and the Bible*, Semeia Studies, vol. 60, 1–6. Atlanta, GA: Society of Biblical Literature Press.

Aune, D.E. (1997–1998). *Revelation*. 3 vols., Word Biblical Commentary. Nashville, TN: Thomas Nelson.

Beal, T. (2023). *Religion and Its Monsters*, 2e. New York: Routledge.

Collins, A.Y. (2001). *The Combat Myth in the Book of Revelation*. New Haven, CT: Yale Divinity School.

Davies, W.D. and Allison, D. Jr. (1988). *Critical and Exegetical Commentary on Matthew*, International Critical Commentary., vol. 1. Edinburgh: T & T Clark.

Durheim, B.M. (2021). Symbolized reality: liturgy and table top role-playing games. *Liturgy* 36 (4): 52–29.

Fehleison, J. and Eurich, A.S. (2019). Reacting to the past and role-playing games in early modern history. *The Sixteenth Century Journal* 50 (4): 1142–1148.

Feltmate, D. (2010). 'You wince in agony as the hot metal brands you': religious behavior in an online role playing game. *Journal of Contemporary Religion* 25 (2): 363–377.

Fewell, D.N. (2003). *The Children of Israel: Reading the Bible for the Sake of our Children*. Nashville: Abingdon.

Howard, M.A. (2018). A game of faith: role-playing games as an active learning strategy for value formation and faith integration in the traditional classroom. *Teaching Theology & Religion* 21 (4): 274–287.

Huizinga, J. (1931). *Homo Ludens: A Study of the Play-Element in Culture*. Boston: Beacon.

Inoles, A., al-Rahman, M.A., and Buckler, P. (2016). A Muslim reflection on *Dangerous Games:* what the moral panic over role-playing games says about play, religion and imagined worlds. *American Journal of Islamic Social Sciences* 33 (3): 138–149.

Inoles, A., al-Rahman, M.A., and Buckler, P. (2018). Bridging cultural divides through fantasy/science fiction role-playing games and fictional religion. *The Muslim World* 108 (3): 387–418.

Laycock, J.P. (2015). *Dangerous Games: What the Moral Panic over Role-Playing Games Says About Play, Religion and Imagined Worlds*. Oakland, CA: University of California Press.

Leeson, W.A.M. and Gibbs, G.G. (2019). Gaming to learn: pedagogical uses of video, board, and role-playing games. *Sixteenth Century Journal* 50 (4): 1129–1134.

Ogden, D. (2013a). *Dragons, Serpents, and Slayers in the Classical and Early Christian Worlds: A Sourcebook.* New York: Oxford University Press.

Ogden, D. (2013b). *Drakon: Dragon Myth and Serpent Cult in the Greek and Roman World.* New York: Oxford University Press.

Ogden, D. (2021). *The Dragon in the West: From Ancient Myth to Modern Legend.* New York: Oxford University Press.

Pagels, E. (1995). *The Origins of Satan.* New York: Vintage.

Porter, A.L. (2008). Role playing and religion: using games to educate millennials. *Teaching Theology & Religion* 11 (4): 230–235.

Pyper, H. and Vander Stichele, C. (ed.) (2012). *Text, Image, and Otherness in Children's Bibles*, Semeia Studies, vol. 56. Atlanta, GA: Society of Biblical Literature Press.

Rossing, B.R. (1999). *The Choice Between Two Cities: Whore, Bride and Empire in the Apocalypse*, Harvard Theological Studies. Harrisburg, PA: Trinity Press International.

Rossing, B.R. (2004). *The Rapture Exposed: The Message of Hope in the Book of Revelation.* New York: Basic Books.

Russell, J.B. (1986). *Lucifer: The Devil in the Middle Ages.* New York: Cornell University Press.

Russell, J.B. (1987a). *The Devil: Perceptions of Evil from Antiquity to Primitive Christianity.* New York: Cornell University Press.

Russell, J.B. (1987b). *Satan: The Early Christian Tradition.* New York: Cornell University Press.

Russell, J.B. (1990). *Mephistopheles: The Devil in the Modern World.* New York: Cornell University Press.

Tolkien, J.R.R.1947). On fairy stories. https://uh.edu/fdis/_taylor-dev/readings/tolkien.html (accessed 27 October 2023).

Vint, S. (ed.) (2016). *Science Fiction and Cultural Theory: A Reader.* London/New York: Routledge.

Wainwright, A.W. (2001). *Mysterious Apocalypse: Interpreting the Book of Revelation.* Eugene, OR: Wipf & Stock.

Wray, T.J. and Mobley, G. (2005). *The Birth of Satan: Tracing the Devil's Biblical Roots.* New York: St. Martin's Press.

**Part III**

**Affective Machines: Deleuze, Cultural Studies, and the Next Wave**

# 8

# Mysteries of the Bible Documentary

The Bible in Popular Nonfiction Documentary Film

In the introduction of this book, we considered the complexity inherent in studying "the Bible in/and popular culture." We asked, What is it that we study when we explore Bible and mass culture together. Are we attempting to better understand the Bible by considering its role in mass culture, or are we exploring mass culture and its effects using the Bible?

In Part I of this book, we looked at three essays exploring the Bible *as* a form of popular culture. These were essays that looked at the *Bible* and cultural studies. What we study in that context is the history of Bible collection, production, dissemination, and use as a cultural expression. "Bible" becomes a cultural product and cipher for identity via the cultural "marketplace" of late capitalism, a cultural market that both creates and reflects class hierarchies and locations. In Part II, we looked at examples of Bible *in* popular culture, of Bible *and* popular culture. These essays explored the Bible as it appears in mass entertainment media and considered how these appearances both create and reflect other ideologies in US culture.

In this third and final portion are three essays rooted more deeply in intertextuality (as understood by Barthes and Kristeva), and the Bible becomes a tether, a sounding line dropped through the cultural depths, letting us explore the tectonics of how culture itself is formed and the machinery of how it functions. The first essay is the most conventional in its content: an exploration of Bible documentaries. On the one hand, the essay explores an element of film theory (defining and describing "truth" and "reality" in film, here via documentary film), but, on the other hand, it asks more fundamental questions about how culture and cultural products mediate what we see as "real" in the first place. The second essay takes up this theme and pushes it further, asking how the Bible intersects with (and inspires?) various discourses on "conspiracy" and hidden reality. The final essay is the most abstract and theoretical and returns to the images of fashion and consumption raised in Part I. That essay asks questions via an exploration of the Bible and the US fashion industry about animate humans and inanimate systems or products. The essay also returns to early discussions of the "viral" Bible when it explores the Bible's "agency" behind its own creation and spread.

All three essays play, in part, with questions of epistemology and cognition. Do our personal assumptions, values, and thinking reflect, adapt, or create reality? How do we use religion, or language, to focus or control irrationality? In what ways do the systems and culture we create operate independently of us, perhaps autonomously? The essays in this third section regard the search to understand or describe the Bible as less an end or goal and more a means; they use biblical studies to study mass or popular culture. Although these essays delve into some of the most current (and complex) areas of contemporary humanities scholarship – critical theory, posthumanism, affect theory – they return as well to the original and fundamental forms of cultural studies: articulating how culture forms and defines the ways we experience "humanness."

## Truth and Representation

As many now do, I incorporate documentary film into my general introductory Bible courses. Despite expanding use and increasing critical interest in Bible in/ and film, until fairly recently, many biblical scholars were a-critical in their approach to or use of film and film theory. How one "reads" a film is analogous to (but nevertheless different from) how one reads a text. Film criticism and theory address the function of basic elements of filmmaking – camera work (including, but not limited to, point of view, shot framing, and traditional camera transitions), film editing, lighting, music, sound, props, costuming, "authorship," and other factors. Film critique should attend to basic questions of the gestalt of the entire film.

Use and critical review of documentary film require even greater attention given the genre's implicit and overt claims about truth, representation, and reality. The analysis or use of documentary film should attend to not only the film's content but the way the film structures and presents its argument as well. It is important to attend to both the structure and the content of a documentary when considering its accuracy and "truth" or articulating its meaning (for a general, introductory overview on documentary criticism and theory, see Aufderheide 2007; McLane 2012; and Nichols 2010).

Several often-unexamined factors influence the effect of a documentary film. The context of consumption of documentary film, for example, affects a viewer's experience(s). Few documentaries – and significantly fewer Bible documentaries – are broadly marketed in popular cinemas. Most viewers consume documentary film either via television or in various instructional and institutional settings. In other words, we often view documentaries either in private or in specific communities; focus is on instruction and this focus often imposes an institutional framework or bias. When viewed in an institutional context (a church, synagogue, campus theater, or a classroom), the general assumptions of that organization affect our expectations and conclusions and most certainly color our perception of the "reality" presented in the film. The content of the film is often processed by pre or post viewing conversation that always has both ideological and didactic interest with implicit institutional endorsement or critique. This viewing context masks the creative and entertainment focus of documentary, fostering the illusion that such films are produced and consumed for didactic – as opposed to persuasive, dogmatic, propagandistic, or entertainment – purposes. Documentary film is always already prone to awaken questions about truth, representation, and reality; these questions make the genre itself difficult to define.

The complexity of issues surrounding "truth" in documentary can be illustrated in William Rothman's survey of Robert Flaherty's *Nanook of the North* (US/FR, 1922), the first, and in many ways paradigm setting, commercially released documentary film (Rothman 1998, pp. 23–39). In the film, Flaherty says he intended to fully and accurately document the life of a particular Inuit family whose existence persists, largely unaffected by the encroachment of modernity. Nanook's story, he insists, is real. Flaherty, however, produced a film that would not meet modern standards of ethnography. What *Nanook* does document is a "real" Inuit in the act of performing "real" and "traditional" native activities and practices. Yet nearly every scene was staged by the director. Flaherty obscured or omitted various marital and home customs that he estimated unpalatable to the norms and morals of his audience. Nanook's life outside the documentary, as Rothman points out well, certainly had been highly influenced by modernity despite the film presenting him as "unspoiled" and primitive. Alas, even the name "Nanook" is an imposition; our protagonist actually had what Rothman calls the "marquee-busting name" of Allakariallak (Rothman 1998, p. 25). Reflecting on how the documentary both is and is not "real," Rothman writes:

> Insofar as he participated in the making of *Nanook*, the "real" Nanook has a relationship to the camera that is part of his reality, part of the camera's reality, part of the reality being filmed, part of the reality on film, part of the reality of the film. *Nanook* is a real expression of real relationships that in turn are expressions of ... both the camera and its subjects. Yet Nanook emerges as a fictional character with no reality apart from the film that creates him. Being filmed has no more reality to

> Nanook-in-his-fictional-aspect than to a character in a fictional film. But this means that the fictional Nanook has no reality to the camera.
>
> (Rothman 1998, p. 25)

Rothman goes on to observe:

> In a fiction film, the camera's revelations about characters are also revelations about the real people who incarnate them, revelations that express and thus reveal the real relationships between camera and human subjects. The prevailing fiction is that the character, not the actor, is real. What is fictional about a fiction film resides in its fiction that it is only fiction. What is fictional about *Nanook* resides in its fiction that it is not fiction at all.
>
> (Rothman 1998, p. 26)

This tension has been readily explored in film criticism beginning with the now-somewhat-seminal work by Bill Nichols (1978, pp. 71–83; 1987, pp. 9–20; 1994) and Michael Renov (1993). As biblical critics, we of course recognize the dilemma of representation and reality, of finding the "reality" beneath or behind a text, particularly one surrounded by a host of institutional and scholarly agendas and needs. This tension is the same tension that lies behind various scholarly quests for the historical Jesus or the recovery of ancient Israel. One of the venerable definitions of documentary, and perhaps still one of the most concise and effective, comes from the 1920s and 1930s Scottish film critic John Grierson. Grierson defines "documentary film" as "creative treatment of actuality."[1] As such, both aspects of documentary film – the creative treatment as well as the "actuality" of content – are integral to intelligent consumption of documentary.

## Modes and Methods of Documentary

A few biblical critics have begun to attend to documentary film with these critical questions in mind, yet the bibliography of such work remains frustratingly short. Of particular interest to biblical scholars engaging documentary theory

---

1 This definition is widely attributed to Grierson yet is notoriously elusive for exact citation in his voluminous writings. Grierson is also often credited with coining the term "documentary." As to the latter claim, it is, indeed, true that Grierson seems to be the first printed use of "documentary" in his review of Flaherty's *Moana* (1926) for the *New York Sun* (8 February 1926), yet he does not use the word in any way that suggests he regards it as a neologism. On Grierson's actual and apocryphal role in the foundation of documentary theory (and assessment of both), see Morris 1987, pp. 20–30 and Corner 1996, pp. 3–8.

are questions of the effect of editing and structure to reflect point-of-view and documentary "mode." (In a brief review of works examining the Bible in documentary film, one might mention Moreland 2009, pp. 77–135; Löwisch 2009, pp. 228–256; and Burnette-Bletsch 2014.)

In a highly accessible and commendably brief primer on documentary theory, Henrik Juel (2006) has outlined a fairly comprehensive list of "points to consider" when viewing documentary. He suggests we must begin by analysis of function for the documentary (what is its goal?). We must attend to the "mode" of narrative strategy present in the documentary. Juel lists six possibilities. Documentaries may be:

Expository: lecturing, overtly didactic, for example, with a personal presenter or an explanatory voice-over.

Observational: like a "fly on the wall," the camera, microphone, and film crew seem not to be disturbing the scene or even to be noticed by the participants.

Participatory or interactive: the film crew takes part in the action or chain of events.

Reflexive: the film exposes and discusses its own role as a film (e.g. the ethics or conditions of filmmaking) alongside the treatment of the case or subject.

Performative: the film crew creates many of the events and situations to be filmed by their own intervention or through events carried out for the sake of the film.

Poetic: the aesthetic aspects, the qualities of the form and the sensual appeals are predominant (Juel 2006; See also, Nichols 1994, pp. 172–211).

Adding to Juel, I would suggest that these categories of "mode" are, of course, neither exclusive nor comprehensive. Individual films may use a variety of modes. Documentary mode could be compared to narrative "voice" and perspective in literature. The mode of documentary establishes the viewer's experience and expectation even as it generates viewer expectations regarding content. The seeming omniscient "voice of God" narrative voice present in expository documentary certainly establishes "truth" for the viewer in ways that participatory modes, which tend much more to providing an experience to viewers that the viewers, themselves, "interpret," do not. Narrative voice or mode is often reinforced by film editing and assembly and often also by selection of sets, camera angle, music and more. Biblical scholars are well aware of the influence of editorial choice and voice (rhetoric) in the construction of meaning. Engaging documentary theory could readily offer both tools for biblical criticism (particularly in terms of redaction, source, and ideological criticism) and a role for biblical critics, in turn, to contribute to film theory.

## A (Very Brief) Introduction and Review
## of Bible Documentary

Bible documentaries are legion. Alongside documentaries produced directly for
academic classrooms are documentaries produced and distributed by various
confessional groups, many marketed via the engine of the media industry and
aimed at the ecclesiastical religious education curriculum market. An increasing
number of documentaries are being produced for the direct-to-consumer
market and distributed or displayed via the web. There are several "channels"
for these documentaries on outlets such as YouTube and Facebook. Bible
documentaries have also been produced for the direct-to-television market,
notably for public broadcasting and cable networks such as Discovery, A & E,
the History Channel, and more. In what follows, I would like to engage a few,
select documentaries on the Bible and biblical interpretation. I have chosen
three that represent a generic survey of the marketplace – classroom, television,
and religious community – and the expectations of the documentary's "viewer."
Two of these documentaries reflect standard professional scholarship, though
aimed at slightly different markets; one is aimed at the general pop market, the
other at the legendary "informed consumer" or "soft-academic" market. The
third film is also marketed to the nonspecialist, but in many ways, violates
conventions of "standard" scholarship. Among these three films, the generic
array of viewing contexts (academic pedagogy, home entertainment,
confessional instruction) is covered, as well. In other words, I have chosen these
three documentaries because in them they aggregately cover the general array
of didactic concern, "mission," and audience found in documentaries about the
Bible. By a survey of all three, I hope to demonstrate how these Bible
documentaries engage viewers and attempt not only to inform but also to
persuade and construct the viewer's sense of what is "real" and "plausible" in
biblical interpretation.

Bible documentaries use a variety of modes, but overwhelmingly they tend to
be didactic and expository. Many documentaries use images indicative of
antiquity – archaeological sites, manuscripts, location; some use images of the
Bible in art or in church/synagogue architecture. These choices are not incidental.
To focus on only period-specific images or location places the Bible in space–
time. The effect of such rooting may be either distancing the Bible from our
contemporary moment or the construction of a sense of academic verisimilitude.
Nearly all feature extensive narrative voice-over and frequent shots of scholars
explicating the film's themes or questions. Occasionally, Bible documentaries
use brief dramatic recreation or dramatic reading of biblical (or other) texts. A
very few documentaries (chiefly those produced on biblical themes by the PBS
series "Nova") use participatory and observational modes, with filmmakers
directly shooting and interacting with scholars or archeologists. I have found

only one documentary (*Jesus Camp*, US, dir. Heidi Ewing/Rachel Grady, 2006) that makes thorough use of observational mode. It seems as if Bible documentary creators have a preference for clear spoken-language exposition with clear credentials of "experts." The Word is best expounded by words.

## Mysteries of the Bible

From 1994 to 1998, the cable channel A & E produced a series of Bible documentaries titled *Mysteries of the Bible* (US, prod. Michael Katz/Bram Roos). This series was exceptionally popular (for a Bible documentary, at any rate), running for 5 seasons with 46 episodes. The episodes in the series range rather widely. Topics include fairly popular or enticing subjects such as the Apocalypse of John, noncanonical ("lost?") Christian texts, and the execution of Jesus but also fairly specific and tangential passages (for general audience, at any rate) such as Cain's murder of Abel.

The formula for each episode is fairly stable. Each program begins with a reading from a biblical text followed by voice-over that poses questions surrounding the reading and its interpretation. Following the opening credits, each program is divided into normally four or five acts. Each documentary is largely expository and didactic. Rare images of dramatic recreation of biblical narratives do occasionally appear among (much more common) images of medieval and renaissance artwork depicting the biblical scene. Above the images runs rather ominous narration outlining the present exegetical quandary or bizarre image from the biblical text. Transitions between shots or images proceed at an often-frenetic pace, in some cases presenting over 15 different shots/images a minute. The narration and artwork are accompanied by orchestral soundtracks that often include staccato string attacks at high, slightly sharped, 16th notes, rapid changes in tonality, modality, and meter, including syncopation. In other words, they visually and audibly cite the soundtrack techniques of dramatic, even horror, film genres in order to heighten tension.

Once these mysterious questions are raised, however, the documentary cuts to (eventually music free) footage of certified, published, well-established biblical scholars. Transitions are often abrupt camera jumps or swipes, accompanied by orchestral soundtrack that shifts to adagio, resolved, major keys. Full title and institutional affiliation are provided in text displays for each scholar, each time they appear. The scholars usually sit in libraries or in quiet suburban homes. These visual footnotes suggest scholarship and knowledge. Location shots (e.g. museums, archaeological sites) in *Mysteries of the Bible* tend to suggest modernity and comfort, stark contrast to the alien, harsh, and often violent images associated with biblical texts themselves. The scholars narrate reasoned, mainstream scholarly views on the passage and its questions, resolving the tensions.

For example, "Cain and Abel: A Murder Mystery" (season 4, episode 6) treats Genesis 4:1–16; it explores the tensions of the "Bible and, perhaps history's, first murder mystery" and, of course, the infamous "mark of Cain." After dramatically depicting the murder of Abel by Cain in both recreation and powerfully moving artwork, both dripping in blood and cringing violence (again, with appropriate soundtrack alongside voice-over describing scholars engaged in deep forensic and detective work to unravel the murder) the documentary transitions to Carole Fontaine, then professor of Hebrew Bible at Andover Newton Theological Seminary, calmly suggesting that the story seems like an allegory reflecting ancient tensions between horticultural and sheep-rearing communities.

Even more exemplary might be "Apocalypse: The Puzzle of Revelation" (season 2, episode 3). Over and over again, the documentary juxtaposes lurid images from medieval doom scenes, frightening and ominous music, shots of roiling clouds, and a narration that asks disturbing questions (e.g. Who are the horsemen and when will their reign of horror begin?). Interspersed with images from Christian art are modern images of warfare and chaos such as atomic mushroom clouds and the burning Branch Davidian compound. Once again, these scenes of horror are followed by shots of mainstream, well-published (and well-identified) scholars all, again, in quiet settings calmly explicating the text by offering mainstream commentary.[2] The repeated effect of these transitions moves the viewer from scandal and mystery into quiet conversation. Lurid, dark images give way to scholars bathed in light in quiet, highly "reasoned" – indeed, almost visually boring – settings, dressed in modern clothing. As narration proceeds and shots transition through these expository documentaries, viewers are taken from the fearful, uncertain, and salacious into the reasoned, explicated, controlled. The mystery of the Bible has been solved.

## From Jesus to Christ

The Frontline documentary (PBS) titled *From Jesus to Christ: The First Christians* (US, dir. William Cran, 1998) focuses on questions of how an ancient movement following Jesus became a world religion. The documentary, in five episodes,

---

2 Including James D. Tabor, identified as "Professor of Religious Studies, University of North Carolina," shot fore-lit in front of a bookcase; Donald Senior, identified as "Professor of New Testament Studies, Catholic Theological Union at Chicago," again forelit but with a PC and array of computer equipment in the background; Adela Yarbro Collins ("Professor of New Testament Studies, University of Chicago") in a brightly lit room, on a couch, with a sun-filled window and bookcases behind, and John J. Collins ("Professor of Hebrew Bible, University of Chicago"), shot with similar light, tightly framed, and with the ever-present bookcase again in the background.

marshals the forces of a veritable "who's who" of historically oriented biblical scholars who, in tandem with the narrative voice-over, present fairly standard academic reconstructions of the historical Jesus and Christian origins. In many elements of its filmmaking narrative, it seems to be aware of, if not borrowing from *Mysteries of the Bible*.

Each episode follows the pattern of the first, titled the "Quest for the Historical Jesus." "Quest" opens with interior shots of a Christian cathedral. With a soundtrack of a distantly heard lector's voice giving way to a more dominant alleluia hymn by a choir, the voice-over poses the initial question: How does a rural, Jewish, messianic movement in the early Roman Empire become a world religion? The camera pans across stained glass windows, pews, and baptismal fonts and comes to rest eventually behind an impressive hardwood pulpit. The point of view is that of the lector gazing out at the pews, an impressive lection-ary Bible lies open to the Gospel of Mark. This sequence is a frenetic series of 16 shots over the first minute and 42 seconds of the episode, none of them static. The camera zooms downward from the roof to pause at floor level facing toward the nave then tours down the narthex in a sequence of nine shots, panning the pews, panning the narthex, pausing and zooming to admire stained glass before centering upon the pulpit, zooming, looking up toward it, zooming, mounting it and panning 180° toward the nave again, before zooming down upon the open lectionary Bible. The room is dark with Caravaggio-like color and shadow. The eye of the camera has just entered the church and toured its way toward the pulpit and found the text. As viewers look across and over an ancient-looking copy of the biblical text, sharply lit from behind camera, out toward a sea of (empty) pews and into a cathedral hall, the documentary proper begins. Mist (of history?) slowly shrouds the open Bible. As the mist fades and the alleluias crescendo, viewers see a Roman period pavement where text and pews once lay. The music shifts abruptly to a Hebrew cantor. The documentary has transported viewers into the world of the Bible.

The rest of the episode alternates between location shots/archeological items and major scholars offering academic commentary. The documentary actively performs the transition espoused by critical scholarship – to interrogate biblical text via historical and literary inquiry without appeal to faith. Visual footnotes that cue "scholarship" and "reason" populate the *mise-en-scène* of academic exposition. Scholars are set in front of libraries of books whose shelf boundaries extend off camera, suggesting, visually, an infinite array of resources. Scholars appear in museums or ancient looking buildings and sets, suggesting an inti-mate, direct experience with the relevant tools of the trade. Scholars are lit, often sharply and from above – the "divine light" radiating downward; they address a figure off camera, making the viewer privy to "overhearing" a conversation in process. Often, the *mise-en-scène* is an open window or atrium, suggesting that the scholarly gatekeepers are bringing viewers "into the light." In at least two cases, the scholarly expert stands or sits before a stairway or an open window set above and behind. The Freudian overtones of this image are overt – in/by their scholarly narration, these experts are leading the viewer up, through the dark labyrinth of time, toward the radiant light of insight, giving birth to knowledge.

## Testimony of the Ark

Yet another example of a biblical documentary is *Testimony of the Ark* (USACOUNTRY, dir. by Rebecca Truraiaire, 2006). This documentary deploys an array of sophisticated film techniques. Largely didactic, it also incorporates observational footage of its central figure, Ron Wyatt, at work on location or touring with camera crews. It incorporates participatory, interactional, and reflectional modes, as well, documenting moments of interaction between the filmmaker and Wyatt. The film uses dozens of different shot transitions. Much of it is clearly shot on location. A number of figures are brought to the fore in expository/didactic "talking heads" roles to evaluate Wyatt's work and its impact; these scholars (as with Wyatt, the film provides no indication of academic affiliation or specific professional credentials) are clearly men (and they are, indeed, all male) of faith. The exposition on the documentary averages a fairly vigorous pace, including around 8–11 shot transitions per minute prior to the opening credits. Once the main thesis of the film begins to unfold, however, this pace reduces dramatically to an almost boring pace of 1.7 transitions per minute, with long stretches of single, stable, fixed camera, in one case for seven minutes. Generally, the camera focuses upon Wyatt expounding his ideas or leading a tour group or college/seminary class (it is unclear which) on location. Wyatt, in these scenes, does not interact with the filmmakers (though, in other scenes, he is occasionally shown as a filmmaker, himself). The film includes interviews with Wyatt's peers who do interact with filmmakers. Some scenes also depict Wyatt addressing questions from someone (though not clearly the filmmaker) sitting off-camera. In part, the film is documenting Wyatt's life, produced and edited after his death.

The film's audio soundtrack is predominantly contemporary Christian music (or music based upon the same). It rarely builds tension, using long sustained adagio in major keys. Nearly every shot is bathed in radiant "divine" light (mimicking, as much as possible, natural sunlight). The narration has no inflammatory or mysterious initial exposition of the type found in *Mysteries of the Bible*. All images are location shots, biblical reenactors, modern scholars, or ancient artifacts. The narration and voice-over address a popular audience directly, arguing that "mainstream scholarship" has turned its back on Wyatt's findings under pressure and resistance from scholars "who don't want to believe in or relate to the living God." Wyatt himself speaks mostly to students or tourists or collaborators who are most often standing partly off-shot. The viewer is, by this technique, immersed in the presentation itself, as if "there" with Wyatt, on location, learning in a contemporary and personal way.

Mr. Wyatt, long obsessed with finding Noah's ark, also claims to have discovered the "grotto of Jeremiah" in Jerusalem. This grotto, a series of chambers beneath construction in Jerusalem's old city, was the final resting place, according to Wyatt, of the Ark of the Covenant. In deep synergy, it is also directly below the supposed location of Jesus' crucifixion, which Wyatt asserts was revealed to him by the Holy Spirit (he is never quite explicit as the means for this revelation). Frustrated at his inability to get skeptics (and unbelieving Jews) to allow him permission to dig, Wyatt, working illegally and alone, claimed to have uncovered a shaft leading to a hidden chamber in which he found the lost ark. Returning later with professional archeologists, the area had collapsed, and the chamber was gone. Frustrated but not daunted, Wyatt continued his investigations, discovering a stone with three shafts that, he asserts, were post-holes for crosses during the early Roman period. Remarkably, the film argues dramatically this turns out to be the very spot of Jesus' crucifixion. The central slot had blood stains (blood would have run through the slot into the chamber below, to drip upon the mercy seat of the Ark of the Covenant), and the blood, when tested, had only mitochondrial DNA suggesting, to Wyatt, that it originated from a person with a mother but no biological father.

The film narration expresses surprise that many of Wyatt's claims have not yet made much headway with mainstream media, biblical scholarship, or Israeli antiquity/archaeology experts. The documentary clearly is attempting to circumvent this resistance (there is a soft push for financial donations to further the work at the film's end, most likely to facilitate the advertising of the documentary and for both more films and research).[3] "Experts" are presented, but institutional affiliation is avoided and titles are rarely used. The sets, props, lighting, and location all are relentlessly "real" and period/location appropriate.

## On the Filming of Documentaries, There Is No End

In *Mysteries of the Bible* the sensational is de-sensationalized. As these documentaries explicate and normalize the sensational, they also diminish the raw edge of biblical literature. *Mysteries of the Bible* corrects puerile and sensational interest in Revelation via what many scholars would consider a highly accurate

---

3 Though limited in general release, the film is readily available online. Copies on DVD can be ordered, the film notes, for personal or "organizational" viewing with appropriate releases and permission, for a small donation. One would assume the push here is to sell copies of the DVD to show at Bible study groups or churches.

historical-critical reading of Revelation. The progress of the documentary draws in the audience by satisfying these expectations, but then inverts them by a return to rationality and "accurate" reading of the text. Yet, this "accurate," text-based interpretation still betrays the essence of the text itself. On some level, how is apocalyptic ever *not* sensational, vulgar, or esoteric? Popular readings of Revelation, steeped in mystery, radiating fear, and pulsing with raw anger are, in many ways, tuned-in to a deep sense of what apocalyptic actually "means." Taking these elements out of Revelation betrays a fundamental quality of Revelation itself.

*From Jesus to Christ* invites its viewers to leave behind ideas of the Bible as religious icon, to stop looking over the text, and, instead, to enter into the world hidden beneath the text. In some cases, Bible documentaries reveal that biblical text still functions in a somewhat a-rational or pre-rational manner in general culture. *From Jesus to Christ* is asking the viewer to leave a context of constructed meaning to view the Bible as it "really was" and to hear what it "really says." Yet, this world, as biblical scholars well know, is in many ways a reconstructed, hypothetical world. The Bible itself – the contents of canon, its social significance, even its very wording – is in more than a few ways a reconstructed and contested document. Within the documentary, the scholarly experts disagree about a host of assumptions concerning Jesus and the history of nascent Christianity. Inviting viewers to leave behind the Bible of the pulpit as a manufactured document detached from "what really happened" pulls readers into a world of the Bible that is equally manufactured, though presented otherwise. This transition is both performed and masked by the contrast of images in the documentary itself. The scholarly reconstruction, the documentary suggests, even if it is fragmented and far away from well-oiled pews, is our only real chance at climbing toward the light of biblical "meaning."[4]

Although *Testimony of the Ark* lacks a level of scholarly rigor that most professional biblical scholars would endorse and revels in an aesthetic that most film critics would find bland, in terms of filmmaking technique, it is rather sophisticated. Again, seeing the film as a whole, it becomes rather clear that the thesis of the documentary is, largely, to construct a world where the film's arguments are seen in the most reasonable light. Indeed, it seems that, from a variety of possible

---

4 One might add, as well, that the scholarly view that emerges from this documentary is, in the end, as singular as the faith-driven readings it attempts to dislocate. The documentary presents a view that the Bible has been "misread" (or, at least, incompletely read) by the church. The "truth" (perhaps even the real "Bible?") is exclusively the history behind/ beneath the actual biblical accounts. In many ways this documentary accepts an argument that there is an origin (event) which has been received (biblical text and faith tradition); scholarship is, properly, the return to the origins of history. *From Jesus to Christ* intentionally raises questions about what the Bible means and about how the Bible relates to history, yet it also indirectly, one senses very unintentionally, raises questions about what a Bible even is, what it should contain, or how (indeed, if) it functions as an authority.

motivations, much of the interest of the Bible documentary is to produce a film whose ideas about the Bible will be seen as "rational" and reasoned. This perhaps betrays a fear that biblical texts or biblical claims are not, inherently, "rational." *Testimony of the Ark* is most likely correct in its assertions that professional biblical criticism will not take its arguments seriously, even if many would debate the reasons the film ascribes. For exactly this reason, it provides an interesting opportunity to reflect upon how we bifurcate between high and low culture, professional and amateur criticism with an eye toward what is at stake – who wins and why? – in that distinction. All Bible documentaries are a form of biblical interpretation. As such, they construct an entire immersed viewing experience where both their arguments and their subject – the Bible – are rational. In many ways, they reveal our own sociological bifurcations between high and low culture, between popular and professional critique, divisions rooted in hierarchical notions and disproportionate power. This hierarchy is one that we would do well to consider.

There is also a fertile insight in the combination of a documentary film – a genre of film that presents thorny questions about representation, truth, reality, ideology, and the artistic/editorial hand – with biblical scholarship. Biblical scholarship, particularly the biblical scholarship exhibited in *From Jesus to Christ* and *Mysteries of the Bible,* foregrounds questions about biblical authors, editors, redactors, canonizers, and critics and the multiple ways these groups in turn problematize biblical representation of history, textual integrity, and the construction of biblical "meaning." The issues surrounding documentary film theory and criticism and those surrounding modern biblical criticism reflect in a continuous loop. The "meaning" of a documentary is more than the sum of its narration and footage and is often deeply intertwined with expectations of authority, hierarchy and the very functionality of religious symbolism – much like the Bible itself. Focusing our own lens on the issues of documentary production and "truth," particularly for "Bible films," not only creates a context of informed viewing but also offers moments for serious reflection on parallel issues and effects of biblical criticism and biblical text.

## Works Cited

Aufderheide, P. (2007). *Documentary Film: A Very Short Introduction.* New York: Oxford University Press.

Burnette-Bletsch, R. (2014). Documentary (Film). In: *The Encyclopedia of the Bible and Its Reception*, vol. 6 (ed. D.C. Allison, C. Helmer, C.-L. Seow, et al.), 1019–1023. Berlin: Walter de Gruyter.

Corner, J. (1996). *The Art of Record: A Critical Introduction to Documentary.* Manchester: Manchester University Press.

Juel, H. (2006). Defining documentary Film. *P.O.V.* (22): https://pov.imv.au.dk/Issue_22/section_1/artc1A.html (accessed 17 October 2023).

Löwisch, I. (2009). Genealogies, gender and the politics of memory: 1 Chronicles 1–9 and the documentary film *Mein Leben Teil 2*. In: *Performing Memory in Biblical Narrative and Beyond* (ed. A. Brenner and F.H. Polak), 228–256. Sheffield: Sheffield Phoenix Press.

McLane, B.A. (2012). *A New History of Documentary Film*, 2e. New York: Bloomsbury Academic.

Moreland, M.C. (2009). Christian artifacts in documentary film: the case of the James ossuary. In: *Resurrecting the Brother of Jesus: The James Ossuary Controversy and the Quest for Religious Relics* (ed. R. Byrne and B. McNary-Zak), 77–135. Chapel Hill, NC: University of North Carolina Press.

Morris, P. (1987). Re-thinking Grierson: the ideology of John Grierson. In: *History on/and/in Film* (ed. T. O'Regan and B. Shoesmith), 20–30. Perth: History and Film Association of Australia.

Nichols, B. (1978). Documentary theory and practice. *Screen* 17 (4): 71–83.

Nichols, B. (1987). History, myth and narrative in documentary. *Film Quarterly* 41 (4): 9–20.

Nichols, B. (1994). *Blurred Boundaries: Questions of Meaning in Contemporary Culture*. Bloomington, IN: Indiana University Press.

Nichols, B. (2010). *Introduction to Documentary*, 2e. Bloomington, IN: Indiana University Press.

Renov, M. (ed.) (1993). *Theorizing Documentary*. New York: Routledge.

Rothman, W. (1998). The filmmaker as hunter: Robert Flaherty's *Nanook of the north*. In: *Documenting the Documentary* (ed. B.K. Grant and J. Sloniowski), 23–39. Detroit: Wayne State University Press.

# 9

# "I (Want to) Believe, Lord; Help Me in My Unbelief"

## Revelation, Raëleans, Mayans, and North American Pop Eschatology

As we saw in the previous chapter, culture, as the means through which we interpret or filter reality, is also, in that role, the means through which we create it. If the physical or material world does not meet our needs or expectations, we use cultural products and technologies to remake it (e.g. air conditioning or vaccines). But just as often, we create social structures that frame (or sort, or describe, or prioritize) reality via language and rhetoric, shared stories and memes, religious acts (or books), and more. As in the production of a documentary film, we plot, frame, shoot, and edit reality to fit cultural narratives and needs. Sometimes we carefully attend to certain facts and patterns, sometimes we dismiss or ignore them.

Religion, especially as defined by contemporary theorist Clifford Geertz, is one of the most potent cultural machines for framing reality. Religion often clarifies what behaviors, customs, roles, and even thoughts and feelings, are expected – or even allowed. This chapter will demonstrate how religion, or, as in this case Bible and biblical interpretation, can be used to construct new realities by defining what is (or isn't) a permissible, or "reasonable," way of explaining or understanding the world. Bible and biblical studies, for many readers, will establish what can or cannot be True, what is worth noticing, or whether or not what seems to be real, actually is real.

When does a pattern become meaningful? What is the difference between visionary insight and mad raving? For many, Bible (and the worldviews many craft using it) function as a tool kit of signs, values, language, and assumptions that place functional limits for understanding the world. To do so, this essay argues, these worldviews often draw on certain "affective" qualities – ways of thinking that both precede and transcend traditional cognition. This chapter will explore the affect and function of "apocalyptic" and the construction of fantasy and conspiracy thinking as modes for constructing cultural expectations and rules for "reality." How we imagine the world will end in the future

*American Standard: The Bible in US Popular Culture*, First Edition. Robert Paul Seesengood.
© 2024 John Wiley & Sons Ltd. Published 2024 by John Wiley & Sons Ltd.

says a great deal about, and may even create, the way we understand the world to be functioning at the present.

As is often the case, so here: discovery begins with a series of visions.

## The Beginning of the End

And it happened, in the days (most likely) of the Roman emperor Domitian, as the ruins and ash of the Jerusalem Temple lay hundreds of miles away, John writhed in visionary throes on the island of Patmos. His seizure of rage was triggered in part by an emperor claiming the title of Lord and God, reigning over a hostile empire with alien gods. The fissures in thought and practice John saw within his own community further enraged him. John paused, lifting his eyes from the text(s) of the Hebrew prophets and Genesis open in his lap. And he looked, and he saw, in the heavens, the real power of the cosmos. John's vision twisted together combat myths from the world around him, visions of redemption and judgment from the Jewish prophets in front of him, animosity to the signs and symbols of the usurping Roman emperor; John wove these strands together with a loom made from a cross and constructed a text both ragged and evocative, binding together cosmogony and eschatology.

The Revelation to John, famously, presents a series of graphic visions regarding John's view of the reality of-and-behind the cosmos. What is unveiled by the Apocalypse, revealed in John's revelation, is the ultimate reality behind civic authority (Rev 4–5). Communities following Jesus that seemed to be weak are really powerful (Rev 2:8–11); communities that seem to be adjusting well to the world are lukewarm toward Jesus (Rev 3:14–22). The Roman emperor, so seemingly powerful and glorious, is a beast, a plaything of more powerful, more sinister forces (Rev 13). The cosmos belongs to God, its creator; such claims are not only ontological, they are also technological. For John's day, control of the sun, moon, and stars is the control of time, seasons, and calendars. Those who seem to be in power, harnessing technology of earth, sky, and water, wielding civil society as a weapon, will soon be drenched in a tide of rage. The end of human history was charging, sword upraised, shouting a guttural cry of doom. The God of creation, the God of Genesis, was initiating change. Destruction would precede re-creation and a new era of utopia, a remaking of primal paradise. John's spectacular text, however, struggled for an audience. Slow to canonization, often marginalized in lectionary and doctrine, it seemed mad. The executioner's ax which John saw rise did not fall. As Tina Pippen has put it, the fundamental problem of Christian eschatology is the persistent refusal of the world to end according to schedule.

John Nelson Darby sat in his study in Scotland (on Darby see Rossing 2005). And he looked and he saw a young girl from his congregation whose visions and dreams unfolded into a system of clearly marked historical dispensations, with ours near the last. The final days would be announced by a rapture of the faithful who would be taken up in a cloud. Those left behind would be left to struggle and turmoil, a Great Tribulation. A final, physical return of Jesus would mark the birth of the final dispensation, 1000 years of utopian peace on earth, the end of which would end earthly history in final judgment. Darby's ideas, spread by an ingenious system of biblical annotations devised by C. I. Scofield to find a ready audience in the New World of America limping from Civil War and Reconstruction, surrounded by new ideas and distressing empirical data about human origins.

## What the Bible Raëlly Says

And it happened in 1947, near Mt. Rainer, Washington, thousands of miles from the rubble and ash of Hiroshima and Nagasaki Japan, that Kenneth Arnold looked, and he saw 10 glowing disks in the sky moving in deliberate ways; subsequent newspaper reports dubbed the objects "flying saucers." The reports played upon a popular fear after the war. Orson Welles's Halloween *War of the Worlds* broadcast terrified millions. Earlier reports of World War II aircraft pilots about trailing lights ("foo fighters." 'foo' = *feu*) or "phantom missiles" were made public. Unrest increased after the 2 July 1947 reports that a flying saucer had crashed outside Corona, New Mexico. The debris was taken by the US Air Force to nearby Roswell where it would spawn generations of conspiracy theory (see Pelock 2001). These few weeks in 1947 gave birth to a modern – and a narrative – phenomenon. Though substantial variation is found in accounts of UFO encounters, much more narrative consistency remains. Scholars of religion, well aware of the potentiality in oral culture, note that sightings of UFOs arise concurrently with public fears about destructive technology, the tensions of subsequent cold war and the "space age" of exploration, commercialization and weaponization of near-earth space. UFO narratives speak to these fears.

On 20 November 1952, George Adamski looked, and he saw a being emerge from a landed flying saucer and later shocked the world with his story of their conversation. Adamski was not the first person to report contact with an alien (Melton 1995; see also Melton 1980), but his was the first recorded account that combined contact with extraterrestrials and flying saucers. The universe, according to Adamski's informant, was populated with various species of advanced beings who had long monitored life on our planet. Recent developments in nuclear weaponry matched with impending environmental ruin were prompting intervention. After Adamski, claims of direct encounters with aliens proliferated that often betray similarity in plot, structure, and memes. Many include a message of warning and a strong eschatological thrust. Scholars have looked and seen that many UFO and contactee movements have evolved quasi-religious organs and structures (Partridge 2003; Eberhart 1986; Denzler 2001; Lewis 1995). Sociologists who track new religious movements argue that many of these traditions have intellectual roots in Victorian spiritualism, the occult, and Swedenborgian theosophy (Melton 1995). Many UFO religions reinterpret Judeo-Christian biblical texts. Biblical scenes such as Ezekiel's famous sighting of God's chariot (Ezek 1–3), Elijah's transmission to heaven (2 Kgs 2:1–15) and Jesus' ascension (Acts 1:9–11) are, for some, evidence of UFO contact (Leslie and Adamski 1953). Erich von Däniken's, *Chariots of the Gods*, knit many of these themes (von Däniken 1980). Von Däniken found evidence of ancient astronauts in Egyptian, Mesopotamian, indigenous American, and biblical myths, positing that legends of the gods were the primitive reactions of ancient humans to encounters with extraterrestrials parallel to Papuans after World War II who made birds out of airplane parts, cleared trees, burned lights, etc. to attract divine visitors who were actually members of the allied air forces.

James Lewis observes that western religion has been fixated on the idea of the "extraterrestrial" and "extradimensional" God. The gods dwell in the skies, in other realms, and visit our own to direct our living. The model is precisely the same as modern UFO mythology. He writes:

> Let us, therefore, invert von Daniken's (sic) hermeneutic and consider how a religious tradition emphasizing sky gods might influence one to invest religious significance in the contemporary phenomenon of unidentified flying objects (xi)...we might say that the deity of Western religions is – in some sense –an "extraterrestrial being."
> (Lewis 1995, p. xii).

Lewis invokes Rudolf Otto's *Idea of the Holy,* particularly its construction of the sacred. UFO encounters are often transcendent and much beyond "normal" experience. This bifurcation could readily be adapted to Durkheim and Otto's definitions of the sacred and the profane.

> According to Otto, one encounters the sacred as a powerful, alien reality that does not belong to the world of ordinary existence. This experience encompasses components of both fear and attraction...it is "uncanny" and "awesome." (xii).... [Religious meaning applied to UFOs] can be manifested less obviously, in the form of certain themes and patterns

that – when cloaked in the guise of flying machines – are not immediately recognized as religious, but which fulfill religious functions.

(Lewis 1995, pp. xii–xiii)

In 1973, while touring the volcanic region of Clermont-Ferrand, the French racing driver and enthusiast Claude Vorilhon saw an extraterrestrial. Taken aboard the alien's craft and to other worlds, Vorilhon was taught the secrets of human origins and religion; he renamed himself Raël and upon his return began spreading his message via a series of books and lectures. At present, the movement following his teachings, the Raëleans, cite a membership of 60 000–70 000 worldwide (mostly in the United States and Canada).

The Bible is central to the teachings of Raël. Raël argues that the accounts it contains are accounts of prior alien contact with humans. Beginning with Genesis 1:1–2:4, Raël argues humans were initially genetically engineered organisms placed on the planet by a consortium of alien scientists called the Elohim. These aliens have guided evolution; creation, Raëleans insist, betrays intelligent design. As humans prospered, members of the Elohim had sexual contact with humanity and have visited us frequently, offering insight and inspiring individuals. Jesus is the product of genetic engineering and in vitro fertilization of Mary; his genetic father was an Elohim named Yahweh. Yahweh shared numerous spiritual insights with Jesus and taught him advanced technologies for healing. At the rejection of Jesus by confused and frightened humans, Yahweh and other Elohim took him away to extraterrestrial safety. Jesus' promise to return was actually a promise that the Elohim will, en masse, return once humanity was ready to understand their potential gifts. John saw as much. Raël, as well, is the product of Elohim/human crossbreeding, also the genetic son of Yahweh. He, and potentially other humans, will be "resurrected" via cloning to live forever. Raël is the (metaphoric) return of Yahweh's son to declare and prepare for the impending return of the Elohim and the initiation of an earthly, technologically driven utopia in 2035 or 2090; the Raëleans restarted the calendar 6 August 1945 with the bombing of Hiroshima and the dawn of what they call the Age of Apocalypse.

The fundamental message of the Raëleans is to clarify biblical teachings and prepare humanity for utopia. Their website (www.rael.org) identifies Raël as "the last prophet." The Raëleans are "intently millenarian" with extensive interest in Revelation (Palmer 1995, p. 80). A small community of 144 000 (Rev 7:1–9 – the Jews are direct descendants of the Elohim) will, indeed, be saved from Armageddon by rapture by the Elohim (p. 94); the sixth seal in Revelation 6:12–16 is a prediction of unavoidable nuclear war. Raëleans have invested extensively in programs studying human genetics and potential cloning as our hope of survival. Raël has (so far unsuccessfully) lobbied for the construction of an embassy to the Elohim in Jerusalem (which they argue would be the third temple prophesied in Revelation) where the alien teachers would reside and that would serve as a repository for alien engineering and medical technology. In Raëlean thought, a new utopian age for humanity is pending, and a prediction (or, better, declaration) of this transformation is found in biblical text, particularly Genesis and Revelation. But the end of the world (or the beginning of the next one) is an interest that is hardly modern or unique to biblical traditions.

## Discerning the *Bak'tun*

And it happened on an unknown, ordinary day in the 1960s, tractors constructing a cement factory shifted the rubble and hillside of a province in Tabasco, Mexico, and uncovered an inscribed stone among material cast aside in a way typical of modern development, a development that has motive to politely ignore stones marking a dead, indigenous past. These hills would turn out to be tels blanketing a long abandoned Mayan city, El Tortuguero, whose heyday was under the reign of the Mayan King Jaguar (Balam Ahau, 644–679 CE). Among the ruins recovered were a series of stelae and monuments, most notoriously Monument 6. Reassembled and translated, the text contains the now infamous lines "the 13th one will end on 4 Ahau the third of Uniiw. There will occur blackness and the descent of the Bolon Yookte' god to the red." Alternative translations are "there will occur a seeing, the display of the god Bolon Yookte' in a great investiture." Neither translation is ideal. The gist seems to be that on the culmination of the conclusion of some significant date cycle there will be a great display/spectacle/darkness in which Bolon Yookte, the "God of the Nine," does ... something.

Scholars are agreed that the "13th" refers to the 13th *bak'tun* or the end of the Mayan long calendar. The Mayans seemed to have initially used both solar calendars (with a 360-day year) and lunar calendars (with a gestational 260-day year). These two calendars merged in the second or third century BCE to form the Mayan "long calendar," which was set to begin (scholars generally concur) on a date roughly corresponding to the western 3114 BCE. The Mayan were vigesimal (using base 20 for counting). The number 13 was considered very significant. The long calendar was a repeating set of major cycles totaling 5126 years "composed of multiple mini-cycles" (Restall and Solari 2011, p. 13). Essentially, the pattern is:

1 *kin* (pronounced "keen," the word for "sun") = 1 day.
20 *kin* = 1 *unial* ("weenal" or 20 days)
18 *uinal* = 1 *tun* ("toon," the word for "stone." 360 days or ca. 1 solar year)
20 *tun* = *ka'tun* (20 years)
20 *katun* = *baktun* (400 years).

The Mayan long calendar begins with the solstice of 3114 BCE and runs for 13 *bak'tun*, ending on a date most commonly calculated as 12 December 2012.

In and of itself, Monument 6 does not predict doom, though it arguably suggests change. The Mayan long calendar does end with 13 *bak'tun*; there is a very real likelihood that the long calendar does not extend further because of a cultural preference for 13 and the sense that, to be honest, 1 872 000 days seems quite long enough for any practical need. 2012ologists (their preferred term), however, combined Monument 6 with other Mayan archaeology and mythology to argue the end of the 13th *bak'tun* would be unusually significant. In Mayan cosmogony (as detailed in *Popol Vuh* and the Books of the *Chiliam Balam*) the universe as we know it is only the present incarnation of a consistently changing cosmos. We live in the "fourth" (or third) age, the "age of Maize" (humans are descended from maize-beings in Mayan anthropology); the cosmos was in different forms before and will be altered into different stages in the time to come. 2012ologists argued that Monument 6 was predicting the end of our age, a moment of cosmic doom that would end human life as we know it. American pop culture became fascinated by the Mayan long calendar, Mayan cosmogony and Mayan apocalypticism and national Mayan subculture emerged largely driven by internet-based publication.

Although Mayanists and specialists in American indigenous cultures were doubtless flattered by the sudden attention to pre-Columbian art, technology, literature, mythology, and language, they quickly became, no doubt, also somewhat exhausted by the demands of clarification (those who study John's Apocalypse can sympathize, even as we are just now catching our wind after Covid-19). Mayanists often point out the obvious difficulty in correlating calendars, not to mention the arbitrariness and inaccuracy of the western Gregorian calendar. We also have less-than-hoped-for data on how widespread the use of a single, long-form calendar was among the Maya. Finally, of course, there is the more esoteric question of any Mayan expectations of a cosmic transition to come at its end (setting aside the even more final consideration: the argument that Mayans predicted future events and the end of the world is simply silly).

In fact, calendrically indicated cosmic transformation is simply not present in Mayan thought. There are a few, minor, indications that a future transformation would accompany the generic end of our age, though there is by no means any indication of what that transformation will be, nor are there any even vaguely uniform notions that this transformation will be cataclysmic. The pre-Columbian Maya had an eschatology, but not a very developed one. Mayan mythology, like most indigenous American mythology, is cyclical and suggests a pattern of repeated solar, lunar, seasonal, life span, and cosmic transitions. Every indication is that even when the pre-Columbian Mayans did look forward to a new age, it was with very hopeful, positive expectation. Describing pre-Colombian Mayan thought, Restall and Solari write:

> [A rise of the new cosmic order] is simply a resetting of the calendrical clock, a milestone to mark time in the distant past. In that past, birth and creation, not death and destruction, were the important events.... No where in this set of concerns is there a preoccupation with the end of the world, the end of time, apocalypse, extinction, or even an exceptional or unusual focus on death.
>
> (2011, pp. 134, 138)

The most difficult challenge to 2012ology raised by Mayanists is the problem of separating pre-Columbian Mayan thought from postcontact Mayan thought. The latter has, of course, been heavily influenced by western notions of Christian faith and practice. It also does seem to possess a more developed, and dire, eschatology. Postcontact Mayan thought at times repudiated all previous ideology and myth as a result of the complex pressures of colonial adaptation and expansion. Again, as outlined by Restall and Solari:

> [I]t is western –not Maya –civilization that contains ...the millenarian mother lode.... *Millenarianism* is the belief that an impending transformation will dramatically change society (3). Concepts of millenarianism and Apocalypse were deeply embedded within the cultures that were brought by Europeans to the Americas. Those ideas first of all reached central Mexico, influencing the Aztecs and their neighbors in the early sixteenth century.... Soon after, influence of Western culture into the cities and towns of Yucatan and Guatemala.... Christian notions of Doomsday and the second coming of Christ were easily appropriated, resulting in the cataclysmic narratives recorded by Maya scribes in the early colonial period. As the centuries passed, those narratives were viewed as an entirely Maya cultural phenomenon. They are often used as the basis for modern, popular interpretations of the Maya worldview and its prophecies.
>
> (2011, p. 5)

Mayan cosmology post contact was heavily influenced by Christian eschatology, particularly apocalyptic varieties. This influence has not only resulted in internet obsession with Mayan prophecy of "doomsday," but it colored pre-Columbian Mayan thought as well. As Spanish conquistadors overrode Mayan territory, biblical memes overrode Mayan mythology, infecting it with a pernicious doomsday virus that fused together cosmogony and eschatology, a virus ironically delivered through a still festering repudiation of the indigenous past.

## Converging Sight Lines

One of the earliest UFO interpreters employing a scholarly psycho-socio-religious perspective was Carl Jung. And he looked, and he saw UFOs as a form of "modern mythology." Though allowing the possibility that something "real" might lie behind many sightings, Jung noted that most reports lack physical evidence and even reports of actual phenomenon or objects were being interpreted via the dire possibility of nuclear war. Humans, as always, "looked to the heavens" for help. Technology had destroyed belief in (G)od(s), but extraterrestrials with advanced technology and deeper wisdom provided a seductive way to recapitulate ancient narrative. Jung refers to this narrative as a collective psychic projection where collective subconscious desires were being mirrored. Jung also combines his highly psychological, naturalistic reading of UFOs with striking language resonate with both New Age and Christian eschatology:

> It is not presumption that drives me, but my conscience as a psychiatrist that bids me fulfil (sic) my duty and prepare those few who will hear me for coming events which are in accord with an end of an era. As we know from ancient Egyptian history, they are manifestations of psychic changes which always appear at the end of one Platonic month and the beginning of another. ...[T]hey are changes in the constellation of psychic dominants of the archetypes, or "gods" as they used to be called, which bring about, or accompany, long-lasting transformations of the collective society. This transformation started in the historical era and left its traces first in the passing of the aeon of Taurus into that of Aries, and then of Aries into Pisces, whose beginning coincides with the rise of Christianity. We are now nearing that great change which may be expected when the spring point enters Aquarius.
>
> (Jung 1964, Vol. 5 pp. 589–590)

A very short space later he continues:

> I am, to be quite frank, concerned for all those who are caught unprepared by the events in question and disconcerted by their incomprehensible nature. Since, so far as I know, no one has yet felt moved to examine and set forth the possible psychic consequences of this foreseeable astrological change.
>
> (Vol. 6 p. 590)

Other modern prophets are creating new burial shrouds for the cosmos woven from strands of multiple alien, indigenous and Christian threads. The charismatic Christian rapture televangelist Jack Van Impe wrote extensively that the

Mayan predictions of doom could correspond to Christian expectations of biblical rapture.

What is it that we see as we review this series of visions and visionaries about ourselves, about biblical text, about our community? We might begin with what we don't see at academic conferences or in scholarly literature. UFO religions frequently engage the Bible and construct their own interpretations of its text and characters, yet biblical scholarship has ignored them. Largely, I think this is because of a dominant paradigm that such forms of interpretation are beneath scholarly attention. John A. Saliba, commenting on the same, observes:

> Biblical scholars are likely to object strongly to the use of belief in UFOs as a principle of hermeneutics. The main reason for this is obvious: the existence of UFOs is a statement of faith and their alleged presence in biblical times is a hypothesis. UFOs, therefore, cannot be the method of eliciting the meaning of the scriptural text, since they themselves are an interpretation of the same text.
>
> (1995, p. 33)

Saliba suggests biblical scholars will not rely on a hermeneutic guide or principle rooted in faith whose only confirmation or justification is (circular) arguments arising from scripture itself. Alas, if only this were the case.

One may well ask if it is more rational or empirical to engage biblical interpretations that are rooted in divine revelation via the Holy Spirit. Biblical scholars eschew modern "new age" exegesis, but readily study biblical exegesis from ancient mystical and ascetic movements. Are Raëleans really less rational than Essenes? Why are there entire conferences and libraries examining ancient Christian Gnostic exegesis, yet modern Gnostic-like UFO religions are unengaged? What we find, I think, is a glimpse at the boundary walls of scholarship. We as scholars are ourselves subject to cultural norming and values. Critical scholars, with advanced university training and often influenced by theology, concede a sense of rationality that would assume, a priori, that extraterrestrial visits to earth by aliens have not happened. As such, biblical interpretations that are grounded on this assumption are also a priori not scholarly and beneath attention. Yet a priori claims of divinity, ancient or modern, are considered worth critique. Sociocultural norming is affecting our scholarly thinking so that we are comfortable engaging scholars who argue that an extradimensional deity created the earth, was incarnated in human form, and rose from the dead, but not those who posit biblical text correlates with extraterrestrial visitors or indigenous American mythology. Using a model of cultural studies that questions the separation of high and low culture as a way of questioning elements of social norming and hierarchical allegiances, we would be forced to concede something is affecting our scholarly attention.

Writing of the Raëleans, Susan Palmer observes:

> It is all too easy to render a new religion in caricature and then dismiss it
> as absurd or pathological. After all, today's "cult" might grow up to
> become the Mormon Church, the Baha'I faith, or the Jehovah's Witnesses
> of tomorrow. The Raelian church might in a hundred years become one
> of those Bible-based Christian minority churches that are well known
> and accepted in society but branded by fundamentalist theologians as
> "heresies" because of their deviant interpretations of Creation, the Fall,
> and the nature of Christ.... Contemporary Prophets are not awarded the
> benefit of the doubt granted the great prophets in history.... Is it because
> a prophet's call must be shrouded in the mists of time before it can be
> awarded dignity?
>
> (Palmer 2004, pp. 14, 15).

Raëleans, in a moment some will likely see as ironic, position themselves as
the rational way to read biblical text avoiding any appeal to supernatural (in the
sense of "above nature") beings. Instead, they appeal to organic creatures using
highly advanced technology, but all subject to the normal rules of physics and
genetics. They are attempting to read biblical text in a way that rises above
superstition and faith in the super(para) normal. This is also the intention
found in quite a bit of biblical scholarship of the last 150 years. Scholarship has
attempted to apply elements of sound lexicography, philology, interpretive theory, social theory, and more as a way of engaging the text on a "rational" basis.
Clearly, there is a broad, cultural tendency at present toward the celebration of
rationality over traditional spirituality.

In our responses to Mayan prophecy, we can see something of the colonial
motivation and cultural resistance that John himself faced. Apocalyptic and
prophecy movements merge ideas from multiple cultural narratives, sacred
texts, and traumas, interpreting and reinterpreting the present, to fashion, ultimately, new forms of religious consciousness. In comparison, we may glimpse
the visceral temptation toward dismissal of the puerile that apocalyptic often
faces from the culture it critiques. We see the always-already linkage in western
thought between cosmogony and eschatology, between utopia and dystopia.
Americans seem obsessed with dispensations, longing to understand their own
place in a New World suspended between a displaced indigenous past and
European hopes and fears.

As in both UFO and Mayan eschatologies, we are presented by the Apocalypse
with a choice: to be madmen or to be their oppressors. This forced dichotomy
and its pressure to reevaluate what we regard as "normal" or "real" lies at the
core of apocalypse, a core laid bare by modern visions and seers. Perhaps the
real revelation lies in looking for who sees this present age as dystopia, and why,

and what possibilities might be unveiled by their visions of eschatological utopia and salvation.

What all these systems and stories and values have in common is that they are rooted in two, fundamental principles: the world is not as it would seem, and we are racing toward a decisive, critical moment of resolution. All affirm a mysterious and consuming power at work in the world, a power seen and understood only by an elite group of insiders. All these ways of thinking are forms of conspiracy thinking. I would argue, they are also, in exactly the same way, forms of apocalyptic logic.

A hallmark of the Anthropocene is human-initiated mass extinction of several of our neighbor species. Since the late nineteenth century (as argued by Vox 2017), the post-Darwin West has imagined a human eschatology that was not divinely initiated but was the result of human activity or general planetary disaster. We have also seen (again, Vox) a rising interest in ancient Jewish and Christian apocalyptic texts and their mysterious images and predictions of doom. In both ancient and modern contexts, the end was nigh, but also the fault of someone else. Apocalyptic, conspiracy, and horror share several characteristics. They each purport to expose the "really real" world, the reality beneath the mundane world we normally see and experience. They are highly visual, "graphic" rhetoric. Finally, they trade in the affects of disgust, anxiety, shock, and fear. They use these affects, in part, to compel readers to emotional and active allegiances. Biblical apocalyptic is so often cited in various sci-fi-, disaster-, and conspiracy-driven worldviews because apocalyptic reasoning is, itself, a type of conspiracy thinking. The affects inspired by this sci-fi/horror genre themselves reveal affects integral to ancient apocalyptic literature; in each affect functions as revelation to create a motivated, active opposition to larger political forces and powers.

## On Conspiracies of Affect(s) and Apocalyptics

In December 2016, a gunman looked up, and he entered the Washington, DC restaurant Comet Pizza and demanded the release of child sex slaves hidden in the restaurant's basement and maintained for the pleasure of DC's political elites. He was responding to an online conspiracy "Pizzagate," an elaborate and arcane story extracted from leaked Democratic presidential campaign emails and pieced together over an array of internet social media communities. The fundamental conspiracy linked political subterfuge with sinister threats of a shadow government motivated by its practice of Satan devotion. Unlike fears of a Mayan doomsday, Pizzagate conspiracy would persist, indeed grow throughout the term of President Trump into the QAnon movement (which entered mainstream political discourse in the run-up to the 2020 election). QAnon (named for Q Anonymous, a collective of internet detectives and pseudo-informants) argued that Donald Trump was secretly leading a war of rebellion against "Deep State" operatives and a satanic, pedophilic conspiracy of professional politicians (most, but not all, Democrats). These intricate conspiracies (beginning in the chatrooms of the 4chan and Reddit websites) only accelerated during the confusions and closures inspired by the Covid-19 pandemic of most of 2020. By October, just weeks shy of November's presidential election, President Trump was tweeting QAnon conspiracies on social media and being asked by reporters if he would disavow the conspiracy as untrue (he would not). The energies behind QAnon and Pizzagate would distill into the various fears and alienation that led many US citizens to be convinced that sinister powers orchestrated a massive, fraudulent election count in fall of 2020, and on 6 January 2021 a few to attack and invade the US Capitol and attempt to overturn the results of that election.

Three features strike me about the Pizzagate scene: first, the extraordinary motivating force of a conspiracy theory discourse to provoke violence. Second, I note how, structurally, the argument and their underlying logics are remarkably similar to fear of UFO invasion, Mayan doom, and John's Apocalypse. Third: the immunity of that discourse to factual correction. This has led scholars working in the field of affect theory (Stewart 2007; Sedgwick 2003, pp. 123–152) to conclude that conspiracy theory is structured according to the logic of affect. This structure is also, we would argue, the structure of apocalyptic. Apocalyptic, like conspiracy, is a discourse aimed at a particular configuration of vivid, highly engaged emotions – fear, exhilaration, and rage. These feelings are what conspiracy theorists and apocalypticists alike seek to express: our world is an overly complex thing that impartially crushes individuals beneath its wheel, and the only escape left for "ordinary" people is to unmask and resist.

Popular use of "apocalyptic" tends to define the word as catastrophic disaster or the end of an era of human history. Scholars of apocalyptic, however, use a much more limited definition. Following the pivotal work of John Collins (1998), apocalyptic is now viewed as having two significant characteristics. First, in apocalyptic literature, a protagonist receives a vision of the future or of the heavens from angelic figures. This narrated vision is often an abstract presentation of symbolic actors who enact, parable-like, the author's thesis on the nature and significance of the political moment or the cosmos. Second, apocalyptic offers a glimpse of the reality behind reality, of the "really real" at work in the cosmos. Powers are revealed as godly or as evil, in league with or against the protagonist and the community they represent. Apocalyptic is, generically speaking, a narrative description of a vision or journey in which the hero discovers or is instructed in the real nature of things.

In early Judeo-Christian apocalyptic, the revealed secret of the universe was often a deep struggle between good, as represented by God and evil, eventually embodied in Satan. Jeffrey Russell and Elaine Pagels have argued that, though possessing ancient near eastern (particularly Babylonian) and Jewish roots, the figure of Satan as a discrete candidate marshaling forces of evil into a war against God, is born in Judeo-Christian apocalyptic (Russell 1987; Pagels 1996). In *The Birth of Satan*, T. J. Wray and Greg Mobley, after a general survey on Satan's development, note the power of Satan as alter-ego to Jesus and God and question what we "need" in this character. Satan's literary home, apocalyptic literature, "takes the deepest, foundational stories of a culture, its myths, and imposes them on the surface of history." (2005, p. 169) Satan and apocalyptic, then, function as "cosmic conspiracy theory":

> The real meaning of history is not apparent, it can only be revealed, and under the surface of everyday life lays a vast nefarious network, a murderous, invisible, universal, and ageless conspiracy dedicated to thwarting happiness and fouling the wellsprings of kindness, to sowing discord and conquering the universe in the name of Death.
>
> (Wray and Mobley 2005, p. 169)

Satan, as Wray and Mobley contend, is the ultimate western conspirator. Wray and Mobley note that a seemingly endless array of both medieval and modern conspiracy theories – anti-Semitism, Freemasonry, Reformers, Papists, Communists – reflect fears of Satan and those secretly in his allegiance as the "powers of the air and principality" (Eph 2:2). Like the bartering-Satan, however, these systems have a strange blend of power and vulnerability. Their sinister control is as impervious as it is secret, except, of course, when it isn't and an average person both unveils and inverts it.

Although Wray and Mobley ask if Satan is "real" in their final chapter, from an affective perspective, their question misses the point of both apocalypticism and conspiracy thinking: the reality of Satan (or UFOs, or Mayan prophecy) is beside the point. Affect approaches to apocalyptic have made a significant mark in recent scholarship precisely by emphasizing the way that affects shape how bodies encounter the world, leaving truth in the dust. Affective approaches to conspiracy, most notably in the work of (and responses to) Eve Sedgwick, whose work reveals how both political critique and a literary "hermeneutics of suspicion" (critical readings attuned to unveiling heteronormative or patriarchal systems, for instance) though valid and valuable, traffic in a paranoid affect that distorts text and context.

The effect, or, better, the affect, of conspiracy theory is the revelry of suspicion, fused to logics of identity, empowerment, and apocalyptic calls to action.

Conspiracy theories are rich in shadowy others who have finally been transfixed by the arrow of truth; hence "belief" in conspiracy produces a feeling of empowerment and control (Bilwicz et al. 2015; Brotherton 2017; Prooijen 2018). Nefarious other-worldly powers have been detected, but their power is victim to its arrogance; they have exposed themselves (to the discerning), and the weak have a moment (often, only one, immediate moment) to defeat the strong. Conspiracy, like apocalyptic, resists logical refutation or analysis. Conspiracy theories, like apocalyptic (perhaps religious language itself) though dressed in a veneer of "fact," are not coherent by intention. Rather, they offer a set of entangled affective parameters that interface with and rewrite systems of power.

## Apocalypse: John's Vision of the (Sometimes Scary) Real World

In the opening chapter of the canonical Apocalypse, the seer John is startled while deep in prayer by a voice from behind. He writes in verse 12, "And I turned around to see the voice." Seemingly a non sequitur, in Revelation the expression is apt; what follows proves to be a relentless blending of literary, auditory, and visual memes. It is filled with disjointed visions of spectacular monsters, cosmic warfare, and esoteric reality drawing copiously from Hebrew scripture and Jewish second Temple literature but also from Greco-Roman art and public spectacle (Frilingos 2004). Revelation is a visual text, meant to be "seen," even if, or as, it is read aloud and heard. Aa series of vivid, confusing visions are mediated to the prophet – and through the words of the written apocalypse to us – by an angelic or divine figure. Apocalyptic revels in juxtaposition arising from a pervasive dualism that drives its narrative and frames its interests; indeed, polar conflict may be a work's only coherent "plot." Apocalyptic asserts history has a *teleos*: the struggle of Good vs. Evil.

Greg Carey observes: "[A]pocalypse inhabits the realms of imagination, of comparison, symbol and vision" (Carey 2005, p. 6). Carey likens apocalyptic to the poetic (p. 13) because it, like the poetic, involves "looking beyond the everyday world" in a text rife with visions, metaphors, and deep affects that "seeks to reshape the imagination" (p. 16). "Like poetry, apocalyptic discourse often aims at affect rather than data, at moving its audience rather than informing them" (p. 13).

The visual nature of John's apocalypse has been a staple of readerly critique for centuries (Frilingos 2004; Moore 2014a). John's text not only mounts a series of show-stopping scenes – the heavens rip open, monsters climb up from the seas, there are wars, graphic nudity, sexual violence, and scenes of amazing destruction – it is a text brimming with eyes. Monsters bear multiple heads, divine spirits are covered with eyes, the slaughtered lamb grotesquely blinks back at the reader with a perfect, prime number of eyeballs. Revelation watches us watching it. (Kotrosits 2014, pp. 474–475). Revelation's embodied eyes and bloody bodies are terrible. Stephen Moore's review of John's images foregrounds their affects of horror (and disgust) (Moore 2014a, b). John's Apocalypse, intending both fear and revulsion, uses sexuality to suggest profligacy and then to elicit disgust (Moore 2014a) and drenches bodies in blood and gore. John focuses on bodies – bodies in torture, bodies in pain, bodies under duress, bodies in rapture, pure bodies, unspoiled bodies, monstrous bodies – bodies often depicted as partial, filled with fluids waiting to be unleashed, bodies that allure at first, but ultimately disgust, bodies that rot and turn into carrion, bodies that are torn to pieces, burned in fire. By their affectual engagement, these images revolt, repel, and terrify.

If apocalyptic literature is the revelation of the world as it "truly" is, the reality that is beneath what appears to be real, Revelation imagines a world filled with rage, disgust, and horror. Revelation is teeming with highly "visual" texts of monsters, terror, consumption and being consumed. Revelation is spectacle, but its graphic imagery, in any other context but Christian canon, would be immediately recognized as a horror show (Aichele et al. 2013; Seesengood 2016). Like horror, apocalyptic not only reveals hidden Truth, its truths are often – very literally – monstrous and capable of violence and rage. Evil and horrible things lie just beneath the surface of reality, waiting to burst through and appear. If Satan is conspirator, could we also say that apocalyptic is a type of horror story?

## Horror Movies: *28 Days Later*…and the Revelation of Rage

Of the making (and interpreting) of apocalypse, particularly as a modern horror movie, there seems no end. Apocalypse lives on, and film is a particularly ready medium for the would-be modern apocalypticist with its inherent emphasis upon the visual, its celebration of the graphic, its giant screen. Recalling Carey and Collins (apocalyptic is mediated vision of another world), film may be inadvertently always-already apocalyptic.

Writing on the intersection of film and religion, specifically upon the way film is/uses/expresses (embodied) rituals, Brent Plate turns briefly to explore the physical nature, the embodied sense, of spectatorship. He writes: "film is never 'merely' image and/or sound but always multi-medial, impacting the various senses of the human body and causing it to shudder or sob, laugh or leap" (Plate 2008, p. 60), "a movement of the body that is pre-conscious, before rational awareness" (p. 60). Film and religion use embodiment and affect to construct alternate world(s) and reality (pp. 3–5; 14–17). Film, with its collective composition, its tendencies toward etiology, its construction of cultural mores and norms becomes contemporary mythology. Film is, in many ways, always-already apocalyptic (Wright 2008).

Of course, some movies are *really* apocalyptic and *really* horror. *28 Days Later.* (UK, written by Alex Garland, dir. Danny Boyle, 2002) is a prime example. The movie opens with animal rights activists invading a primate research facility with the intent to liberate some lab-test chimpanzees. As they enter the lab housing an array of clearly distressed (and tormented) animals, they utter the film's first lines and announce their arrival into a macabre, high-tech underworld: "Fucking Hell."

The activists release a clearly distressed chimp, realizing too late they have unwittingly released a deadly contagion. Known as "Rage," the virus causes vicious aggression in primates; ignoring food or other needs, "the infected" become zombie-like, attacking other humans with clawing hands and rending teeth. The virus is blood-born and fast-acting overpowering a new host within seconds.

The movie's protagonist, Jim (Cillian Murphy) awakens from a coma in a hospital room, 28 days after the release of the virus. Wandering a deserted London, he is soon attacked by packs of the Infected then saved by Selena (Naomie Harris). *28 Days Later* is graphic, violent, and graphically violent. The infected are covered in open wounds and blood; they vomit pints of black blood and pus. They scream in rage and pain. They tear and bite and rend. Jim and Selena eventually join forces with a father–daughter team to seek out the last surviving military outpost, outside Manchester (they have heard a beacon over the wireless). On arrival, they discover that the remnant military are safe and well supplied but have also conspired to attract and rape women. Further, the entire world has not been destroyed. Britain is under quarantine by world governments allied in a conspiracy of containment. The apocalypse of the film is the revelation that our own (government-funded) technology has created an unstoppable, contagious Rage, but also that government solutions are fatal and horrific.

A film whose premise is that human technology and environmental arrogance will result in an apocalyptic plague of infectious rage begs for an affective reading, particularly in a post-2020 United States. In the oft cited description of Steven Shaviro (1993; see also Shaviro 2004) affect-influenced film theory is moving from psychobiological and social understandings of viewer response into "visceral, affective responses to film, in sharp contrast to most critics' exclusive concern with issues of *form, meaning, and ideology*" (Shaviro 1993, p. 38; my italics). Shavario argues emotion is the after-effect of affect. Affect in its Deleuzian sense, is a transfer of will and of consciousness via mechanisms and forms that produce that a/effect.

One of the most erudite and engaging studies of affect and film, particularly of horror movies, is Eugenie Brinkema's 2015 *The Forms of the Affects*. Brinkema argues affect is (in a Foucaultian sense) a "fold," the exterior made complex by the discovery of its attached interior. She advocates for a "radical formalism" that, for film criticism and literature, "would take the vital measure of theory for form *and* take the measure of form for affectivity" (Brinkema 2014, p. 37). Form produces affect. The meaning of affect in film is that interstitial, preconscious moment of the transfer itself: the jolt at a sudden sound, the wince at the sight of blood, the aroused crossing of the legs, a transfer that eludes (or elides) because it precedes (or evades) conscious cognition, yet which is also embedded in form.

The affect(s) of horror vacillates between excitement (at times quasi-sexual) and disgust. Horror discloses and reveals even as it obliterates both surfaces and superficiality: bodies are ripped open, and the reality (of evil) is exposed and foregrounded. Horror, like affect, requires bodies: the fearful eye, the rigid hand, the open mouth, torn flesh blood, but also, like apocalyptic, discovery and reflection. Horror, as a genre, has affective forms of both the disembodied and unseen, the fearful abyss beneath the surface or skin. Ultimately the affect of horror is the Freudian *Unheimlich*, and the membranes between the *Unheimlich* and the sacred are precariously thin. Bruce Kawin (2012, pp. 360–361) notes the descent into horror is a ritual descent beneath the surface, into the underworld and the superego.

Criticism of horror movies, in terms of affect, often focuses upon disgust and powerlessness, both seen in the dismemberment of the body (Brinkema 2014, pp. 152–181). Freud famously associated the uncanny not only with the embodied sensation of repulsiveness but also with (unwanted) discovery and revelation. Disgust and other (crude, consumptive) embodied actions (expectoration, regurgitation, defecation, urination, mastication, flatulence, gestation – things within bodies now bursting out) are the antithesis of reason and thought; disgust is triggered by (what are considered) baser forms of embodiment: viscera, foul odors, excrement, blood.

Often seen as the antithesis of aesthetics (as well as of reason), horror and disgust not only have influenced criticism of biblical apocalyptic (e.g. Moore 2001, pp. 173–199) but also have influenced film studies on horror and pornography (Pomerance 2003; Carroll 1990; Freeland 2000. See also Adams and Yates 1997 for an early work fusing literature on the ugly and disgusting and religious discourse). Mikita Brottman argues that horror and disgust arise most acutely not just from images associated with refuse but particularly with consumption, rending, and dismemberment (and exposure) of bodies (Brottman 1997). As bodies are torn and fragmented, particularly *human* bodies, we are aroused to disgust and repulsion. Horror, as a film genre, exploits this primal reaction, often blurring it into highly sexualized images and violence. Violence becomes a cipher for possession and control (or its loss). As Brottman points out, there is an inherent element of consumption and of being consumed (or torn), of implicit cannibalism. We are reacting to a fear of bringing impurities into our bodies, even as we fear being torn and eaten ourselves. The affect of horror is, on one level, a fear of *both* eating and being eaten; it is a fear of *both* being torn and becoming cannibal. Horror also violates the barriers between concealment and exposure, interior and exterior, skin and depth. Horror is revelation; revelation is horror. Both revel in the affects of rage, fear, and disgust. Both apocalyptic and horror reveal (re)constructed worlds. They expose hidden, bursting interiors. They are graphically disgusting and fearful. They are fundamentally the encounter of a world beyond our control. But this new world is not random. Horror arises from the discovery that it is very much under control of someone and something – just very much not under ours. Horror presumes, as does Apocalyptic, that "something is out there," in control if unseen, breaching our mundane world via some other space, as chaos threatening order, evil to combat good. To survive horror – or apocalyptic – one must know the secrets being kept. Of course, all this is also the same logic of conspiracy thinking. Revelation can open the gates of Hell that many a monster has walked through; the monsters, and their masters, plot against us perpetually. Every horrible apocalypse is also a terrifying conspiracy.

## Conspiracy

Conspiracy literature, and literature on conspiracy, has grown at a rapid pace in the past decades fueled by the ubiquity of social media and our present era of "fake news." As a (now) largely internet-text phenomenon, conspiracy literature revels in the potential of hypertext. Webpages facilitate rapid cross-reference; they are multisensory, integrating video, audio, and image (Landow 1992, 2004). Like John's Revelation, web documents are hyperlinked, hyper-referenced visual texts; indeed, conspiracy often relies upon minute, close review of photos and images. Both apocalyptic and conspiracy are narratives of the discovery, but both are also driven by affects of disgust, anxiety, and anger. Conspiracy is world creation via "real world" revelation whose graphic rhetoric tends to focus upon embodiment, disgust, and the revelation of what lies beneath surfaces and skins.

Issues of food, consumption, and viscera are never far removed. For example, arising late in the American presidential election of 2016, the "Pizzagate" conspiracy certainly coalesced Alt-Right, anti-Democrat sentiment at a critical stage of the election process and continues into fears about secret government (or tech industry, or Jewish) plans to secret microchips into Covid-19 vaccines (or, more mundane, to exploit the pandemic in order to increase government control). Not to mention belief in stolen elections and conspiracies of the Illuminati (or whomever) who effected it. According to online conspiracy groups, chiefly the website Reddit, photos and emails released as part of a broad hack of Democrat Party email revealed a brimming network of child sexual slavery among government and political elites, orchestrated by Clinton campaign chair John Podesta. Tracing out the significance of restaurant signage and architecture (and making much out of Podesta's admiration of the performance artist Mariana Abramović) the conspiracy argued a world beneath the apparently family-friendly city block where Satanic "soul cooking" rituals abounded. Other conspiracy and neo-Nazi sites, such as Andrew Anglin's *Daily Stormer*, linked the conspiracy to Jewish blood-libel tradition (and invoked Anglin's previous conspiracy obsession: the human-infiltrating subterranean race, the Reptillians).

Both apocalyptic and conspiracy literature function by exposing the "real" cosmos, a trait also in common with horror. These three genres also share characteristics of shock, exposure, violence; they are graphic in every sense and function affectively, changing the way their readers feel about and interact with the larger world. The resulting, cumulative affect within both apocalyptic and conspiracy literature, both genres that trade in the affects of horror, is disgust and terror but also manipulation and motivation. Consumers are motivated to emotional and physical response, not mere agreement or compliance. Indeed, this affective allegiance is the literature's intent. The goal of apocalyptic and conspiracy rhetoric (and, arguably, affect) is the articulated fears of powerlessness but also the motivation of action alongside the declaration (or exposure) of the "real" world. What both apocalyptic and conspiracy communicate is a sense of identity, a vigorous subjectivity, and the polarization of that identity into action (even if only emotional resistance). They attempt to motivate via fear, disgust, and anger into allegiance and identity modification.

Apocalyptic, film, and conspiracy literature have a powerful spectatorial "reality" (which result in the perception) to create a diegetic "reality" that is fundamentally affectual – really, it seems, in ways that other forms of storytelling (prose literature, say) cannot quite achieve (perhaps because of the viscerality and universality – the preliteracy – of engagement with image). Film, in its (overt and intentional) creation of alternate worlds (Plate 2008, pp. 3–9) seems to share uniquely in apocalyptic literature. It also captures much of what apocalyptic – with its emphasis upon visions, signs, "seers," and "seeing" – is attempting to create, affectually, in prose. Revelation has an always-present conspiratorial element. Truth is "out there," but hidden until revealed. The universe aligns and coordinates in secret places, hidden beneath seemingly innocent or ordinary surfaces.

As we draw from recent affect-oriented film criticism on horror (Brinkema 2014; Brottman 1997; Carroll 1990; Pomerance 2003) we can profitably understand both apocalyptic and conspiracy discourses in a new light. They are forms of horror and draw from horror's affective form. Similarly, horror is a means of world-revelation and meaning creation. All three – apocalypse, conspiracy, and horror, revel in the affects of fear, rage, disgust, and shame.

What is hidden – secret worlds, demonic antagonists, aliens, ancient religions, agents of the deep state, the Illuminati, Jews – are exposed, just as horror reveals what is in the body – blood, organs, vomit, urine, feces. Hidden things are exposed and forcefully expelled, ripped from beneath. Affect links viewer and film; affect links religion and film; affect links horror and revelation; surfaces link, via the fold, to depths; affect links cognition and embodiment. Like rituals, movies are the affective embodiments of narrative and sign. All flow in succession to create meaning.

## Works Cited

Adams, J.L. and Yates, W. (1997). *The Grotesque in Art and Literature: Theological Reflections*. Grand Rapids, MI: Eerdmans.

Aichele, G., Pippin, T., and Walsh, R. (2013). Revelations of the dream. *Bible and Critical Theory* 9 (1–2). https://www.bibleandcriticaltheory.com/issues/vol9-no1-2/vol-9-no-1-2-2013-revelations-of-the-dream/ (accessed 27 October 2023).

Bilwicz, M., Chichocka, A., and Soral, W. (ed.) (2015). *Psychology of Conspiracy*. New York: Routledge.

Brinkema, E. (2014). *Forms of the Affects*. Durham, NC: Duke University Press.

Brotherton, R. (2017). *Suspicious Minds: Why We Believe Conspiracy Theories*. London: Bloomsbury.

Brottman, M. (1997). *Offensive Films*. Nashville, TN: Vanderbilt University Press.

Carey, G. (2005). *Ultimate Things: An Introduction to Jewish and Christian Apocalyptic Literature*. St. Louis: Chalice Press.

Carroll, N. (1990). *Philosophy of Horror, or Paradoxes of the Heart*. New York: Routledge.

Collins, J.J. (1998). *The Apocalyptic Imagination: An Introduction to Jewish Apocalyptic Literature*, The Biblical Resource Series, 2e. Grand Rapids, MI: Eerdmans.

von Däniken, E. (1980). *Chariots of the Gods: Unsolved Mysteries of the Past* (trans. Michael Heron. New York: G. P. Putnam's Sons.

Denzler, B. (2001). *The Lure of the Edge: Scientific Passions, Religious Beliefs and the Pursuit of UFOs*. Berkeley, CA: University of California Press.

Eberhart, G.M. (1986). *UFOs and the Extraterrestrial Contact Movement*. Metuchen, NJ: Scarecrow Press.

Freeland, C.A. (2000). *The Naked and the Undead: Evil and the Appeal of Horror*. Boulder, CO: Westview.

Frilingos, C.A. (2004). *Spectacles of Empire: Monsters, Martyrs and the Book of Revelation*, Divinations: Rereading Late Ancient Religions. Philadelphia: University of Pennsylvania Press.

Jung, C.G. (1964). Flying saucers: a modern myth of things seen in the sky (trans. R. F. C. Hull). In: *Civilization in Transition*, Bollingen Series. Collected Works of C. G. Jung, vol. X. Princeton, NJ: Princeton University Press.

Kawin, B.F. (2012). *Horror and Horror Films*. New York: Anthem Press.

Kotrosits, M. (2014). Seeing is feeling: Revelation's enthroned lamb and ancient visual affects. *Biblical Interpretation* 22 (4): 473–502.

Landow, G.P. (1992). *Hypertext: The Convergence of Technology and Contemporary Critical Theory*. Baltimore: Johns Hopkins University Press.

Landow, G.P. (2004). *Hypertext 2.0: The Convergence of Contemporary Critical Theory and Technology*, Parallax: Revision of Culture and Society. Baltimore: Johns Hopkins University Press.

Leslie, D. and Adamski, G. (1953). *Flying Saucers Have Landed*. London: Neville Spearman.

Lewis, J.R. (ed.) (1995). *The Gods Have Landed: New Religions from Other Worlds*. Albany, NY: State University of New York Press.

Melton, J.G. (1980). UFO contactees°–°a report on work in progress. In: *Proceedings of the first international UFO conference* (ed. C.G. Fuller, B.L. White, J. Clark, and M.M. Fuller). New York: Warner Books.

Melton, J.G. (1995). The contactees: a survey. In: *The Gods Have Landed* (ed. J.R. Lewis), 15–64. Albany, NY: State University of New York Press.

Moore, S.D. (2001). *God's Beauty Parlor and Other Queer Spaces in and around the Bible*, Contraversions: Jews and Other Differences. Stanford, CA: Stanford University Press.

Moore, S.D. (2014a). Retching on Rome: vomitous loathing and visceral disgust in affect theory and the apocalypse of John. *Biblical Interpretation* 22 (4): 503–528.

Moore, S.D. (2014b). *Untold Tales from the Book of Revelation: Sex and Gender*, Resources for Biblical Studies, vol. 79. Atlanta: Society of Biblical Literature Press.

Pagels, E. (1996). *The Origin of Satan: How Christians Demonized Jews, Pagans, and Heretics*. San Francisco: Vintage.

Palmer, S.J. (1995). Women in the Raelian movement: new religious experiments in gender and authority. In: *The Gods Have Landed* (ed. J.R. Lewis), 105–136. Albany, NY: State University of New York Press.

Palmer, S.J. (2004). *Aliens Adored: Raël's UFO Religion*. New Brunswick, NJ: Rutgers University Press.

Partridge, C. (ed.) (2003). *UFO Religions*. New York: Routledge.

Pelock, K.T. (2001). *Roswell: Inconvenient Facts and the Will to Believe*. Amherst, NY: Prometheus Books.

Plate, S.B. (2008). *Religion and Film: Cinema and the Re-Creation of the World*. Short Cuts. New York: Wallflower.

Pomerance, M. (2003). *Bad: Infamy, Darkness, Evil & Slime on Screen*, The SUNY Series, Cultural Studies in Cinema/Video. New York: SUNY Press.

Prooijen, J.-W. (2018). *The Psychology of Conspiracy Theories*. New York: Routledge.

Restall, M. and Solari, A. (2011). *2012 and the End of the World: The Western Roots of the Maya Apocalypse*. New York: Rowman & Littlefield Publishers.

Rossing, B. (2005). *The Rapture Exposed: The Message of Hope in the Book of Revelation*. New York: Basic Books.

Russell, J.B. (1987). *Satan: The Early Christian Tradition*. Ithaca, NY: Cornell University Press.

Saliba, J.A. (1995). UFO contactee phenomena from a sociopsychological perspective: a review. In: *The Gods Have Landed* (ed. J.R. Lewis), 207–250. Albany, NY: State University of New York Press.

Sedgwick, E.K. (2003). *Touching Feeling: Affect, Pedagogy, Performativity*. Durham, NC: Duke University Press.

Seesengood, R.P. (2016). A world of feeling: the affect of Lars von Trier and/as biblical apocalyptic. In: *Close Encounters Between Bible and Film: An Interdisciplinary Engagement*, Semeia Studies, vol. 87 (ed. L. Copier and C.V. Stichele), 209–232. Atlanta: Society of Biblical Literature Press.

Shaviro, S. (1993). *The Cinematic Body*. Minneapolis, MN: University of Minnesota Press.

Shaviro, S. (2004). The life, after death, of postmodern emotions. *Criticism* 46 (1): 125–141.

Stewart, K. (2007). *Ordinary Affects*. Durham, NC: Duke University Press.

Vox, L. (2017). *Existential Threats: American Apocalyptic Beliefs in the Technological Era*. Philadelphia: University of Pennsylvania Press.

Wray, T.J. and Mobley, G. (2005). *The Birth of Satan: Tracing the Devil's Biblical Roots*. New York: Palgrave.

Wright, M.J. (2008). *Religion and Film: An Introduction*. New York: I. B. Tauris.

# 10

## Bespoke Words

### The Bible, Fashion, and the Mechanism(s) of Things

This chapter hopes to weave conversations from all the various threads spun so far in the book – agency, the definition of culture and cultural studies, class and hegemony, mass market culture, meaning-making, cultural signs/ciphers, media, intertextuality, and (of course) Bible – in an examination of biblical passages on-and-about clothing and fashion (and the array of scholarly and interpretive communities arising from them). Biblical passages about clothing regulations, body ornament and body display are significant to many confessional readers and to many feminist and queer biblical scholars and manifest in pious, but also sharply economic and material, ways. As I read biblical text and survey some of its interpretation, I will argue that, like the clothing that we wear, the Bible is an active Thing, creating, through an assemblage of materials, concepts, affects, social order, and subjectivity. The chapter will juxtapose a series of "garments" of argument. An outfit is composed of several separate but complimentary pieces, assembled to create a meaningful, aesthetic, final whole; as follows, we shall see the final outfit of this argument emerge from disparate pieces that "mean" via assemblage.

## Theoretically Naked

We start off with the bare essentials, with the skin that touches the body and bone that become the animate "dressed" self. It may seem silly, in what follows, to think so much of clothing, given the importance of the body and the Self. Indeed, though, for many Bible readers, it would be equally trivial to attend to the body (and not cultivate the soul). In Matthew 6:25, Jesus advises "[D]o not be anxious about your life, what you shall eat or what you shall drink, nor about your body, what you shall put on." He continues "Is not life more than food, and the body more than clothing?" (RSV). I would quickly agree to that latter

*American Standard: The Bible in US Popular Culture*, First Edition. Robert Paul Seesengood.
© 2024 John Wiley & Sons Ltd. Published 2024 by John Wiley & Sons Ltd.

question, with a boisterous "Yes! Lots!" even as I would arrive in agreement by a route that completely ignores his initial advice. Indeed, this chapter will obsess over bodies, food, drink, clothing, and a host of other material and found objects and how Bibles and Bible readers use, engage, create, adapt, adopt, transform, and transcend them all.

Elizabeth Chin's (2016) elegant *My Life with Things: The Consumer Diaries* is late-capitalist and new materialist review of Things and their accumulation and assemblage into complex systems of consumption which fuse subjectivity and materiality. Theories of seamless materiality and subjectivity are also critical to Deleuze's idea of "assemblage," and Chin tacks this pattern to her reading of Marx, the politics of anthropology, and her relationship to the material things near and around her. As she does, she also, via cultural studies orientation, patches into an emerging conversation in twenty-first century theory and continental philosophy.

In her Oxford Bibliography entry on new materialism (2017), Susan Yi Sencindirer defines the "material turn" and new materialism as an "interdisciplinary, theoretical and politically committed field of inquiry emerging roughly at the millennium as part of what may be termed the post-constructionist, ontological, or material turn." She continues, "Spearheaded by thinkers such as Karen Barad, Rosi Braidotti, Elizabeth Grosz, Jane Bennett, Vicki Kirby, and Manuel DeLanda, new materialism has emerged mainly from the front lines of feminism, philosophy, science study, and cultural theory." In general, new materialism is a collection of work and thinking focused on renewed attention to matter, systems, and material aspects of Things. It is dissolution or interrogation of the binary between actor and agent, sentience and "matter."

More interdisciplinary work oriented around common questions and theme than method or organized approach, new materialism returns philosophical attention to the Things around us. As a part of a general "nonhuman" turn (Grusin 2015b) this material turn, and drawing from various twentieth-century philosophical renegotiations of accepted western philosophical foundational axioms (anthropocentrism, Cartesian dualism, poststructuralist antibinarism, and vitalism), new materialism reexamines the "thingliness" of Things and the arbitrary binary between animacy and inanimacy, human and animal/floral, agency and inertness, volition and action, thought and affect. To put it simply: Things do Stuff, and biological animacy is actually the aggregation of an array of nonmaterial, "inanimate," chemical and physical properties, agents, reagents and "actants" (Bennett 2010). To put that simply, whatever any Thing does, it gets it done by Stuff. New materialism intersects with and often draws from, but is not precisely identical with, other theories of inquiry such as animal/animality studies, affect theory, computer/artificial intelligence and artificial thought, economic theory, ecological theory, and more. Much work has spun outward from the near endlessly provocative *1000 Plateaus* of Deleuze and Guattari (1987), particularly the Deleuzian concept of "assemblage." (For a general, beginning review of new materialist and posthuman critique, see Alaimo and Hekman 2008 on the intellectual history of the question and general outline of its question; Bennett and Joyce 2010 for interdisciplinary and political aspects to the work; and Coole and Frost 2010 and Dolphijn and van der Tuin 2012 for a survey of pivotal essays and authors). Material approaches to the field of religion owe much to the work of S. Brent Plate (particularly Plate 2014 and his work with the journal *Material Religion: The Journal of Objects, Art and Belief* from 2004 to present).

New materialism also can be expanded with an array of thinking, loosely categorized as "object-oriented ontology," to expand and encompass not just material items (and the mutual interaction between Things and animate beings) but even inanimate conceptual or systemic structures or processes that emerge from the nexus of various forms of materiality and activity. Rather than emerging from Deleuze, object-oriented ontology develops out of Heidegger's *Being and Time*, in particular his challenge to an anthropomorphic separation of the categories of human and nonhuman. It is a resistance to the privileging of special pleading for human cognition, as Quentin Meillassoux (2008) has termed "correlationalism" or the argument that thinking and being are, necessarily, congruent and cannot be separable. Timothy Morton (2010) has applied this idea to ecological systems and Graham Harman (2002) to human tool-making, social systems, and the role of both in human evolution. The most natural point of connection between object-oriented ontologies and new materialist thought sits squarely in affect-infused studies, what Jane Bennett (following Bruno Latour) calls the "actant" – a term or category for the active "agency" of inanimate objects (Bennett 2010; Latour 2005).

## Boxers and Socks

With the burgeoning of scholarship on the Bible and "affect," one hesitates to use the word. First, it is fairly certain that, in biblical studies, "affect theory" will be "methodologized," read about more than read, overapplied. Second, and more substantively, is the risk of being positioned among work equating "affect" with "emotion."

Affect, as I'm using it, began in the social sciences tracking responses and reactions that are automatic, precognitive but persisted, in a second incarnation, in work engaging or emerging again from Giles Deleuze but also from feminist/queer critics such as Eve Sedgwick (on a quick-and-ready review of Affect, see Koosed and Moore 2014; Kotrosits 2016; Koosed and Black 2019; and Schaeffer 2019). Attending to affect is attending to how Things affect us, the automatic, involuntary, pre/pan-cognitive ways we regard or respond and how those responses are a form, themselves, of meaning. Affect is a corrective to centuries of philosophical inquiry that has stressed intent and logic, the primary mediators of agency and sentience. Affect is automatic. Affect, as I use it, is "meaning" or cognition without (or prior to) awareness (Massumi 2009). Affect is pan-human. Images, texts, music, architecture, film, animals, materials, environments, systems, theories, technologies, and beyond all have affect. So, affect, as I'm using it, not only includes, but is focused on "in-betweenness" or "becomingness." Affect is the connection – between human and non-human animals and plants, between systems and individuals, between Beings and Things. In short: Things affect us. Indeed, merging affect and nonhuman studies (animal studies, assemblage theories, new media, new materialism, systems theory, speculative realism, neo-vitalism, and object-oriented ontology to name a few) quickens an array of complex questions about agency.

Few Things in the world touch or affect us more frequently or more intimately than clothing (Seigworth 2016). We dress to inspire (or inhibit) affect when we dress in ways to conceal aspects of our body that we deem publicly shameful, to perpetuate modesty. Clothing is public intimacy. Clothing both expresses and shapes a sense of the self. Clothing and fashion are not only economic, and class creating/demonstrative, but are also fundamentally affectual.

## Shirt and Trousers

The Bible speaks to clothing, making it, for many, not just an affectual or political act, but specifically also one of religious devotion. In general, one might divide biblical language on clothing into three categories: liturgical purpose; articulation of social rank (and metaphorically a symbol of distress or salvation); and concern for "modest" clothing.

Liturgically, for example, priests wear clothing to indicate their holiness and dedication to God (including headgear and underwear; Exod 28:1–5; 29:5–6; 31:10; 39:1; Lev 8:7–9; Num 20:26; Ezek 44). Clothes (particularly fringes) and priests and (male) laity wear fringes to recall their Jewish identity (Num 15:38; Deut 22:12; Zech 8:23 – a practice continued in the second Temple era: Matthew 9:20; Luke 8:44). Biblical law contains a prohibition against mixing fabrics, very likely a contemporary pagan practice (Lev 19:19; Deut 22:11). The cleanliness of liturgical garments is stressed (not a trivial matter in an age of animal sacrifice). Though a distinct element of modern Jewish practice, male head covering is not really present in biblical text. The current liturgical use of yarmulke or kippot is medieval. Women veil in the Hebrew Bible, but not liturgically (e.g. Tamar in Genesis 38). Indeed, the only Hebrew Bible veiling for religious cause is Moses who veiled his face after its resulting alteration arising from a spectacular encounter with God (Exod 34:35). Ruth 3:15 (see also Isa 3:22; 25:7; 28:20) indicates women could and did veil for social reasons. Transvestitism (for either sex, liturgical or otherwise) is forbidden (Deut 22:5).

Perhaps, in part, because clothing conceals bodies but reveals identity. Clothing reveals an individual's status and, as such, is also a metaphor for joy, grief, corruption, or salvation (Gen 37:3; 41:42; 1 Sam 24:4–5; 2 Sam 13:18; Ps 45:13–14; Isa 3:22; Ezek 27:24; Dan 5:7, 29, 25; Esth 6:8; 8:15; Eccl 9:8; Job 22:6; Mark. 12:38; Luke 15:22; 16:19; Acts 12:21). Clothing also demonstrates grief (Gen 44:13; Lev 10:6; 2 Sam 3:31; Isa 2:2–4; Ezra 9:3). Grand clothing, particularly spotless white clothing, is a symbol for luxury and wealth, but also of salvation. Jeremiah enacts a symbolic prophecy by wearing, burying then exhuming the same linen undergarment (Jer 13:1–11). Zechariah has a vision of the high priest clothed in filthy before God's accuser, Satan (Zech 3).

Certainly, a central theme surrounding clothing in Hebrew Bible is the issue of modesty. Nakedness is regarded as shameful in Genesis (Gen 3:7, 21, perhaps also, in the New Testament, the reason Peter dresses when he sees Jesus, John 21:7), and a euphuism for sexual congress is to "uncover the nakedness" (Lev 18), yet concern over immodest clothing in Hebrew Bible is concerned primarily with concealment of *male* genitalia (e.g. Gen 9:20–27; Exod 28 or 2 Sam 6:20).

Fine clothes in the New Testament can be a sign of God's favor but are more often about haughtiness or exploitative wealth (Matthew 6:28; Luke 16:19; Acts 12:21; Jas 2:3; 1 Pet 5:5). Missionaries are forbidden to carry two cloaks, and disciples are urged to "consider the lilies" and not worry about clothes (Matthew 10:10; Mark 6:9 and Matthew 6:25–34; Luke 12:22–32). Cloaks are to be surrendered in lawsuits, much like Hebrew law forbade keeping an overcoat as loan collateral (Matthew 5:40; Exod 22:26). Clothing is never considered negatively, per se; Paul the apostle is a fabric worker, as are early converts (Acts 18:3; Dorcas in Acts 9; Lydia in Acts 16). The forgiveness of sins is likened to clothing being "washed" pure in "the blood of the lamb" (2 Chr 6:41; Neh 9:21; Job 29:14; Ps 149:4; 132:16–18; Isa 50:9; 51:8; 52:1; 61:10; 66:10; Ezek 16:10; Zech 3:4; Eph 4:22–24; Col 3:12, 26; Rev 3:5, 18; 4:4; 7:9; 19:18).

Within the New Testament there is a new disinterest in (disregard for?) fine clothing that is nearly always coupled with an interest in preservation of "modesty." There is no specific liturgical garb commanded for followers of Jesus, apart from head covering for women in 1 Cor 7 (which is connected with issues of gender submission generically). Also, alongside a broad shift in attention to modesty and gendered hierarchy over liturgy is a shift in attention to women's dress. The two most notorious passages on clothing and modesty – 1 Tim 2:9–10 and 1 Pet 3:3 – enjoin women to modest dress specifically against *excessive, secondary adornment* (as per Rev 19:18, a motif not inconsistent with Hebrew Bible Ps 31:30; 2 Kgs 9:30; Prov 5 and 7).

Most contemporary Christian groups recognize the New Testament is interested in "modest clothing," but interpret "modest" as clothing that inhibits (generally male) sexual desire. This is only a partial understanding of biblical modesty. Indeed, read closely, quelling or checking sexual desire does not appear to be the primary focus of New Testament imperatives for modesty at all. Biblical injunctions toward modesty are instead found in contexts concerned with gender submission and with socioeconomic status, so restraint dressing in ways that garner inappropriate notice or that seem unsubmissive.

## Shoes

"Biblical modesty" in dress is an attempt to separate adornment and display of wealth. It is economic and social. Alongside the food production and media industries, the clothing industry has undergone remarkable and dramatic change in the past 50 years. Fashion is intentionally ephemeral, of course, but the changes in industry are not merely changes in taste. As Elizabeth Cline discusses, the rise of low-cost, mass clothiers has altered both industry and patterns of consumption (Cline 2012; see also Cline 2019); at present, manufacturers dictate public tastes and access in unprecedented ways.

In the nineteenth century, clothing was expensive. Durably made, garments were intended to last despite heavy wear. Only the wealthy owned several unique outfits. By the twentieth century, modern manufacturing changed this. In the 1950s the average American family spent 10% of its annual income on clothing (Cline 2012, p. 22) and owned several dozen items. By our current standards of consumption, the average US consumer owns some 300 items of clothing and purchases over 100 items per year, though clothing is more cheaply made and significantly less durable. Notably, though consuming more and more items, we are paying less and less (per increase in median income rate). "According to annual statistics compiled by the US Bureau of Economic Analysis, individual spending on clothing is now just less than $1000 a year. Families spend about $1700 a year" (Cline 2019, p. 22). Consumption has increased, but spending has dropped just as precipitously.

Clothes are now made much more cheaply and rapidly. The bulk of the difference is the global effects on labor costs. (Cline 2019, pp. 42–43). Overwhelmingly, the cost of a garment is labor and mechanization matched with low-wage international production, which has reduced that capital investment in manufacturing; low-cost clothing has become an expectation, but it is an expectation enabled by exploitative employment practices (piecework, sweatshop work conditions, etc.) and disastrous environmental and secondary costs. Cheap fashion is, in many ways, as nefarious as factory farming and industrial monoculture agriculture.

Fashion, as a burgeoning industry, has also recently become both a social and scholarly interest. Clothing is both individual and collective, public and private. Somewhat counterintuitively, fashion and clothing are not just about the garments we put on, but on a more fundamental level, they are about the bodies we dress and the systems (economic and political) that surround us. Fashion, as an act (or an art) is non-verbal communication (Damhorst et al. 2000). This is particularly true for clothing as religious symbol and as means of religious expression (Damhorst et al. 2000 have an entire section on religion. Foster 1997, p. 4). Yet, like many strategies of subjectivity, fashion does all this interanimated by-and-with other social systems.

Fashion is both signifier and signified. Clothing and fashion are, I would argue, not merely a burgeoning manufacturing industry but also are Deleuzian machines, produced by an industry and regulated by social order, that in turn produce or manufacture Identity; what we put on when we dress is a complex system of meaning-making symbols. When we dress, we participate in that system manipulating it, and manipulated by it, and this participation has real social, political, economic and environmental effect and consequence. Fashion, at least in the United States, frequently weaves the threads of religion and capitalism into the fabric of subjectivity.

## Jacket

For example: Christian thought until the medieval era argued "to dress in excessive luxury was considered sinful, and to be dressed soberly was to be 'impeccably' dressed which comes from the Latin for 'without sin'" (David 2015, p. 16). Fashion, however, "encouraged lustful behavior and was associated with pride and vanity, as well as the sensuous, earthly pleasures of the flesh. Such thinking is much more reflective of biblical text. Garments that distorted body shapes came in for torrents of vitriolic rhetoric... In Christian eyes, humans should accept their God-given bodies" (David 2015, p. 16). The industrial revolution sparked Enlightenment, Colonial, and later Victorian interest in the care of the body, hygiene, and in self-decoration, shifting attention back to bodies and the things "hidden" by clothes (which, in the Victorian era, certainly, themselves, demonstrated much about public and economic status). Clothing was covered in complex layers of embodiment (David 2015, p. 16).

As cheap fashion has industrialized, so have the ways religious sensibility interacts with it. Contemporary protestant Christianity, for example, has sparked a burgeoning subindustry in Christian and Bible-themed clothing, particularly casual wear decorated with Bible or Christian-themed messages or imagery. According to an oft cited statistic, in 2009 that subindustry accounted for $4.6 billion in sales (note, for example and review, Nussbaum 1996), a number made more startling when one realizes the US t-shirt market as a whole was around $11 billion. As an industry, the explosive growth is most frequently ascribed to entrepreneur and believer Michael Edwards who in 1990 started in his apartment silk-screening shirts with Bible verses and, by 1995, was cofounder of Exodus Productions with $1.2 million annual sales (Dressler 1996; Nussbaum 1996). Within five more years, the industry had the attention of not only apparel insiders but the business community as a whole, according to one survey (Jonsson 2007).

Evangelical Christians often rhetorically position themselves outside traditional fashion markets (indeed, as outsiders to many traditional markets such as music, entertainments, and film) and often avow "secular" or "worldly" products, fashions, and goods are antithetical to their values (and that secular marketing ignores them). Yet the Christian apparel industry is not just performing resistance to signals of wealth or cultural awareness (or "fashion"), it is, at times, using these systems to articulate counter identity, using models from popular "secular" culture to articulate a counterculture and mark oneself as outsider (e.g. the "God's Gym" design logo for casual wear). Whatever the spiritual motives, the practice is fiscally quite lucrative. Christians looking to make a public witness of their alienation from popular culture do so via consumption and purchase of pop reframed pop culture items and spend significantly in the process. They use fashion as a mechanism for deviation from – and protest of – popular culture and the fashion industry itself.

## Tie

Religion (from *religare*, "to tic, bind; to knit") is an organized communal way to react to what humans regard as awe-inspiring or "sacred" according to standard definitions à la Durkheim, Geertz, or Eliade; it is, however, also a way of mediating and regulating affect. Religion is also a system producing and ordering Things in the world around us. Religion shapes, and is shaped by, material culture and technology.

So also Bibles. As we discussed earlier in Chapter 1, perhaps written tongue in cheek but anticipating many of the current questions behind speculative realism and object-oriented ontologies, Hugh Pyper mused about the Bible as a selfish gene or meme (specifically in the sense of Richard Dawkins, but perhaps more broadly Pyper 1998). After considering the history of Bible preservation and transmission and surveying the burgeoning rate of Bible publication (a trend marked even more by Timothy Beal 2012), Pyper draws from Richard Dawkins's assertion that "an organism is a gene's way of making other genes" Pyper asks: What if Judeo-Christianity is a Bible's way of making more Bibles?

Questions such as these resonate with the current "turn" to the nonhuman, which Richard Grusin defines as "the human ... characterized precisely by their indistinction from the nonhuman" (2015a, p. ix). Such a shift includes Latour's Actor-Network theory, Affect Theory, Deleuzian "assemblage" readings, artificial intelligence and technology/networks, new materialism (feminist, Marxist, or otherwise), systems theory, and speculative realism.

Gilbert Simondon has written forcefully on the latter, specifically the congruence of human evolution and technology (2016). Humans do not biologically evolve to respond to environmental shifts or changes (or evolve much more slowly. Note the development of this idea for popular readers by Harari 2015, 2017. See also Hayles 1999). Rather than natural selection producing the human equivalent of an elongated beak, as in Darwin's famous finches, we develop new tools. Systems and structures and technologies – languages, religion(s), economies, political theory – are arguably also complex tools for our adaptation and growth. Witness, for just one example, our global alteration of social norms, patterns, behaviors, and technology use in the wake of the unique Covid-19 coronavirus. Its (very real) biological threat was met much more (certainly much more rapidly) by changes in social order, structure, and tool use than by genetic selection. Via similar responses, over time, humans have created the material world as it currently is; we have as bio-appendages to human evolution. To be human is to be cyborg (as per Clark 2003). These tools and systems integrate into our lives and enhance our physiology, reaching critical junctures where we both cannot live without them and cannot fully control them. They become affective and autonomous. Simondon argues the evolution of the human is the coevolution of the tool, but it is also via adaptation of social behavior and all that goes with that – including systems and structures such as economics, politics, kinship, consumption, and religion, with all their various subsystems, "machinery," and "tools."

## Glasses

Consider again, then, the field of fashion. This essay has noted how clothing is integral to human society and organization, pivotal to many human activities in religion (a cultural act that many would argue is uniquely human), and, in doing so, is also in our present age highly industrialized, economic. Clothing has wrapped itself around almost all our major social systems. Were clothing a domestic or native biological organism, plant or animal, even viral, we would have absolutely no hesitation observing how wonderfully successful it was in its growth and expansion (genetically), and we would immediately credit this success to its ability to live symbiotically with humans and coevolve (guided or influenced, perhaps, by human systemic intervention). Were my English-tailored suit my Irish setter, we would see all that it represents – where it "evolved from," how it functions, what cultural and social mores it reflects or reinforces – would be seen in very different ways. We would see, at once, the false binary of being either Thing (solely) acted upon or with (at least genetic) "autonomy," and with that glimpse, we would see the complexity of the agency of Things, the limits of the categories of "animate" and "inanimate."

My point (in this essay, at least) is less to assert an autonomy of Things or Thing-ness (though that's a fine line of thought), but more about the autonomy and agency of culture and *Systems* – in this case human participation with matter to form networks of meaning *as constituent parts of* technologies of survival and adaptation and to note the complicated ways that systems (capitalism, fashion, religion) interanimate and, like systems such as evolution, geological change, celestial mechanics, take on a form of sentience. If nothing further, our definitions of sentience, structure, agency, and autonomy are in need of clarity, and arguments for human uniqueness or privilege need review. What if clothing, or at least fashion, *does* make the man?

So, again, to Bibles. Deleuze and Guattari famously argue for the book as machine, a device for making meaning created by an author, left for readers, an assemblage that incorporates all the author's desires and intent (both known and subconscious), the context of its own narrative, and the circumstance of the reader.

> As an assemblage, a book has only itself, in connection with other assemblages and in relation to other bodies without organs. We will never ask what a book means, as a signified or signifier; we will not look for anything to understand in it... A book exists only through the outside and on the outside. A book is a machine.
>
> (1987, p. 2)

Books, Bibles, are machines, made of multiple parts (contexts, language, history, reader) for creation of other meanings, other machines. They are affective systems, not, in the end, unlike the clothing we might wear as/while/if we read them.

The Bible, and fashion, are similar meaning machines. Like clothing, like fashion, the Bible is (after Deleuze and Massumi) a machine producing more machines, and biblical criticism, like communities of religious devotion that also read Bibles (perhaps, even, as a sort of subset of the same) is an industry of consumption and display not unlike fashion; in a strange fusion of materiality and agency, Bible and biblical interpretation shroud our body in affective tapestries, weaving themes of concealment and display, stitching and altering the material and social worlds we inhabit.

## Works Cited

Alaimo, S. and Hekman, S.J. (ed.) (2008). *Material Feminisms*. Bloomington, IN: Indiana University Press.

Beal, T.K. (2012). *The Rise and Fall of the Bible: The Unexpected History of an Accidental Book*. Boston: Houghton Mifflin Harcourt.

Bennett, J. (2010). *Vibrant Matter*. Durham, NC: Duke University Press.

Bennett, T. and Joyce, P. (ed.) (2010). *Material Powers: Cultural Studies, History and the Material Turn*. New York: Routledge.

Chin, E. (2016). *My Life with Things: The Consumer Diaries*. Durham, NC: Duke University Press.

Clark, A. (2003). *Natural Born Cyborgs: Minds, Technologies, and the Future of Human Intelligence*. New York: Oxford University Press.

Cline, E.L. (2012). *Overdressed: The Shockingly High Cost of Cheap Fashion*. New York: Penguin.

Cline, E.L. (2019). *The Conscious Closet: The Revolutionary Guide to Looking Good While Doing Good*. New York: Penguin Random House.

Coole, D. and Frost, S. (ed.) (2010). *New Materialisms: Ontology, Agency, and Politics*. Durham, NC: Duke University Press.

Damhorst, M.L., Miller, K.A., and Michelman, S.O. (ed.) (2000). *The Meanings of Dress*. New York: Fairchild Publications.

David, A.M. (2015). *Fashion Victims: The Dangers of Dress Past and Present*. New York: Bloomsbury.

Deleuze, G. and Guattari, F. (1987). *A Thousand Plateaus: Capitalism and Schizophrenia* (trans. B. Massumi). Minneapolis, MN: University of Minnesota Press.

Dolphijn, R. and van der Tuin, I. (ed.) (2012). *New Materialisms: Interviews & Cartographies*. Ann Arbor, MI: Open Humanities.

Dressler, C. (1996). Apparel makers honor God and bottom line. *Los Angeles Times* (29 February).

Foster, H.B. (1997). *"New Raiments of Self": African American Clothing in the Antebellum South*, Dress Body Culture. New York: Oxford.

Grusin, R. (2015a). Introduction. In: *The Nonhuman Turn*, Center for 21st Century Studies (ed. R. Grusin), vi–xxiv. Minneapolis, MN: University of Minnesota.

Grusin, R. (ed.) (2015b). *The Nonhuman Turn*. Minneapolis: University of Minnesota Press.

Harari, Y.N. (2015). *Sapiens: A Brief History of Humankind*. New York: HarperCollins.

Harari, Y.N. (2017). *Homo Deus: A Brief History of Tomorrow*. New York: HarperCollins.

Harman, G. (2002). *Tool-Being: Heidegger & the Metaphysics of Objects*. Peru, IL: Open Court.

Hayles, N.K. (1999). *How We Became Post Human: Virtual Bodies in Cybernetics, Literature, and Informatics*. Chicago: University of Chicago.

Jonsson, D. (2007). Christian clothing becoming the latest fashion in the US. https://www.fibre2fashion.com/industry-article/2902/christian-clothing-becoming-the-latest-fashion-in-us (accessed 3 November 2023).

Koosed, J.L. and Black, F.C. (2019). *Reading with Feeling: Affect Theory and the Bible*, Semeia Studies, vol. 95. Atlanta: Society of Biblical Literature Press.

Koosed, J. and Moore, S.D. (ed.) (2014). Affect theory and the Bible [special issue]. *Biblical Interpretation* 22: 4–5.

Kotrosits, M. (2016). *How things feel: biblical studies, affect theory and the (Im)personal*, Brill Research Perspectives in Biblical Interpretation. Leiden: Brill.

Latour, B. (2005). *Reassembling the Social: An Introduction to Actor-Network-Theory*. New York: Oxford University Press.

Massumi, B. (2009). 'Technical mentality' revisited; Brian Massumi on Gilbert Simondon. Interview with Arne De Boever, Alex Murray and Jan Roffe. *Parrhesia* 7: 36–45.

Meillassoux, Q. (2008). *After Finitude: An Essay on the Necessity of Contingency*. New York: Continuum.

Morton, T. (2010). *The Ecological Thought*. Cambridge, MA: Harvard University Press.

Nussbaum, D. (1996). A business of the cloth finds a surge in demand. *New York Times* (28 January).

Plate, S.B. (2014). *A History of Religion in 5½ Objects: Bringing Spirituality into the Senses*. Boston: Beacon Press.

Pyper, H.S. (1998). The selfish text: the Bible and memetics. In: *Biblical Studies/Cultural Studies: The Third Sheffield Colloquium*, Journal for the Study of the Old Testament, Supplement Series, vol. 266; Gender, Culture and Theory, 7 (ed. J.C. Exum and S.D. Moore), 70–90. Sheffield: Sheffield Academic Press.

Schaeffer, D. (2019). *The Evolution of Affect Theory: The Humanities, the Sciences, and the Study of Power*, Cambridge Elements: Histories of Emotions and the Senses. Cambridge: Cambridge University Press.

Seigworth, G.J. (2016). Wearing the world like a debt garment: interface, affect and gesture. *Ephemera* 16 (4): 15–31.

Sencindirer, S.Y. (2017). New materialism. Oxford Bibliographies. http://Oxfordbibliographies.com/display/document/obo-9780190221911/obo-9780190221911-0016.xml (accessed 29 October 2023).

Simondon, G. (2016). *On the Mode of Existence of Technical Objects* (trans. C. Malaspina and J. Rogone). Univocal, vol. 39. Minneapolis, MN: Univocal Publications.

# Conclusion

2020 Visions: Why the Bible and Popular Culture Matter

## Prelude to a Riot

Living and working at a small, independent college in the United States during 2020 was a strange, daily cocktail of anxiety and boredom. In March and April, Covid-19 forced many home, often in isolation (perhaps, at times, *wishing* to be isolated), even as it left others overwhelmed and at risk as "essential workers." During the course of the year, (tested) infections would reach over 19 million leaving over 332 000 dead by late December, sadly not even a third the toll Covid would come to take.[1] Unemployment roiled throughout the year, rising as high as 14.7% in April and ending (in December) at 6.7% (though with a staggering 853 000 claims for unemployment assistance). Over 40% of the US workforce transitioned to remote work and learning, which had additional economic ripples. Even after three vaccines were racing toward general approval for the US market, the nation still faced an array of shortages in products and services, a wildly unpredictable labor, and escalating inflation.

Racial unrest and election year politics frothed the public health crisis and its economic repercussions even further. Thousands flouted stay-at-home guidelines and protested "government intrusion" upon their liberties (regulated mask wearing, school/business closures, limiting public assemblies, and travel and quarantine regulations). In response to video footage of Minneapolis police choking to death George Floyd, US cities erupted in Black Lives Matter protests, and public conversation turned to issues of systemic racism, police violence, and inequity. A close and contentious election for president was complicated by mail-in ballots and baseless claims of election fraud. On 6 January 2021 as Congress assembled

---

1 Those, of course, are direct deaths. Overwhelmed hospitals and deferred preventative care no doubt cost additional lives. By some measures, 2020s "death index" was up around yet another 300 000 for the year, suggesting these might be indirect casualties of the health crisis.

*American Standard: The Bible in US Popular Culture*, First Edition. Robert Paul Seesengood.
© 2024 John Wiley & Sons Ltd. Published 2024 by John Wiley & Sons Ltd.

to recognize lawfully certified state election outcomes and electoral votes (and conclude the process of Biden's election as President), President Trump appeared at a rally outside the White House calling on his disgruntled followers to "take back our country" after weeks of prior, baseless claims of election fraud and using speech many regarded as incitement to insurrection (and for which he would face his second impeachment trial).

It's difficult not to imagine that the volatility of political and social divisions of 2021 were at least exasperated by the uncertainty and isolation of 2020. The United States tends to respond to anxiety via religiosity (at least via its rhetoric. Note, for example, Poole 2010), and, unsurprisingly, 2020 was a year punctuated with appeals to the Bible. Many sought religious exemptions for vaccine and mask mandates, often citing the "mark of the Beast" in Revelation 13 as their justification (Firebaugh 2021) whereas others opposed vaccines as generic betrayal of trust in God (Colarossi 2022). As the virus swelled through the population unchecked, religious communities were often included in state-mandated closures or crowd restrictions, prompting protest and court action (Redjai 2020). Popular faith healers took to social media rebuking the Satan of Covid-19 in the name of Jesus (Woodward 2020). Covid-19 was seen by some as a plague sent by God to rebuke and humble the United States for sexual sins (Sippell 2020). President Trump, on 1 June 2020, following a speech intended to reassure Americans, famously strode across a riot-littered capital street to pose in front of St. John's Church (awkwardly) holding a Bible aloft (upside down); unsurprisingly, religious ideology and symbolism (Christian, overwhelmingly) permeated the 6 January 2021 protests (see Berlinnerblau 2022 and the remarkable scholarship and digital archive of Altman and Copulsky 2021).

This tumultuous year was frequently dubbed "apocalyptic." The internet was brimming with (only partially joking) memes about impending disaster or plague – murder hornets, UFO invasion, zombie hoards, megastorms, volcanos, and more. Of course, most who used the term simply meant global (cosmic?) disruption and doom. As we have reviewed in Chapter 7, "Apocalypse" as scholarly genre means "unveiling" or "revealing" of the world as it "really" is, often with its cosmic or spiritual implication and significance. Even in that sense, however, 2020 was arguably apocalyptic for Bible and US pop culture. It revealed, again and again, where and how Bible fosters the American imagination. The United States is a nation whose State mythology and fantasy life is integral to its fascination with the Bible. In the coming years, I am certain volumes will be written examining the role of religiosity – particularly protestant Christianity – in US popular rhetoric and political response to the anxieties posed (revealed) by 2020 (for the moment, note Jones 2016; Butler 2021 and Stewart 2022). Americans intertwine religiosity, nationalism, and culture – using biblical image and text – a strategy that is neither antiquarian nor merely academic in its importance.

# Race, Bible, Mass Culture, and US Politics

The year 2020 saw boisterous conversations about politics, religion, and race in a divided nation, but not for the first time. Conservative pundits and politicians roused public ire (and campaign funding) via denunciation of "critical race theory." In 2021, these protests evolved into (astroturfed?) "grassroots" local government candidacies and appeals to school boards regarding curriculum and student reading lists, particularly surrounding US history. Black Lives Matter advocates turned their attention to public monuments venerating Civil War partisans and Confederate military, many erected during the early twentieth-century Jim Crow era.

As the nation has become increasingly polarized, comparison with the heated division and rhetoric of the years prior to and following the US Civil War are almost irresistible. Indeed, the association of race and political division to Bible reading has influenced US public life and citizenry for centuries. In the antebellum United States, race, economics, political affiliation, and religion fused in debate over the Fugitive Slave Act of 1850. Abolitionists had long argued slavery was immoral. There was no "good" or ethical way to own another human being, and any slave seeking freedom should be aided. Proslavery advocates, however, argued slavery was permissible morally, because it was not condemned in the Christian Bible. Further, they argued, Paul's letter to Philemon demonstrated that the Christian, moral response to a fugitive slave was to return the slave to the slave owner.

Philemon is one of the shortest documents in the New Testament and the shortest writing to have survived from Paul.[2] Scholars say this letter was written by Paul to one of his friends and former students, a fellow named Philemon. As the letter unfolds, we learn that Paul, under some form of (house?) arrest by the (Roman?) authorities, has met another man named Onesimus. Current scholarly consensus is that Onesimus has had some falling out with Philemon but also that Onesimus, after meeting Paul, has converted to Christianity. Philemon and Onesimus are somehow estranged; Paul is sending along news of his current condition in the letter but also sending back Onesimus to Philemon, expressing hopes that the two can reunite. Paul hopes that the fact that the two are now both believers in Jesus can form the basis for a restoration of their ruptured relationship.

Philemon was hotly debated in the early decades of the nineteenth century in America. Slavery was widely practiced in the Roman Empire, Paul's geographic and political context. Ancient Christian interpreters (perhaps most instrumentally

---

2 On Philemon, the history of its scholarship, and the intersection of that history with cultural context, see Seesengood 2017.

John Chrysostom) argued that the breach between Onesimus and Philemon was the result of Onesimus, a slave, escaping from Philemon (note, again, Seesengood 2017). Some would suggest that Onesimus, arrested as a fugitive slave, met Paul in prison where Paul then explained the gospel to him, converting him. Paul, the ancient interpreters argued, was sending back Onesimus while also asking Philemon not to beat or murder Onesimus.

Antebellum abolitionists argued Philemon wasn't about slavery at all. In Philemon 1:16, Paul writes that he is sending Onesimus back "no longer a slave but more than a slave, a beloved brother- especially to me but how much more to you, both in the flesh and in the Lord." (NRSV) "In the flesh," they argued, meant that Onesimus and Philemon were biological siblings. "Slave," they argued, was to be understood as a metaphor. As one might imagine, slavery defenders took the exact opposite argument; "brother," they said, was metaphoric (despite Paul's modifier of "in the flesh," a phrase normally meaning "literally" or "actually") whereas "slave," was to be taken literally. The issue could not be more significant. Millions of lives hung in the balance of the interpretation of one verse in one chapter of one (very short) book of the Bible.

Except, of course, that it didn't, really. I would argue that the cultural needs and a political issue – whether or not to endorse or oppose slavery in antebellum America – actually shaped both the methods of biblical scholars and the very verses that they read, and rarely did it occur the other way around. For example, Deuteronomy 23:15 (a key text from a key book of the Bible) expressly forbids the return of an escaped slave. Oddly, this verse was largely absent in the debates over Philemon waged in the American south (many simply disregarding it all together, nearly everyone failing to note that the traditional Christian interpretation of Philemon meant Paul, born and educated as a devout Jew, was in overt and deliberate violation of that text without any explanation at all). Cultural values did not arise exclusively from Bible reading, despite what anyone claimed. Bible reading (and interpretation) was shaped by cultural context.

## Bible, Culture, Race, and Scholarship: 2020 Correcting Our Vision

Attention to how political need, social location, and race affect a biblical critic's work has been a long-time staple of modern biblical scholarship. Cain Hope Felder's edited collection, *Stony the Road We Trod* (1991) showcased a number of scholars offering informed and determined reappraisals of biblical text and, perhaps more centrally, the scholarship and cultural norms which had emerged around them. Felder noted in the introduction "there are today just a little more than thirty black North Americans who have completed Ph.D./Th.D. in biblical studies." (p. 1). That, happily, has changed (resoundingly), but, despite that growth, Felder described a biblical scholarship and intellectual landscape in terms that the subsequent 30 years seem scarcely to have noticed, let alone addressed. He writes:

> At the beginning of this century, the prolific black historian, political philosopher, and educator W. E. B. Du Bois in his *Souls of Black Folks* asserted that "the problem of the twentieth century is the problem of the color line." Now that we are near the end of this century, it is woefully apparent that white racism is, at least for African Americans, the most pervasive problem. For many of us, it remains not only unresolved but is often quite subtle, thus all the ore pernicious. This is so because, more often than not, white racism is *denied* or *trivialized* by those who perpetuate it through their family socialization, the mass media, corporate life, curricular emphases, and religious separatism... Some would say that it is not so much that whites are against blacks; rather, whites are just so completely for themselves that, by any means at their disposal, they will protect their privileges in a society designed to work for them. In this reasoning, all blacks have to do is to deny their own history and identity and thus to act like they are part of the American dream so that "the system" can work for them too. Yet for African Americans, this type of reasoning has more often than not led only to a nightmare of self-abasement, a valuation of all other racial and ethnic groups except their own, and a crisis of expediency overwhelming integrity. (p. 3)

Felder's critique sounds remarkably familiar to anyone reading contemporary social critique by historians and scholars such as Derrick Bell, Alan Freeman, Kimberlé Crenshaw, Richard Delgado, or Cheryl Harris.[3] Critical race theory emerged from work in critical theory, and particularly through the root structure of Marxist/Gramscian cultural studies. Beginning as it did via legal studies influenced by critical theory (particularly poststructuralism), critical race theory argued law (like "culture") was a construct and was built to both create and perpetuate white privilege. In the case of US history, with an economic system and Constitution "stamped from the beginning" (Kendi 2016) in racial difference and discrimination, both race/racism and capitalism are necessary descendants of colonialism. Much more than politely "listening to other voices" (as if only the "other" voices are being influenced by race and its constructs, as if "traditional"

---

3 Those interested in something beyond polemic, popular (mis)characterization of Critical Race Theory should consult Delgado and Stefancic 1984. For an anthology of pivotal texts, see Crenshaw et al. 1996.

biblical scholarship is not racialized), biblical scholarship that attends to core ideas of race and its ties to economic/class difference and political/legal power becomes instead a glimpse into the mechanisms of how biblical text has been used to create those economic and political structures of oppression or protection. It becomes, in other words, the inevitable culmination of cultural studies approach to scholarship of the Bible. In 2020 key scholarly works again fused race, Bible, and American popular culture. There will, absolutely, be more to come. Three, however, roughly map on to the areas of scholarship exemplified in this volume.

Lisa Bowens's *African American Readings of Paul: Reception, Resistance and Transformation* examines the history of Paul on-and-by Black scholars and clergy (Bowens 2020). Paul's letters (in addition to Philemon) have been particularly fraught spaces for African American readers, particularly Paul's celebration of "slavery" as a metaphor for faith and the instructions found in the Epistle to the Ephesians for slaves to "obey their masters" in everything and I Corinthians 7:21–22's declaration that slaves should not attempt to gain their freedom (which is tossed off as a trivial matter). Bowers details the ways African American readers sought to redeem, circumvent, or reclaim these troublesome texts (as well as how they document the ways these texts were used, often selectively, by white scholarship and church to oppress them).

Esau McCaulley's *Reading While Black: African American Biblical Interpretation as Exercise of Hope* takes the role of the Black church and its influence on African American biblical scholarship seriously (McCaulley 2020). As Felder and others noted, African American biblical scholarship has long been integrally tied to communities of faith (and also to faith-driven calls for social justice and transformation). Critical biblical scholarship (following conventional European modes) has often been dismissive of the spiritual aspects of Bible reading – indeed, has often set itself principally as the rational, scientific counterweight to popular readership. McCaulley works to integrate both ecclesiastical tradition and critical text, bringing both to bear on issues such as systemic economic racism, unequal policing, and racial discrimination.

Finally, 2020 also saw the appearance of Nyasha Junior and Jeremy Schipper's *Black Samson: The Untold Story of an American Icon* which explores the use of the character Samson as cipher for Black (male) bodies and their struggle against oppression (Junior and Schipper 2020). Later liberation reading focus on Moses. African American readings, however, had deep roots in the celebration of Samson – a character taken prisoner, ridiculed, abused, and debased to merely a strong body but who was also paradigmatic trickster and who ultimately defied his chains, summoned his strength, and destroyed his oppressors.

As US population demographics trend, within 20 years white populations will be the national minority. White/European males represented only about 31% of the US population in the 2020 census, suggesting their strong majority among biblical studies PhDs does not represent US society and is likely unsustainable. Long before 2040, following trends in college enrollment trends perhaps by 2025, the majority of students in higher education in the United States will be non-white. There is simply no debate: biblical scholarship in the United States will eventually address and incorporate the questions and issues raised by scholars of color and critical race theory. Doing so, as critical race theory is the apex of cultural studies, biblical scholarship will also foreground cultural studies approaches and questions. This is not a question of what US biblical studies *should* do; it is a simple acknowledgement of what the field *will* do, as the nation and academic structures which nurture change. Understanding cultural studies approaches to biblical scholarship – scholarship that foregrounds how Bible readers (including scholarly and clerical ones) were influenced by culture and how culture was influenced by Bible readings – is going to be integral for understanding the discipline as a whole. As this quick survey on US culture, race, and biblical studies has shown, there are real-world implications to how we read and construct culture and increasing attention to how culture intersects with our readings is inevitable.

## A Final Review

As we have seen, scholarship of the Bible and popular culture has a distinct intellectual genealogy. Cultural studies is not synonymous with "reception criticism"; the latter is a subset of the former, heavily oriented around history of scholarship and practice. Nor is cultural studies reducible to "media studies"; again cultural studies can include analysis of mass or popular media, but it is also deeply invested in how culture functions – producing and being produced by its mass consumed items and media.

Cultural studies is concurrent with critical theory, presuming cultural realities are constructs but turning attention to how (and why) the construct functions. Conventional cultural studies criticism was in origins largely anglophone and presumptive of Marxist ideas (largely as mediated through Althusser) of cultural hierarchy (hegemony), a momentum which reached an inflection point in the late twentieth-century work of the Birmingham Centre for Contemporary Cultural Studies.

Along its development – and via its mediation from UK into US academic discourses via Yale and other bastions of North American critical theory – cultural studies was infused by critical insights of Barthian/Kristevan intertextuality – a flipping of script, somewhat, to inquire how an individual, formed by culture, approached both culture and text. This move was both precipitated by, and demonstration of, an interentanglement between cultural studies and (Jamesonian) late capitalism (likely also a residue of its Americanization).

In its most recent iterations, cultural studies has turned, as have the humanities in general, to inquire the limits of culture and toward the posthuman. New work on materialism, assemblage, affect, animality, and technology complicate both simple understanding of "culture" and "human." As human communities interact, cultural studies sits side by side with critical race theory as useful tool; indeed, the two are arguably differentiated only by nuance and interest. Finally, given the critical role of the Bible in the development of US origins, discourse, law, economics, art, entertainment, and, well, culture, biblical studies intersecting with cultural studies has a unique contribution to make to the study of US religion, history, and scholarship.

In this book we have seen the Bible itself as an element of American popular culture. The Bible has emerged in various forms of US media, from humble comic books to high-art film. It has become an item of consumption and identity production unlike any other. We've also seen the Bible appear as instigator or model for American popular culture. Biblical tropes form the narrative logic of our national imagination. The Bible is a key – and common – text for allusion in film and other media. Biblical structures of thinking (and suspicion) frame our national narratives of self and sense. Finally, we have seen that the tables may turn, and Bible itself can be better understood when read alongside popular culture. We can see Bible in new light – as a radical text, as a moment of (colonial) religious syncretism, as a Book that becomes a (re)productive machine.

Early summer 2021, my family and I piled into our car and began a two-week-long road trip from our home in eastern Pennsylvania westward to the vast interior of the United States, looking to visit family, many we'd not seen face-to-face in two years. As exhilarating as it was to be away from our house, the tensions of 2020 were not gone. We scanned the news, marking the number of Covid-19 infections in the states we traversed, particularly watching the news of the Delta variant (unnerved at its reported ability to "break through" and infect even the vaccinated). We heard continued reports (and saw conversation on social media) of low vaccination rates and the politicizing of public health conversations. We saw firsthand the uneven application of masking guidelines. The rural highway roadsides were occasionally decorated with signs declaring "Trump Won," urging votes against abortion, and at least once advertising a White Power satellite radio station; urban streets were marked by "Black Lives Matter" graffiti, signs urging masking and vaccination, and pro-LGBTQ and Pride Month sentiment. We remain a nation very divided, as well as a nation where perception of reality, authority of information sources, and even basic recognition of facts are heavily mediated by ideology.

Along the highways of America one readily finds billboards urging Christian devotion – "No Jesus, no peace; Know Jesus, know peace;" "Lost? Reach out to Jesus" – signs urging repentance before Judgment. More recently, these signs have taken on themes from conservative US politics – identifying Trump as God's chosen leader, challenging the legality of abortion, asserting that God will abandon the United States if they do not turn to conservative political politics.

Professional Bible scholars know the feeling of driving past these signs, firm mouthed, embarrassed in a way. The urge to distance oneself from these readings – to describe them as "unscientific," unlearned, unequal to one's own – is overwhelming. And, in many ways, not unreasonable. Bible scholars have often spent decades developing skills with ancient languages, textual criticism, the sociohistorical context of the Bible, the history of interpretation, the precision of methodology. It is tempting to argue that these roadside readings are not "reasonable" readings, and even more that analysis of them or engagement with them is more sociology than biblical criticism.

The argument of critical cultural studies, particularly the one presumed by this book, differs from both of those urges. These road sign readings fundamentally *are* a form of biblical scholarship, and their engagement and analysis *are also* biblical criticism. To argue otherwise is to reimpose the barriers between high and low culture, barriers that are arbitrarily drawn in order to preserve hierarchy. Certainly, all readings are not equally convincing, equally informed, equally reflective, or equally ethical. Yet, this volume argues, all are equally *expressions of* biblical criticism. In many ways, these road sign readings both reflect and create the Bible's influence on the average US citizen in ways that far outstrip the influence of professional biblical scholars. To ignore them as "low" or unfit is a serious misstep and, I would argue, irresponsibly isolationist. Biblical scholars need to engage the public Bible and popular media. And, to be clear, not merely to "correct" popular misconception. Seeing the full array of popular bible reading can reveal or highlight new ways of thinking about the Bible that are useful to all readers.

The history of biblical transmission – its redaction, collection, transcription, and manuscript preservation – is an early and often difficult to absorb lesson for novice Bible scholars. One realizes, sometimes painfully, that the Bible is more fossil record than historical artifact, that it is the collection of cultural accretion surrounding its oral stores and history of readership, that we read a reconstruction and, in that reconstruction, miss more than we know and must live with the possibility of amendment and revision in even that paltry amount. As our novice scholar matures, they soon learn the effect of ideology on reading and upon every (re)construction of biblical "meaning." Like lenses, our methodologies and the agendas that often both create and emerge from them filter out what we see. And, to continue the metaphor, as our "eyes" change over time, new lenses will be needed, again and again.

To read the bible attuned to cultural studies is to realize yet another level of mediation. We read the Bible in-and-through culture, resisting some points, seizing upon others. No one truly reads the Bible for the first time. It is as if we read and inscribe the Bible in a mirror, watching ourselves write, even as we read and revise our own words. Reading the role of the Bible in-and-on the history of US politics and racial difference makes clear, however, these are not simple intellectual points. Real lives and real human suffering hang in the balance.

Driving across Appalachia, between the road signs the highways often pass through mountains, the exposed layers of sandstone and bedrock creating small canyons on either side of the turnpike. Beginning readers of the Bible often think of it as unchanging Rock, a steady, firm, and timeless touchstone or anchor. But, of course, rocks are not unchanging, nor, even if ancient, are they timeless. Rocks came to be in the form that they did by clear and understandable processes, and rocks can persist through an array of dynamic forces, but not unchanged. Rocks are shaped by the relentless effects of wind and water, even as jutting stones shape and change the flow of water and wind, in turn. In a similar way, reading the Bible alongside cultural studies reads the Bible itself as part of the cultural landscape, the narrative of cultural flow and creation; it reads the Bible as a complex cocktail of energies – as creation of culture, as creator of culture both at once. The way one reads the Bible is always shaped by culture, just as the readings one produces shape culture in turn.

## Works Cited

Altman, M.J. and Copulsky, J. (eds.) (2021). Uncivil Religion: January 6, 2021. www.uncivilreligion.org (accessed 29 October 2023).

Berlinnerblau, J. (2022). After Jan. 6, secularism is the crucial 'guardrail' – and it's fatally weak in America. *Salon* (7 January) https://www.salon.com/2022/01/07/after-jan-6-secularism-is-the-crucial-guardrail/ (accessed 29 October 2023).

Bowens, L.M. (2020). *African American Readings of Paul: Reception, Resistance and Transformation*. Grand Rapids, MI: Eerdmans.

Butler, A. (2021). *White Evangelical Racism: The Politics of Morality in America*. Durham, NC: UNC Press.

Colarossi, N. (2022). Right-wing pastor blasts Trump for vaccine support. *Newsweek* (10 January). https://www.newsweek.com/right-wing-pastor-rips-trump-supporting-vaccines-he-going-lose-his-voter-base-1667714 (accessed 3 November 2023).

Crenshaw, K., Gotandaa, N., Peller, G., and Thomas, K. (ed.) (1996). *Critical Race Theory: The Key Writings that Formed the Movement*. New York: New Press.

Delgado, R. and Stefancic, J. (ed.) (1984). *Critical Race Theory: An Introduction*, Critical America, 2e, vol. 59. New York: New York University Press.

Felder, C.H. (ed.) (1991). *Stony the Road We Trod: African American Biblical Interpretation.* Louisville, KY: Augsburg Fortress Press.

Firebaugh, T. (2021). Covid-19 vaccines: why some Christians deny them as 'the mark of the beast.' *Religion & Politics* (11 October).

Jones, R.P. (2016). *The End of White Christian America.* New York: Simon & Schuster.

Junior, N. and Schipper, J. (2020). *Black Samson: The Untold Story. Of an American Icon.* New York: Oxford.

Kendi, I.X. (2016). *Stamped from the Beginning: The Definitive History of Racist Ideas in America.* New York: Nation Books.

McCaulley, E. (2020). *Reading While Black: African American Biblical Interpretation as an Exercise in Hope.* Grand Rapids, MI: InterVarsity.

Poole, W.S. (2010). *Satan in America: The Devil We Know.* New York: Rowman & Littlefield.

Redjai, I. (2020). Coronavirus: churches are essential. If protestors can assemble, so should people of faith. *USA Today* (8 August). https://www.usatoday.com/story/opinion/voices/2020/08/08/coronavirus-pandemic-churches-essential-businesses-open-religious-freedom-column/3323082001/ (accessed 3 November 2023).

Seesengood, R.P. (2017). *Philemon: Imagination, Labor and Love,* T & T Clark Study Guides to the New Testament. New York: Bloomsbury.

Sippell, M. (2020). Trump-supporting televangelist who blamed COVID-19 on premarital sex dies of COVID-19. *The Wrap* (5 November). https://www.thewrap.com/irvin-baxter-televangelist-covid-19-dies/ (accessed 3 November 2023).

Stewart, K. (2022). *The Power Worshippers: Inside the Dangerous Rise of Religious Nationalism.* London: Bloomsbury.

Woodward, A. (2020). Coronavirus: televangelist Kenneth Copeland 'blows the wind of God' at Covid-19 to 'destroy' pandemic. *Independent* (6 April). https://www.independent.co.uk/news/world/americas/kenneth-copeland-blow-coronavirus-pray-sermon-trump-televangelist-a9448561.html (accessed 3 November 2023).

# Index

Note: this index omits most modern scholars cited throughout the work. Please refer to the bibliographies at the conclusion of each chapter for a systematic listing. Please refer, as well, to the table of contents for a general review of subjects treated.

*American Standard: The Bible in US Popular Culture*, First Edition. Robert Paul Seesengood.
© 2024 John Wiley & Sons Ltd. Published 2024 by John Wiley & Sons Ltd.

*Nanook of the North* (documentary film), 155–6
neoliberalism, 7
new historicism, 12
new materialism, 191–2

object-oriented ontology, 192
Ostwalt, Conrad, 72, 77–8
Otto, Rudolf, 170

Paley, William, 42
Pekar, Harvey, 59
Pizzagate (conspiracy theory), 178–9, 186
posthuman, posthumanism, 18–19
postmodernity, 8, 75
  defined, 8–9
  and metanarrative, 8–9, 75
poststructuralism, 13
Prothero, Stephen, 52
Pyper, Hugh, 67–68, 198

Qanon (conspiracy theory), 179

Räel (Claude Vorilhon), 171–2
  as a biblical interpreter, 177
reception criticism, 15–17
religion, definition of, 15–17
Religious Book Club (RBC), 47

Sacks, Daniel, 82–3
Satan (biblical character)
  in biblical text, 139–40
  and conspiracy, 180–1
  development of, 140–3
  and God, 148
Scofield, Cyrus I, 46, 169
  Scofield Bibles, 47–8, 169
Scott, A. O. (film critic), 98

Sedgewick, Eve, 18, 192
Segovia, Fernando, 3, 12–15, 95
"selfish genes," 67–8, 198
sexualized depiction of women, 65
Sherwood, Yvonne, 15
Stewart, Lyman and Milton, 46
"strange woman" *('isha zara)*, 123–4
structuralism, 13
superficiality (as substance and significant), 16, 50

Tanach (Torah, Navi'im, Kethuvim– Jewish Bible), 96–7
Taylor, Mark C., 49–51
Teubal, Savina, 62–3, 65, 68
Tolkien, John Ronald Ruel (J.R.R.), 130, 132–3, 137, 145
Tompkin, Silvan, 18
Tompkins, Jane, 112
Trump, Donald J., 203–4, 210–11
"two woman motif" (Proverbs), 122–4

Unidentified Flying Objects (UFOs), 169
  in/and the Bible, 170
  modern mythology, 175–6

Van Impe, Jack, 175–6
vegetarianism, 72, 81, 85
"virtuous wife motif" *('ishah hayil)*, 124
virus, viruses, 2–3

"war in heaven motif," 141–3
Weigh Down Watchers, 83–84
Welch, Richard, 72, 82
Wellhausen, Julius, 62

# Index of Biblical Citations

*American Standard: The Bible in US Popular Culture*, First Edition. Robert Paul Seesengood.
© 2024 John Wiley & Sons Ltd. Published 2024 by John Wiley & Sons Ltd.

Printed and bound by CPI Group (UK) Ltd, Croydon, CR0 4YY

26/02/2024

14459636-0001